CONTEMPORARY CHURCH
ARCHITECTURE

CONTEMPORARY CHURCH
ARCHITECTURE

Edwin Heathcote and Laura Moffatt

1807 WILEY 2007

WILEY-ACADEMY

Front Cover: Private Chapel, Almadenejos, Spain, Estudio Sancho-Madridejos
Frontispiece: Jubilee Church, Rome, Italy, Richard Meier & Partners
Right: Christ Church, Donau City, Vienna, Austria, Heinz Tesar

Published in Great Britain in 2007 by Wiley-Academy, a division of
John Wiley & Sons Ltd

Copyright © 2007   John Wiley & Sons Ltd, The Atrium, Southern Gate,
Chichester, West Sussex PO19 8SQ, England
Telephone (+44) 1243 779777

Email (for orders and customer service enquiries): cs-books@wiley.co.uk
Visit our Home Page on www.wiley.com

Anniversary Logo Design: Richard Pacifico

Other Wiley Editorial Offices

John Wiley & Sons Inc., 111 River Street, Hoboken, NJ 07030, USA

Jossey-Bass, 989 Market Street, San Francisco, CA 94103-1741, USA

Wiley-VCH Verlag GmbH, Boschstr. 12, D-69469 Weinheim, Germany

John Wiley & Sons Australia Ltd, 42 McDougall Street, Milton, Queensland
4064, Australia

John Wiley & Sons (Asia) Pte Ltd, 2 Clementi Loop #02-01, Jin Xing
Distripark, Singapore 129809

John Wiley & Sons Canada Ltd, 5353 Dundas Street West, Suite 400,
Etobicoke, Ontario M9B 6H8

Wiley also publishes its books in a variety of electronic formats. Some
content that appears in print may not be available in electronic books.

Executive Commissioning Editor: Helen Castle
Content Editor: Louise Porter
Publishing Assistant: Calver Lezama

ISBN 978 0 470 03156 8

Cover design © Artmedia Press Ltd, UK
Page design and layouts by Artmedia Press Ltd, UK

Printed and bound by Conti Tipocolor, Italy

CONTENTS

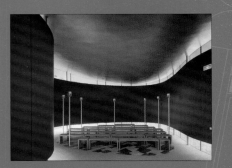

THE 20TH-CENTURY CHURCH
THE ENIGMA OF SACRED OBJECTIVITY

Edwin Heathcote

I. A MATTER OF MORALITY

About 1835, in England, Augustus Welby Pugin (1812–52) transferred the equation of Christianity and Gothic into architectural theory and practice. With him, to build in the forms of the Middle Ages was a moral duty. And he went further. He contended that, as the medieval architect was an honest workman and a faithful Christian, and as medieval architecture is good architecture, you must be an honest workman and a good Christian to be a good architect.[1]

With this Aristotelian syllogism, Nikolaus Pevsner dealt with the issue of the basis of the Gothic Revival in simplistic Puginian terms. Note the appearance of the words 'moral' and 'honest'. These two words have underpinned the great majority of the literature that deals with the fundamental change in architecture that emerged from the 19th century to inform the architecture of the early 20th century. As Robert Furneaux-Jordan states in his summation of *Victorian Architecture*: 'Architecture, thereafter [after Pugin] ceased to be a matter of taste, it became a matter of morality'.[2]

As Furneaux-Jordan points out, this removal of architecture from the realms of the aesthetic to the ethical persists to this day in a lingering trace of the moralising nature of criticism from which the modern artistic and architectural spheres have never recovered. Pugin and, later, John Ruskin were credited with this change in spirit, whereby it was claimed that the Gothic was the only moral style for churches, the classical style having been derived from the pagan civilisations. This was combined with a nascent Functionalism (a rejection of the classical language as a system devised for timber which had been transposed to stone) regarding structure that had been inspired by the French 18th-century position and an aspiration for *architecture parlante*:

> The great test of architectural beauty is the fitness of the design to the purpose for which it is intended, and that the style of the building should so correspond with its use that the spectator may at once perceive the purpose for which it was intended.
> *AWN Pugin*.[3]

Gothic alone was perceived to be a style that had derived from the desire to build for God. For Pugin, the verticality of the Gothic was an 'emblem of the resurrection'. What other style could a church possibly be? God was on the side of the Gothic.

This was not merely a stylistic debate, however. The plan of the English church, derived from the Protestant preaching house and the currency of all British church architecture from Christopher Wren onwards, was abandoned in favour of a plan that could accommodate the fundamentally Catholic ritual espoused by the ecclesiologists. The emancipation of Catholics and a spate of high-profile conversions, including John Henry Cardinal Newman, Pugin himself and Friedrich Schlegel in Germany, prompted a reassessment of Catholic liturgy and the perceived shortcomings of the Anglican mass. The ecclesiologists and the Oxford movement essentially rediscovered the sacraments (particularly communion) and sought spirituality through the continuity of the historic ritual of the church.

The arrangement of chancel, aisles and side-chapels became as important as the Gothic ornamentation. This was Gothic as generator of the plan, not merely as a stylistic device. The principal proponent of this approach was William Butterfield, a Functionalist Gothicist (not necessarily a paradox). His buildings revelled in their ugliness, yet they have lasted well; All Saints, Margaret Street, London (1849–59), was a key structure, a bold piece of urban infill design and an important example to others.

Although it is easy to see a rational route, as many have done, between Pugin's writings, Ruskin's plea for honesty and the happy craftsman, Butterfield's modern Gothic idiom and William Morris' idealistic medievalising socialism through to the Bauhaus and Functionalism, the path is in fact much less clear cut. Le Corbusier's *Vers une Architecture* (1923) is bristling with studies of the

Anglican Cathedral, Liverpool, UK, 1903–78, Giles Gilbert Scott

Parthenon while the neoclassicists of revolutionary France and, later, Karl Friedrich Schinkel in Germany exerted a great influence on the emerging Modernism, just as did the British Arts and Crafts. The most admired British classicists, Wren and Nicholas Hawksmoor, lingered in spirit, if not in language, close to the Gothic. No Athenian or Florentine building ever had steeples like those that defined London's skyline.

Britain was not alone in the debates that were raging about style and morality at the end of the 19th century. Goethe encouraged the lyrical in architecture ('It is the poetical part, the fiction, that makes a building into a work of art')[4] in a manner that was also close to the French revolutionary architects. However, his heart lay with Johann Joachim Winckelmann; he greatly admired the world of antiquity and expounded his views with great authority and learning to an eager audience. Goethe was fundamentally of a different age to Pugin and Ruskin. He was perplexed by the completion of Cologne Cathedral in a Gothic style after the original plans had been found; he tried but failed to appreciate it and could not bring himself to understand the passion for the medieval.

Schinkel appreciated the Gothic as the language of spirituality and inspiration, but remained firmly neoclassical in his convictions, while GWF Hegel saw in Gothic, or 'romantic', architecture, that which 'is peculiarly appropriate to the Christian rite, together with a harmony between the architectural form and the inner spirit of Christianity' (*Vorleisungen über die Ästhetik*). Arthur Schopenhauer, however, advocated neoclassicism as an unsurpassable architectural language and saw the many Gothic projects as 'trying to embalm the dead body of Christianity'.[5]

Gottfried Semper, one of the key names in 19th-century architectural theory, concerned himself with a symbolism of construction, material and colour and, although often cited as a proto-Functionalist, remained unable to find a new style. He condemned neo-Gothic largely because of its associations in Germany in the second half of the 19th century with Catholicism and the conservatism, which he saw as a suffocating influence on German culture.

Although there was a proliferation and high level of architectural debate in the German-speaking countries, many of the actual innovations in ecclesiastical architecture during the 19th century (and those that would have the greatest influence in the next century) came out of France. Despite the pervasive influence of the École des Beaux-Arts and the preponderance of a neo-Renaissance language on the French architectural scene, some remarkable and visionary leaps were made. The romantic Byzantine language of the Sacré Coeur at Montmartre, Paris (1875–7), by Paul Abadie, predates JF Bentley's Westminster Cathedral by a couple of decades, and the age saw the predominance of one of Europe's great 19th-century architectural theorists, Eugène Viollet-le-Duc.

Victor Hugo's novel *Notre Dame de Paris, 1482* (1831) featured the eponymous cathedral as its central character; the other figures appeared like humorous gargoyles existing within the great structure's shadow (it is interesting to note that Hugo believed that printing and reading by the masses would lead to the end of the church building as a text in stone as people's ability to read its language would be lost). In his novel Hugo analysed the architecture of the city and its relationship to the cathedral, discussed attitudes towards conservation and also interpreted the Gothic as an expression of the liberty and fulfilment of the French nation:

> Upon the face of this ancient queen of French cathedrals, beside each wrinkle we constantly find a scar. *Tempus edax, homo edacior* (time is destructive, man more destructive) – which we would willingly render thus – Time is blind but man is stupid.

But as Hugo bemoaned the insensitive 'restorations' of the great Gothic buildings, a tide of such work was about to engulf the northern European countries. In France the inspiration behind many of these schemes (if not the actual work itself) came from Viollet-le-Duc. He was responsible for setting apart the Gothic as *le style* among *les styles*. His 'restorations', which now seem dubious, were based not on an actual past stage in the building's life, but on an idealised model.

For Viollet the Gothic was a celebration of technology and was 'flexing, free and questing like the modern spirit', in contrast to the classical which was static and immobile. His *Dictionnaire raisonné de l'architecture française* (1854–68), an encyclopedia of French Gothic architecture, and *Entretiens sur l'architecture* (1863–72), were seminal works. Despite his medievalising *oeuvre*, his rational theories and faith in technology (he appreciated machines in a way that was unheard of in England where they were the preserve of the engineer and the philistine, not 'high art') are a direct predecessor of the worship of technology and its use as a paradigm in Le Corbusier's *Vers une Architecture* and, once the stylistic trappings had been disposed of by his pupils, a fundamental impulse for the growth of Modernism. For a modern espousal of Viollet's views it is worth reading Jean Gimpel[6] who also advocated the theory that Western civilisation reached its greatest moment in the Middle Ages, and that the Renaissance merely saw the artist lifted to demi-god status and art replacing religion as the fundamental impulse.

The use of technology and new materials was the impetus that led to drastic changes in architecture. In England, while Deane and Woodward were building the Oxford University Museum using structural ironwork and Gothic decoration on the structure with the help of Ruskin, Louis-Auguste Boileau was building an iron church in Paris. At the Church of St Eugène (1854–5) Boileau used iron columns and iron vaulting ribs to create a Gothic structure of a lightness and slenderness that the medieval church builders would have greatly envied. The church was in a poor area of Paris and iron was used for reasons of economy rather than theory and, although it was not the first time that iron had been used for ecclesiastical architecture, it was the first time it had been used so visibly.

At the same time Victor Baltard was building Les Halles Centrales with its magnificent iron structure (comparable to the Crystal Palace in London), often cited as an early example of Rationalism. Yet his Church of St Augustin in Paris (1860–71), which also utilises structural iron, is a tragic blend of styles that dress the building in an eclectic sauce, disguising the flavour of its structure (which even features an iron dome). The Rationalism that could be brought to bear on a station or a market hall rarely made it intact through to churches.

This timidity when applying modern principles to church architecture prevailed until around the turn of the century when the crucial jumps were made. In France two buildings best illustrate the spectacular progress. The first of these is the Church of Notre-Dame-du-Travail, Paris (1899–1901), by Zacharie Astruc which finally utilised the unsentimental iron structures that had been defining the stations and sheds of the last half-century. The result is a powerful and light interior, bold and expressive, and a highly influential building that is completely articulated by its unadorned structure. But as this building was rising, another Paris church was in progress that would have even greater repercussions.

The mantle of structural innovation was moving from iron to concrete and Paris was firmly in the vanguard. Work had begun on St Jean de Montmartre in 1894. Although it was not finished until 1904 it proved a sensational building with which to open the century. Not only was it the first church to use reinforced concrete, it was perhaps the first building of any type to display its concrete structure so boldly and so proudly. Anatole de Baudot, a pupil of Viollet-le-Duc, designed it, and its execution is closer to a 20th-century Art Nouveau *oeuvre* than it is to neo-Gothic. The pointed arches are still apparent, but so are rounded arches. The architectural vocabulary expresses the structure more than the style. The use and celebration of structure remains faithful to Viollet-le-Duc's Gothic principles, and the use of new structural technology is also sympathetic to his ideals, but Baudot managed to shed the clutter and stylistic baggage that had bound architecture to the 19th century and ecclesiastical architecture to the Middle Ages. While François Hennebique pioneered concrete structures in the ensuing years in Paris it was left to Auguste Perret to take these developments in ecclesiastical architecture to a truly modern conclusion.

The scene in Europe at the turn of the century was cluttered with styles. Gothic, classical and neo-Renaissance vied with each other and innovation in ecclesiastical architecture was rare. The emerging Arts and Crafts Movement in Britain had a powerful effect on European architecture and encouraged architects to explore the vernacular, resulting in a spate of National Romantic buildings, while new styles emerged to take their place next to the established ones. Many fine churches had sprung from the Arts and Crafts Movement in an almost direct line from Butterfield's All Saints, Margaret Street, while a vein of largely stultifyingly dull Gothic continued to dominate British ecclesiastical design, along with a few other historical styles that cropped up less frequently but nevertheless regularly.

John Ninian Comper's uncluttered Gothic carried on the style and approach of his master, GF Bodley, resulting in some fine, simple spaces such as St Cyprian's, Clarence Gate, London (1901–3). He continued building in Gothic until the middle of the 20th century: St Mary's in Wellingborough, Northamptonshire, UK for instance, was not finished until 1950. Gothic was blended with Arts and Crafts to good effect at Holy Trinity, Sloane Street, London, by JD Sedding (1888–90) and other churches across the country with varying effects; some innovations were made, but usually only the familiar motifs and vernacular details were added to an already overcrowded stylistic catalogue of features.

Two huge cathedrals defined the turn of the century in Britain. The first of these was the Catholic Westminster Cathedral (1895–1903) designed by JF Bentley, a convert, as had been Pugin before him. Despite Pugin's zeal, the Catholic establishment and many of the new converts had been wary

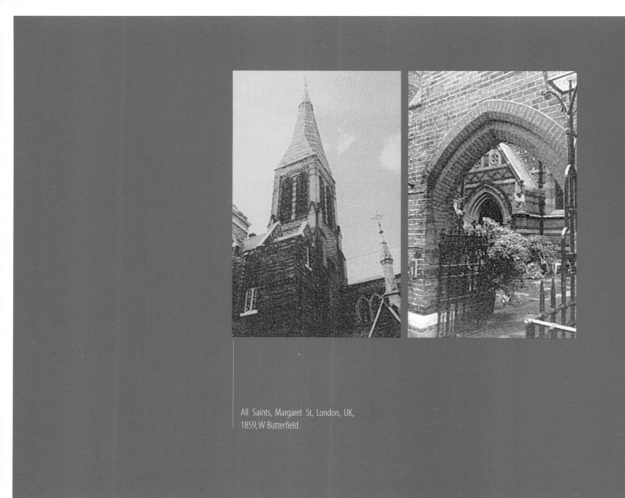

All Saints, Margaret St, London, UK,
1859, W Butterfield

of the Gothic that had become so associated with the Church of England over the past half-century. At Westminster a compromise was found between the Italian baroque of Herbert Gribble's Brompton Oratory and the nearby Westminster Abbey in the shadow of Pugin's Gothic parliament, the symbol of the established Anglican state. That compromise was a monumental Byzantine, perhaps influenced by Abadie's Sacré Coeur but wholly different, taking its cue as much from Norman Shaw's nearby Scotland Yard and its stripey bricks, the Hagia Sophia and Ruskin's beloved Venetian Gothic. It was a substantial building, boldly massed and with dark, cavernous interiors and a huge campanile.

The other structure that was taking shape was Giles Gilbert Scott's precocious design for Liverpool Cathedral. Scott, the grandson of Gilbert Scott (maltreater of many medieval churches and prolific architect), had entered a competition of which the rules decreed that all entries must be Gothic in execution. A wave of protest had ensued from architects to whom the idea of imposing a historical style seemed anathema. The 22-year-old Scott won and his design, a powerful composition in a stripped, stark, free Gothic matured as he developed until his death in 1960. It was only completed in 1978, probably the last cathedral to be made fully of stone and a fine epitaph to the great age of Gothic revival.

Although impressive these last great sighs of historicism proved a dead end. The historical revivals were no longer a part of any living theological impulse and lacked the vitality inherent in a movement that comes from within. Churches continued to be built all over the continent and the US in every conceivable revived style, but the energy and the future lay with the French structural innovators and the architects of the late Arts and Crafts in England. These were the link to the next phase, the century of Modernism.

II. ARTS AND CRAFTS

> The modern way of building must be flexible and vigorous, even smart and hard. We must
> give up designing the broken-down picturesque which is part of the ideal of make believe.
> The enemy is not science but vulgarity, a pretence to beauty at second-hand … Much has
> to be done; it is a time of beginning as well as of making an end.　　*WR Lethaby* [1]

William Morris could not be envisaged without John Ruskin, just as Lethaby owed a huge debt to Morris, but there was a century and a world between them. Morris' socialism and his violent reaction to the vulgarity and uselessness of the objects at the Great Exhibition led to his Arts and Crafts vision, a vision that inspired many pupils and followers. But whereas some of those followers became stuck in the pleasant pastoral and paternalistic idyll of Morris' *News from Nowhere*, Lethaby and a few others were able to free themselves from the vestiges of historicism and project their architecture into the 20th century.

Apart from Lethaby, the other critical figure in the move to a modern church idiom was Edward Prior. Prior designed two churches that embody a simplicity and clarity of intent that is in stark contrast to the highly decorated, fussy structures of even the Arts and Crafts architects, let alone the Gothic revivalists. The first of these was Holy Trinity, Bothenhampton (1884–9). The forms of the Gothic were retained in the pointed arch of the building's structural ribs and in the windows, but this was a powerfully elemental church. The structure alone defines the form of the building, which was the inspiration behind Prior's next church – St Andrew's, Roker.

This church (built 1906–7) was a response both to Prior's own rational architectural convictions and the new spirit of the Anglican Church that had, in places, begun once more to comprehensively examine its liturgy and rites in the wake of the excessive medievalism that had swept the country through the pervasive influence of the ecclesiologists. It had led to a heightened awareness of the word and the corporate nature of the mass. The excessive segregation of the clergy and the congregation which had resulted in chancel arches, half invisible altars shrouded in mists of incense, screens and choirs acting as barriers between the laity and the ordained was increasingly seen as unacceptable.

Prior's response was an austere church, devoid of distracting decoration and clearly focused on the altar. The space created is a stark barn defined by the huge structural ribs that form arches across the nave. All questions of style and decoration had been banished. The pointed form of the arches may be reminiscent of Gothic, and the architect was almost certainly influenced by Saxon forms, but these are abstracted to the extent that they melt into an organic image. Prior wrote that 'Church architecture, least of all, has been able to go beyond the trivial efforts of traditional picturesqueness; least of all our buildings has it been monumental'.[2] The sentiments precisely correspond with those of his friend, Lethaby, whose quote begins the chapter.

LEFT St Mary's, Wellingborough, Northamptonshire, UK, 1950, N Comper

RIGHT Westminster Cathedral, London, UK, 1903, JF Bentley

At St Andrew's, Prior made no effort to prettify the building. It is a tough church for an industrial, dockside community, and monumentality and presence is achieved through its scale and the solidity of its construction. Prior also used reinforced concrete in the arches and the roof structure in an early application of the material in English ecclesiastical work (Bentley was in fact using concrete for the domes at Westminster Cathedral at the same time). The only relief to the rough-textured austerity of the interior is the painted chancel ceiling, executed 20 years after the building's completion. An electric sun at its centre and a cosmological scheme of stars, creation and representations of the tree of life and Eden echo Lethaby's preoccupation with symbolism and the archetypal temple, a 'Ceiling like the Sky'.

This phrase is taken from Lethaby's book *Architecture, Mysticism and Myth* (1891), in which he attempts to survey the ancient civilisations and cultures and derive a typology of symbolic elements which he subsequently splits into common themes that run universally across cultures. It is a lyrical exploration of architecture as the embodiment of *Weltanschauung* and can help us understand the impetus behind his remarkable *oeuvre*

Lethaby, like his contemporary Adolf Loos in Austria, was concerned with the stripping down of ornament and a rational approach to building and construction. His writing presages Modernist manifestoes:

A gothic cathedral may be compared to a great cargo ship which has to attain a balance between speed and safety. The church and the ship were both designed in the same way by a slow perfecting of parts; all was effort acting on custom, beauty was mastery, fitness, size with economy of material.[3]

The comparison with the ship is reminiscent of Le Corbusier while the following leaves Loos ringing in our ears:

We must remember that beauty may be unadorned and it is possible that ornamentation, which arises in such arts as tattooing, belongs to the infancy of the world, and it may still be that it will disappear from our architecture as it has from our machinery.[4]

Loos' *Ornament and Crime* (1908) echoes these sentiments in precisely the same terms. But Lethaby is also something of a paradox. His writing is lyrical and exposes a depth of knowledge into primitive symbolism and archetypes that is more than a peripheral interest, yet his attitude to architecture is firmly practical to the extent that he preferred the term 'building' as it did not carry the same connotations as 'art'. It has often been pointed out that despite regarding himself as a humanist he advocated a severe and joyless architecture. But *Architecture, Mysticism and Myth* can be interpreted as a search for meaning in architecture that is independent of ornament but relies on a Jungian collective unconscious as the basis of a language of archetypal elements, the use of which will lead to a freeing of architecture from historicism and sham detailing due to the universal nature of the typology of the structures' fundamental elements. 'Old architecture lived because it had a purpose. Modern architecture, to be real, must not be a mere envelope without contents.'[5]

Of all his buildings, that which illustrates this point of view most clearly is his of All Saints, Brockhampton, of 1902. The building lies at the start of the 20th century and ushers in a new mode of thinking and a new architectural epoch. Lethaby's architectural swan song was his masterpiece. After the completion of this church he devoted himself entirely to teaching. The church is left to speak of his architectural vision and it does so eloquently. The space inside is one of primeval simplicity and is imbued with a curious sacrality that could belong to the temple of an ancient cult. It is a powerful expression of Lethaby's conviction that a truly Modern architecture could only emerge from a developing tradition in an evolutionary rather than a revolutionary way. Although his writings may lead the reader to assume that he would have become an ardent Modernist, this was not the case and he condemned Functionalism as 'a *style*, instead of seeking the truly modern, which expands and forms itself'. This church is his interpretation of the fruitful union of an evolving vernacular tradition, new building technology and his own symbolic leanings.

The first of these is addressed by a building – which very obviously fits into its Herefordshire vernacular context – the local medieval churches (and secular buildings such as barns) with their broad thatched roofs (Lethaby used thatch for its insulation, not for its picturesqueness) and muscular, squat, stone structures. The issue of technology is addressed by the building's construction, which consists of mass concrete vaulting with the marks of the formwork left proudly on show between the subtly curving triangular arches (derived from the same source as Prior's structures), which spring from low in the building's thick walls so that the building encloses the congregation like a great tent – the fabric of the canopy of the sky.

With this symbolic gesture Lethaby begins to address the third of the issues – that of symbolism. Perhaps most obviously the building is composed of a series of Platonic solids that come together

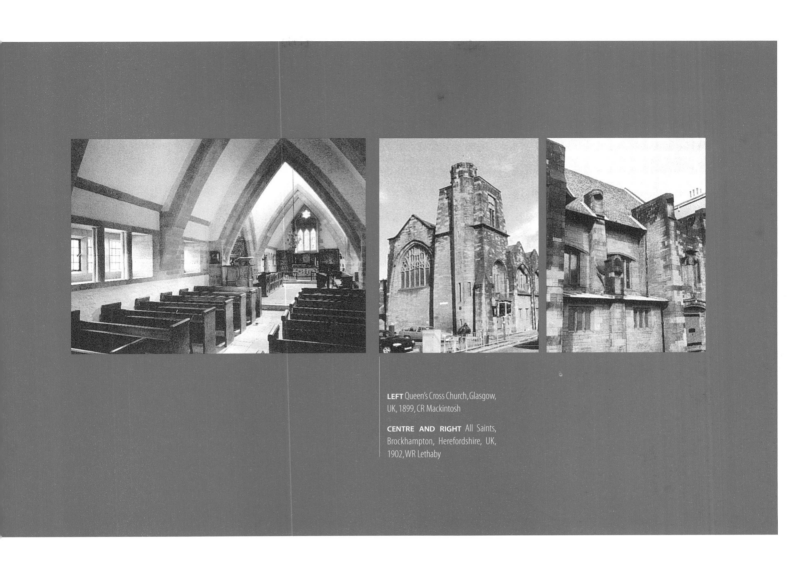

LEFT Queen's Cross Church, Glasgow, UK, 1899, CR Mackintosh

CENTRE AND RIGHT All Saints, Brockhampton, Herefordshire, UK, 1902, WR Lethaby

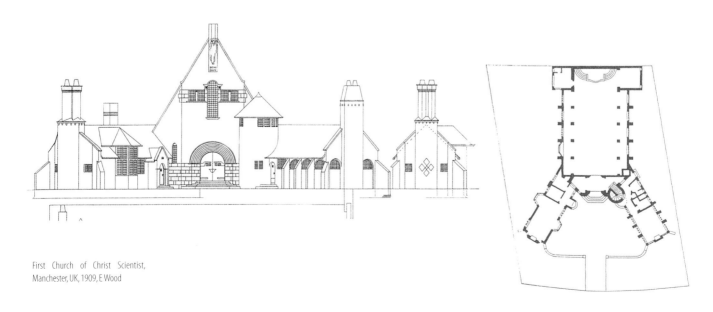

First Church of Christ Scientist, Manchester, UK, 1909, E Wood

like universal building blocks. The stumpy tower is formed by the stacking of two cubes crowned by a pyramid – all recurring forms which Lethaby explores in *Architecture, Mysticism and Myth* – the square as the symbol of strength and of the world itself. The tower, too, forms a cube, penetrating the roof, while the triple lancet window at the east end uses more conventional Christian imagery – giving parity to all parts of the trinity – and this is surmounted by a star, the symbol of Christ's birth and of the heavens themselves. A light fitting at the centre of the church (now removed) reinforced the cosmological theme as a visual representation of Lethaby's 'Jewel Bearing tree', or tree of light, while a robust stone font is carved with a tree of life or a sacred vine. Other aspects of the building contain the same attention to detail and relation to universal cosmological archetypes and world models that would constitute a book in themselves.

Lethaby explored these themes in two other ecclesiastical schemes. One was his competition entry for Liverpool Cathedral (1903), a cooperative effort with Henry Wilson, Halsey Ricardo, FW Troup and R Weir Schultz. This was a remarkable entry that defies classification except to say that it is an embodiment of Lethaby's symbolic preoccupations, incorporating elements of Byzantine, Islamic vernacular, and a bizarre Babel-like tower all intended to be executed in concrete. By far the most original of the entries and probably the least likely to win in view of the Gothic brief, it nevertheless remains an enigmatic image from a route that may have generated a whole new architecture.

The last of Lethaby's ecclesiastical works to be mentioned here was in fact his first: the Chapel of St Colm and St Margaret at Melsetter House on Hoy in the Orkney Islands. Lethaby designed Melsetter House in 1898, a scheme that involved the conversion of an old laird's house and some outbuildings. In 1900 he built a remarkable chapel for the house that incorporated many of the ideas he would later use at Brockhampton, including the use of the concrete roof (here covered in the local slate) and the triangular form of the structure. The font features a wavy relief symbolising the water, while sun, moon and cross adorn the keystone of the arched doorway in a simple display of Lethaby's preoccupation with cosmic and universal symbol systems. Structurally and architecturally it was an advanced design that incorporated elements of the local vernacular, the local prehistoric stone monuments, and modern building technology, a very successful and thoughtful scheme that could have augured well for a new direction in church building.

Of the other entries for the Liverpool Cathedral competition, the most interesting was that of Charles Rennie Mackintosh. Unlike Lethaby's entry, Mackintosh's was in a Gothic idiom and was a far less original design. It was, however, interesting in that it shed light on Mackintosh's regard for, and skill at using, the Gothic language to inform his own individualistic style. The architect managed to inject the subtle feel of the Secession into the gently tapering buttresses and the fine, modernised Gothic detail.

Mackintosh did in fact get a church built at Queen's Cross in Glasgow between 1897 and 1899. In this building can be seen the same respect for tradition and continuity that is apparent in his designs for the cathedral. Yet the design dates from a period when some of Mackintosh's greatest innovative masterpieces (hailed as precursors of Modernism by a maverick genius) were behind him, including the Glasgow School of Art. There are similarities between the art school and the church: both are plain and functional and relieved by thoughtful and exquisite detail. The modernity of Mackintosh's church lies in its simplicity and its bold, forthright structure. The church's tower is elegantly battered, which gives an attenuated Art Nouveau feel to an otherwise plain Gothic church, although Mackintosh's fine detailing is in evidence throughout (including the extruded flying buttress). A simple vaulted roof defines the internal space while the walls are tied together with riveted steel I-beams and the unfussy nave has an uninterrupted view of the altar with few distractions within the building.

The roof bears great similarity to another fine church by a less–known architect, the Unitarian Church, Middleton, by Edgar Wood, designed in 1892. This building is more highly decorated than Mackintosh's with exquisite symbolic carvings, a tree of life on the organ screen, and an idyllic agricultural mural engulfing the whole east end. This is very much a *fin-de-siècle* creation, unlike Wood's other important ecclesiastical commission, the First Church of Christ Scientist, Manchester (1903–9). Described by Pevsner as Expressionist, the building is an eclectic blend of influences from the US to Germany and Austria, which probably found its way back to influence architects in all those countries in turn.

The building is defined by a Y-shaped plan that is reminiscent of the 'Butterfly' plan that was popular with Arts and Crafts architects working in the domestic field. The arms of the Y outstretch to embrace the outside world and gather the congregation into a basilica-shaped church. The building's exaggeratedly high gable amplifies the domestic message (that this is a house of God), while a Venetian window set into it defines a cross at its centre. This is mixed with a Richardsonian Romanesque entrance arch and a curious, fairy-tale turret set to one side. It is a building that would be at home next to the most avant-garde developments on the continent, and despite its curious vernacular idiom it remains bold, sculptural and modern.

Other churches that grew from the Arts and Crafts Movement in Britain tended to be either spectacular bursts of fantasy, which were never followed up, or sober and worthy experiments that blended the muscular Gothic, that had garnered such a following with the Functionalist simplicity of Morris and his followers. Examples of the latter can be found in WH Bidlake's St Agatha's Church, Sparkbrook (1899–1901) and in the stark, modern vernacular of Lethaby's pupil, Randall Wells, particularly at the Church of St Edward the Confessor, Kempley (1903), where he develops the language of the diagonal grid windows seen at All Saints, Brockhampton. Edwin Lutyens used a stylish but ephemeral mix of Gothic and Arts and Crafts at St Jude's, Hampstead Garden Suburb (1909–13), in a pleasing piece of dramatic and picturesque folly wholly appropriate to its garden city location.

The other category – the explosive and visually stunning dead end of English Art Nouveau – is encapsulated in two spectacular churches both highlighted in Pevsner and JM Richards' book *The Anti-Rationalists* (1973). The first of these is Great Warley Church, by Charles Harrison Townsend (1904), architect of the Whitechapel Art Gallery, a seminal influence on European Art Nouveau. The church's rather unremarkable exterior gives way to an exuberant expression of the fecund organicism and swirling tendrils that define continental Art Nouveau but is usually only seen in a more restrained fashion in England. It is an embodiment of the symbolism of the tree of life executed with a lightness of touch that allows the church to breathe and remain a sacred space.

The tree of life and a less restrained palette of *fin-de-siècle* ornamentation overgrow the other building's interior: the Watts Chapel, Compton (1896) by Mary Watts. Built as a memorial to her husband, the artist GF Watts, the chapel is a symbolist fantasy; every inch of its interior covered in relief gesso work, an interminably intricate pattern of organic overgrowth. Curved walls inside give the impression of a fully circular building and of being engulfed in a grotto with walls of jewels. It is the symbolism and poetry of Lethaby's writing tempered by none of the restraint and rationalism of his architecture. The memorial chapel of an artist, in retrospect it may as well be the epitaph of a beautiful few years in architecture which died away later like the flame from a match, but which set souls on fire in Europe in what would prove an unstoppable blaze.

III. SECESSION: RATIONALISM AND NATIONALISM

After Friedrich Nietzsche had declared God dead, Otto Wagner executed the most eloquent epitaph. His Catholic Church of St Leopold am Steinhof in Vienna of 1907 is a Functionalist response to a brief that has become the generator of the building. The building was begun in the year Einstein published his special theory of relativity; it was a time of unprecedented rational and scientific questioning, of fundamental concepts being upturned, and new perceptions of time, space, God and man's place in the universe were emerging. Wagner had slowly lost his own faith in God over the preceding years;

> Up to my fifty-fifth year I believed in an unknown God. Later this God was forced to yield to an implacable fate until eventually the idea matured in me that man can have no faith and that after death his body simply returns to the earth … There is something extremely distressing about my theory concerning life after death but my reason obliges me to adhere to it.[1]

Ironically it was that very lack of faith that enabled him to interpret the brief in a rational and objective manner and consequently make the great leap forward into the 20th century. Church architecture had been shackled by the unquestioningly accepted language and clichés that were applied before the building's function had been seriously examined. With this detached analysis of the problems presented by the building of a Rational church, Wagner the unbeliever came closer to anticipating the reforms that swept continental church design in the 20th century than did any of his contemporaries. It is perhaps all the more ironic that the capital which produced Freud, the figure who exposed the hypocrisy and the dark depths of the subconscious of *fin-de-siècle* Europe, would play host to this church – in the grounds of a mental asylum and sanatorium.

Nietzsche (who himself ended his days in just such an asylum) had argued in *The Use and Abuse of History* (1873) that modern man was loaded down by the weight of history and that he was powerless to create or to express his individuality under this great burden. Otto Wagner was one of the first and possibly the most important architects to advocate the same abandonment of historicism in building:

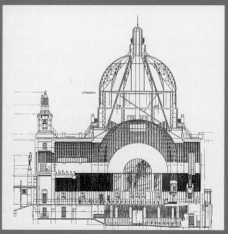

LEFT St Francis of Assisi, Šiška, Ljubljana, Slovenia, 1930, J Plečnik

CENTRE AND RIGHT St Leopold am Steinhof, Vienna, Austria, 1907, O Wagner

The task of art, and therefore also of modern art, has remained what it has been in all times. Modern art must offer us modern forms that are created by us and that represent our abilities and actions … All modern creations must correspond to the new materials and demands of the present if they are to suit modern man.[2]

Wagner successfully moved away from the historicism which was so characteristic of Vienna (although he himself had worked for Ludwig Förster on Ringstrasse buildings) and transcended the raging stylistic debates to create a clean, 'Modern Architecture' the aims of which are proclaimed in his book of that name. The Church of St Leopold am Steinhof was among his most important designs and is roughly contemporary with his Post Office Savings Bank, a building revolutionary in its clarity, simplicity, the modernity of its elevations and its light, airy interior. The church is very much its ecclesiastical counterpart, a breath of fresh air between the formulaic Gothic and baroque creations that dominated European church building at the time. This is a practical not a mystical church. JA Lux wrote in his biography of Wagner (1914): 'Whoever believes that the mystical-religious impulse is nurtured in the semi-darkness of a poorly ventilated, cold, damp interior is brilliantly contradicted by Wagner's building.'[3]

The church consists of a single central space defined by a Greek cross plan (with an extended vestibule), as did his earlier chapel in Währing (1895) and his plans for the conversion of a Capuchin church (1898). The structure is a single span crowned by a great cupola, which gives a volume free from structural interventions and distractions. All pews subsequently have a good view of the raised altar and the floor is very slightly raked to improve visual contact further. The pews are designed in rows of four so that patients can be quickly removed in case of illness or fits. Male and female patients entered through separate doors on either side of the church and a first-aid room and toilets were planned in the basement. A gallery allows relatives to attend Mass segregated from the patients.

The space is light and white inside; Koloman Moser's stained glass provides much of the lighting and the presbytery is lit from the side to avoid glare. The holy water stoup takes the form of a fountain of running water as a device to stop the spread of infection; a gesture typical of the architect's approach to a hygienic building. The decoration is entirely integral to the building; mosaics, metalwork and chandeliers combine in a great Viennese *Gesamstkunstwerk*. An intricate copper baldachin highlights the altar while a profusion of angels in every media looks on. Outside, more angels are perched atop four columns which define the main entrance, while above a gilded dome glitters, flanked by a pair of sculpted saints elevated on twin towers so that the effect of the church, which already stands upon a hilltop, is even more magnificent. The church achieves the monumental and the modern, beauty, practicality and even economy. Wagner calculated the costs of various church plans and thus came to the conclusion that the 'gasometer' design was the most economical in terms of visibility of the altar and construction cost. It was a conclusion that others would come to again later in the century.

Vienna was undoubtedly the heart of Modernism at the turn of the century. Although the original impulse may have come from Britain, it had lost its way, shambling back into conservatism, and only a few lonely figures retained any semblance of innovation. Vienna's position at the hub of a cosmopolitan empire ensured a constant flow of talent into the capital and the best of these young architects gravitated to Wagner's progressive studio. Of these, by far the most original in terms of ecclesiastical design was a young Slovene, Josef Plečnik. Unlike the master, Plečnik retained his faith, to the extent that he devoted his life to God and architecture as if he were a monk. In fact he compared the role of an architect to that of a priest doing good work for the congregation.

Plečnik's first important church was a commission he obtained while still in Vienna in 1908. The Church of the Holy Spirit (1910–13) was to be a meeting place and chapel for Christian Socialists in a poor Vienna suburb. In plan, the church was not innovative: a standard rectangle with the altar at the far end, its section roughly that of a basilica, although the galleries are cantilevered rather than being supported on arcades creating the familiar aisles, but Plečnik's use of concrete was to prove highly influential.

The elevation is an abstracted Greek temple; the language of the columns has been further simplified into a blocky mass. The crypt is supported on angular columns which were to prove a pivotal influence in the development of a Cubist language in architecture in the Czech lands in the years before the First World War. (This itself was the impetus for a number of interesting church designs which, although resembling a form of Expressionism, were mainly confined to elevational modelling exercises). It was an important early use of concrete as a building material and an acknowledgement of its potential as a raw finish.

ABOVE Church of the Sacred Heart, Prague, Czech Republic, 1933, J Plečnik

BELOW St Michael's, Barje, Ljubljana, Slovenia, 1938, J Plečnik

His next church, however, was a more complete project. He was called upon to build a church at Šiška in Ljubljana (1925–30), his home town. The building shows a development of Plečnik's classical vocabulary, which he used in such an intense and individual way that it cannot be called neoclassical or eclectic and certainly bears no relation to the facile wit of Postmodernism, of which he has been hailed as one of the first proponents.

The Church of St Francis of Assisi is based on a square plan with no distracting side chapels and the altar reaches into the congregation to bring them closer to the celebration. The raised altar is an echo of Wagner's functional preoccupation with view but there is none of the cold aloofness that is so apparent with Plečnik's old professor. Outside, the church is a curious blend of Palladio and a Slovenian Mannerism that Plečnik was developing. His work at Prague Castle had shown his incredible talent with composition and detail; every facet of the building was treated with equal reverence resulting in an infinitely satisfying, organic whole. By the time the church was finished, Plečnik had almost completed his ecclesiastical masterpiece, the Church of the Sacred Heart in Prague (1922–33).

This building has an almost absurd presence on the Prague skyline. Its immense belfry protrudes like a looming headstone, a massive *memento mori* with an over-scaled clock at its heart counting away the seconds of our short lives, flanked by two attenuated metronomes.

The sheer brick walls are relieved only by a pattern of shadow caused by raised stones, apparently in an effort to mimic ermine, an emulation of the sacred robes and perhaps a nod to Gottfried Semper's symbolic typology of wall as textile or skin. Inside, the plain walls are relieved by tiny golden crosses, which echo the patterns outside, yet do not distract from the monumental unity of the space. Here, too, the sanctuary and the altar are brought into the body of the church; the space that remains before them is a square. The walls of the church are plain brick while above, a row of windows is set into the frieze. The altars too are plain; veined pale marble articulated using Plečnik's favourite device, the column.

 The altar itself is a slab of marble supported on those same columns and enclosed at the sides and back. The device of the columns as legs alludes to the altar's role as table (and the open space behind to its role of reliquary), while to Plečnik the column represented the body, the humanist notion of man as the mark of all things, so it is appropriate that the mensa is supported on columns; as Rudolf Schwarz pointed out, the altar used to be regarded as the body of Christ. Side altars are set diagonally into the corners, each supported on a single column placed at its centre – a recurring device of the architect (and his successor Otto Rothmayer) and one that symbolises his eccentric and distinctly anti-Rational approach to the classical language. Another columned altar appears in the tunnel-like crypt, a space defined by one continuous vault creating both ceiling and walls, like the canopy of the encompassing sky.

These are Plečnik's most urbane churches. Those further from the city centres speak another architectural language, a pan-Slavic vernacular blended with his own quirky classicism. For Plečnik, architecture was a language which, like the spoken word, expresses the nature and character of the people. He was concerned to articulate a Slovenian artistic expression in his buildings and consequently referred to those influences that he saw as best defining the local character. His obsession with Ionic columns derives from crude vernacular capitals that can be found on ancient Slovenian buildings, which show an abstracted but instantly recognisable Ionic order. This is blended with the characteristic steep pitched roofs and the misleadingly naive mix of classical and local vocabularies that form the language of his work. This expression is exemplified by his Church of the Ascension, Bogojina (1925–7), the 'gasometer' Byzantine of his St Anthony of Padua, Belgrade (1929–32) and exquisite interventions into existing structures including the Church of St Michael in the Marsh, Crna (1938–9).

Apart from these, one of Plečnik's other works that stands out is the remarkable Church of St Michael, Barje (1937–8), a church planned so that it is much wider than it is long. The space has the intimacy of a log cabin and the altar is placed at the heart of the congregation in a move which presages some of the changes that would be advocated two decades later. The church is approached by a symbolic, long stair and entered through an oddly punctured bell tower of rough rubble. Lined with columns/banisters the ascent is reminiscent of the processional route of the Via Appia in Rome, its culmination the steps which rise to the altar.

Finally, mention must be made of Plečnik's necropolis. After having as much effect on a city (Ljubljana) as any one architect ever has, he created a city for the dead nearby. His unusual necropolis can be read like a history of architecture and entombment. It is a surreal realisation of Loos' contention in *Architecture* (1910) that: 'Only a very small part of architecture belongs to art –

tombstones and monuments. Everything else that serves a particular purpose must be excluded from the realms of art'. In those terms this becomes an absurd art gallery, an anti-Rational manifesto and a place of immense beauty and power.

Plečnik was not alone in his desire to create an architectural language which could encapsulate a national character. It was a fundamental concern of many architects across the continent at the turn of the century. Again, the impulse can be seen as having sprung from the Arts and Crafts Movement in Britain with its incessant longing for a style which was both functional and derived from local conditions, traditions and materials. It can be seen as a rational development, one which relied on a Darwinian response to the environment. But often it was more a yearning for national expression and a defiance of a foreign authority. The achievements of these National Romantic architects were often greatest where there was most to rebel against. Plečnik's example makes an ideal beginning; countries come little smaller than Slovenia. But many others had architects keen to develop a new National Romantic vocabulary and while the movements produced much architecture that was whimsical and irrelevant, much was also created that was of lasting value and great innovation.

Like Plečnik, István Medgyaszay had worked in Otto Wagner's office. Also like Plečnik, he later strove to find an architectural expression of his people's existence. Medgyaszay was a Hungarian who made his life's mission the creation of an architectural language which was derived from the folk art of his nation but which used new techniques of construction to carve out a modern architectural genre. He had also worked in the offices of François Hennebique, the leading French advocate of reinforced concrete. Medgyaszay became an important (though largely forgotten) innovator in concrete design and specifically the use of prefabricated elements.

His church at Rárosmulyad (1909–10) – now Mul'a, Slovakia – is a masterpiece of modern church design. Built entirely from reinforced concrete and to an octagonal plan which ensures the full participation of the congregation, it is a remarkable and prophetic edifice. The tower evokes the image of the spires of the timber folk churches of the area while the shallow dome of the church (surrounded by sculpted angels) recalls Wagner's planned chapel at Währing of 1898. That same church was the inspiration for Vjekoslav Bastl's design for the Church of Saint Blaise at Zagreb of 1901, although the design of Viktor Kovačič which was finally realised (1912) evokes a more Byzantine feel, perhaps closer to the intense Orthodox feeling of the period which saw the outbreak of the First World War in the Balkans.

Three other Hungarians made a significant impact on church design; Ödön Lechner, Károly Kós and Aladár Árkay. Lechner's churches at Kőbánya (Budapest, 1893–8) and Bratislava (Saint Elisabeth, 1907–13) are further explorations in his search for a Hungarian national style, comparable in their extravagance and originality to his contemporary Antoni Gaudí. The Church of Saint Elisabeth features an oval plan and a single, impressive domed space with an eccentric strap-work belfry at its side. Kós worked in a National Romantic genre which was inspired by the British Arts and Crafts Movement and designed a subtle, folky church in Zebegény (1908–9) in a self-effacing vernacular; a handsome building. Árkay dealt in a more monumental national style very much influenced by Lars Sonck in Finland and developments towards a Byzantine Modernism in the US. Árkay's masterpiece, the Reformed Church in Budapest (1912) is a true *Gesamstkunstwerk* in the vein of Otto Wagner: a single great space with a domed roof, adorned with abstracted folk motifs centred firmly on a raised pulpit set into a recess beneath the organ. Every detail of the church is thoughtful and convincing.

The Finnish architect who was an inspiration to many of the Hungarians was at the forefront of the search for a national style along with his contemporary Eliel Saarinen. Lars Sonck's Tampere Cathedral (1902–7) is an abject essay in mass and material, a robust mountain of stone and a highly influential work, while Saarinen was to come to prominence in church building later. Elsewhere in Scandinavia two buildings in Stockholm stirred much interest. LI Wahlman's Engelbrecht Church (1904–14) was a kind of ecclesiastical answer to Berlage's modern handling of brick to contain monumental yet functional spaces which presaged the romantic yet rational work of Raynar Ostberg. Inside, huge parabolic brick vaults anticipate the forms of the Expressionists in Germany. Its elegant tower is clearly based on northern European precedents yet its stark simplicity recalls the Arts and Crafts; a fine landmark building.

Ivar Tengbom's Högalid Church (1918–23) explores similar territory but with references to an attenuated brick baroque. Most remarkable of all the Scandinavian churches is undoubtedly the Grundtvig Church in Copenhagen. Designed by PV Jensen Klint in 1913 and built 1921–6, it spans the periods of Arts and Crafts, National Romanticism and Expressionism in a single great stride. The rugged, stepped massing is derived from traditional Danish models but appears like a looming exaggerated organ. The building's sheer verticality and physical expression of the ascent towards the heavens is clearly Gothic in emotion but not in style. The building becomes a kind of stylised mountain in an interesting parallel to the visions of the early Expressionists and their obsession with crystal mountains as the palaces of a new society. It is a wonderful creation that bridges the centuries and augurs a new approach to mass, monumentality and form.

IV. GAUDÍ: A RATIONAL EXPRESSIONISM OF PIETY

Gaudí's incredible Expiatory Church of the Sagrada Família in Barcelona combines the mysticism and structural rationalism which defined the Gothic and an expressionism, piety and nationalism which was purely his own. Its genesis was as a neo-Gothic church but, in the hands of Gaudí, it became the most noteworthy monument to the turbulent cultural and intellectual upheaval that occurred at the turn of the 20th century. The church is very much in the tradition of the *Gesamstkunstwerk* from which Wagner's St Leopold am Steinhof also sprang but even closer to the impetus which spurred the construction of the great Gothic cathedrals, not the rational, functional response of Wagner but a desire to create a monument reaching for heaven, a Bible in stone.

Gaudí, who took over the project in 1884, had been heavily influenced by the writings of Viollet-le-Duc and his quest for a reinterpretation of Gothic forms using modern technology to overcome the structural problems that the medieval builders were unable to conquer because of the limitations of stone. In the Sagrada Família he applied the principle of the parabolic arch as a successor to the Gothic flying buttress, a superior form, stronger with an inherent strength and which could be constructed with the skill of the stonemasons who Gaudí admired. But as well as

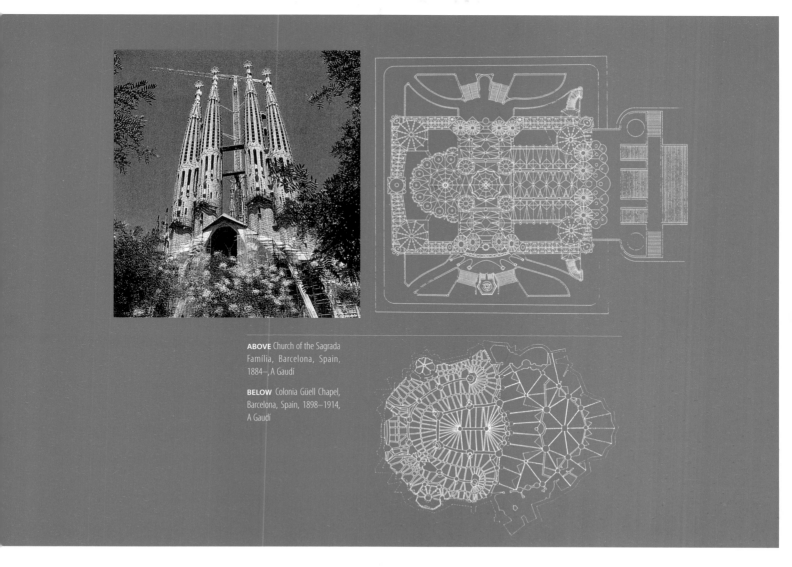

ABOVE Church of the Sagrada Família, Barcelona, Spain, 1884–, A Gaudí

BELOW Colonia Güell Chapel, Barcelona, Spain, 1898–1914, A Gaudí

the structural impetus, Gaudí was driven by an intense passion for God and for his Catalan nation. In this he stands close to Josef Plečnik who carved out a Slovenian architecture from his religious fervour and his monk-like devotion to his nationality. Thus, the Sagrada Família has become a land-mark and an icon that both defines and is defined by Barcelona.

The first religious building in which Gaudí's approach becomes clear is the Chapel at the Colonia Güell (1898–1914), a writhing mass of twisted stone in which each element is unique and sculpted according to its position in the overall scheme and the loads and stresses which are imposed on it. It acts like a great organism adjusting its body until it finds the most comfortable position and, as in an organism, each part fulfils a function, nothing is superfluous. The ideas reach fruition in the Sagrada Família, which mixes its metaphors between skeleton and forest temple. The structural elements appear like the bones of the building while the columns of the nave lean in towards the centre like the canopy of trees in the romantic interpretation of the origin of the Gothic arch. The church is a *Biblia Pauperum*, a whole language of symbolism fossilised in a stone that looks like it might burst forth into life at any moment. The 12 soaring spires represent the apostles, their twisting forms metamorphosing into trees, mitres and crucifixes *en route* to the heavens. Sculpture, text and organic decoration envelop every surface in a fantastic recreation of the Gothic spirit.

It is an unprecedented construction: from some angles it can look like the sticky mess of chewing gum on a shoe straining to stretch between the sole and the earth; from others like a cry of genius rising from the soul to the heavens. Its mere presence cannot but exert an influence on anyone who sees it. The ambition and wild expressionism, which stemmed from a fanatical piety, would have a lasting effect on architecture from Le Corbusier to South America and the wonderful work of Felix Candela and Eladio Dieste.

Cathedral of Socialism, 1919, L Feininger

V. GERMAN EXPRESSIONISM
The Star and the Sacred Mountain

When Walter Gropius' Bauhaus manifesto appeared in 1919, Lyonel Feininger's *Cathedral of Socialism* adorned its cover; a fragmented, sparkling image of a Gothic cathedral, the shining stars of the trinity burning brightly atop the three spires and emitting rays of light to illuminate the world. It was a metaphor for the enlightenment which was to be found in this new movement, this new school of thought.

The background against which this manifesto appeared was one of chaos and a crumbling society. Germany had lost a crippling war, had suffered a crushing blow to national pride, and its economy was spiralling out of control towards oblivion. There was a frantic search for a model, a utopia to be aspired to. Encouraged by the success of the Russian Revolution, socialism was gathering popularity as a response to a desperate situation. Artists began looking both at the alienation of the individual, the scream from within characterised by Munch's masterpiece and Søren Kierkegaard's existentialism, and the coming together of individuals to create a society and an art which was greater than the sum of its parts; an achievement which would express the unity of mankind in a single, synchronised outburst of artistic creativity moulded into plastic form, an ambition embodied for some in the Gothic cathedral.

Just as Pugin had envisaged his utopia on the frontispiece of his *Apology for the Revival of Christian Architecture* (1843) as a medieval city, an idealised urban landscape punctuated by a proliferation of spiky Gothic towers, so the Bauhaus used the image of Gothic architecture to personify their vision of a utopian ideal. It is a northern European ideal, a picture of the medieval society that created the Gothic cathedrals as a high point of Western civilisation, free of the Machiavellian cynicism of the Renaissance and the notion of the artist as inspired demi-urge, a lone maverick genius. The Gothic represents the ideal of art as a communal achievement; the individual subsumes his will into the work until it becomes one great collective cry of creativity.

The Bauhaus itself was created in the image of a medieval guild, partly inspired by the English model of the Guild of Handicrafts and Lethaby's Art Workers' Guild. (Lethaby, who we have already encountered here, had said that 'No art that is only one man deep can be worth much'.)[1] The socialism of the pioneers of the Arts and Crafts Movement in Britain, from Morris to Lethaby himself, can also be seen as a direct influence on the emerging German idealists. The peculiar blend of Gothic imagination and imagery, which constitutes the Expressionist language and the Functionalist aesthetic that emerged from the Bauhaus and from the nascent European Modern Movement, seems paradoxical but the two are inextricably linked.

There are two parallel strands which permeated German architecture around the period of the First World War and which would have resounding repercussions in the emergence of Modernism. There was the rational architecture of Peter Behrens, whose workshop was a breeding ground for some of the most forward-thinking young architects (including Le Corbusier), which, despite its popular associations with Functionalism, was perhaps more closely related to Schinkel's classicism than to Lethaby. This was an *architecture parlante* in the vein of the French revolutionary architects; it could evoke power when needed, or strength and reliability, or the rational process of a factory production line.

The other vein was a plastic Expressionism. This approach generally had little affinity with Functionalism and, as a concrete proposition it is perhaps best exemplified by the work of Hans Poelzig. His was architecture close to the Expressionism of the artist's canvas, architecture as experience, a sculptural and emotional response. What is surprising is that the two approaches met in a brief union. What is perhaps more surprising is that the arena in which they met most fruitfully was sacred architecture.

We have seen that the image of the church, or more precisely the cathedral, was one that helped to define the early Expressionism of Modernism. The image can be seen in its Expressionist manifestation at the heart of Fritz Lang's film *Metropolis* (1926): a nightmare society is saved from doom through cooperation of workers and bosses brought about by love and basic human contact. Technology and Rationalism brought to their extremes by a wicked overlord constitute the enemy. Redemption is found through a heroine who preaches from an underground chapel; the finale takes place on the roof of the great Gothic cathedral, image of the city itself (see Victor Hugo, p 10), while reconciliation takes place outside its doors.

The genesis of this vision of Gothic and the centrality of the cathedral to man's mystical yearnings can be traced back in artistic terms to the Romanticism of Caspar David Friedrich. His painting *Cross and Cathedral in the Mountains* (1813) shows an image in sympathy with the prevalent

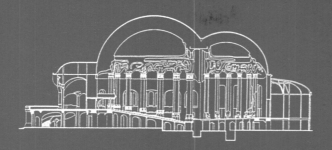

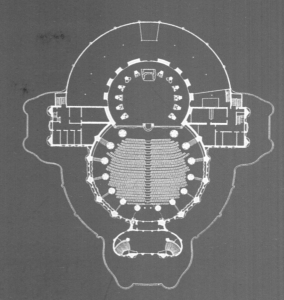

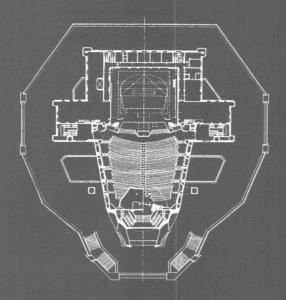

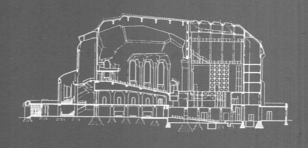

TOP Goetheanum, Dornach, Switzerland, 1920,
R Steiner

CENTRE Goetheanum, Dornach, 1928

BOTTOM Sternkirche project, 1922, O Bartning

mysticism of German Expressionism. Nature, the landscape, the trees and the soaring Gothic spire combine in an image that is both overtly Christian and dubiously pantheistic.

In *Abbey under Oak Trees* the Gothic in question is a ruin, a single lancet window standing as a testament to a lost civilisation and to the permanence of God as a fragment in the landscape, at once within it and part of it. Like Plečnik's rogue single columns (like the cross, the column represents the figure of man, a humanist reaction to Wagner's Rationalism), the image is always centred, the cross, the spire always define the focus, just as the spire dominates the centre of Feininger's woodcut *The Cathedral of Socialism*. This is an expression both of the centrality of the church as a binding force in a society that finds itself increasingly decentred and alienated, and as a reinforcement of the idea of mysticism at the centre of creation, an unknowable force.

This mysticism included elements from Indian cults and from the highly influential cult of theosophy. The oriental ideal of an architecture that embodied a fusion between the inner yearnings of the soul and the form of the building, an existential sculpture, was particularly attractive to the Expressionists. Also attractive to them was an oriental spiritualism, which was woven into Rudolf Steiner's cult of anthroposophy, a development of theosophy. The aim of Steiner's cult was in essence to allow man to discover new levels of spirituality and to open up new worlds beyond the physical plane through adherence to the principles of anthroposophy. Steiner was not himself an architect but he nevertheless designed two buildings that would have a lasting influence on both ecclesiastical and secular architecture. The buildings took the form of temples dedicated to Goethe, who was seen as a spiritual father of the cult.

The first of these (Dornach, 1913–20) was a timber building of two great domes on a concrete structure, the columns and elements of which featured variations in form on a pattern attributed to Goethe's theories of metamorphosis. The walls are created in such a way that they dissolve into the whole and cease to be barriers. The plan-form of the circle was adopted because of its symbolic representation of the whole and of completeness. The second circle was added to interlock with the first and create a resolved directionality which would avoid the tensions inherent in straight-sided forms, or the incessant revolution implied by the unbroken circle. His experiments with the circular form would have an influence on other architects who began to address the problem of the plan-form of a building to express both spirituality and community.

The first building succumbed to fire and a second Goetheanum was erected, also at Dornach, between 1924 and 1928. Radically different in conception from the first building, this was a sculptural creation in reinforced concrete. Steiner used to mould clay with his hands to create models, and the appearance of the building is precisely as if it had been formed in such a way. It is an organic architecture in that each piece relates to the others and the orthogonal; the straight-sided and any trace of angularity have been banished. It is a remarkable display of what can be achieved

LEFT Circumstantes project, 1923, D Böhm

RIGHT Church of Christ the King, Mainz-Bischofsheim, Germany, 1926, D Böhm in the medium of concrete and an immensely powerful building which has exerted an effect on architecture comparable to the curiously organic effect of its elephantine mass on the landscape. Steiner claimed his architecture was an illustration of 'the spiritual evolution of mankind'. It was this evocation, the expression of an inner spirituality, which would have such a far-reaching influence.

Steiner's structures derive from the same impetus as the early visionary sketches of the Expressionists. At the centre of these visions is a single structure, usually of crystalline or vaguely Gothic form, the function of which is often unclear. The one type of building which crops up in these sketches most frequently is the church. As a building type it has a mysticism and an elemental quality which was an attractive image. But these early pioneers saw the task as deeper than one of merely using the church as a convenient and universal archetype. It was used as a metaphor for the community, a single building that would express the will of the people. It is a Platonic vision of the cathedral as a representation of a higher order, the collective will. It also conveys a pure Platonic beauty, the embodiment of a detached, ethereal ideal. As Bruno Taut wrote in *Alpine Architecture* (1919):

> The cathedral and its side aisles are filled with cool daylight. At night, however, its light shines forth into the Mountains and the Heavens … The purpose of the Cathedral? None – if prayer in the midst of beauty is not sufficient.[2]

One of the first and most successful architects to translate these disparate and often incohesive ideas into a body of work that contributed significantly to the development of ecclesiastical architecture was Otto Bartning. In the same year as the Bauhaus manifesto appeared, Bartning wrote that a pious person found his way to church out of:

> a conscious or unconscious need to immerse his ego in the great melting pot of the community – in the hope, not only to unite his voice with a thousand other voices in the same words but to lend his outcry from the depths of despair a thousand tongues and a thousand mouths.[3]

Thus the mysticism (the faith in an unknown and unknowable force), the socialism (the immersion of the individual into the greater being of the community) and the visionary new form of architecture with which to express the new ideals in the new shapes and materials (the glass architecture of Paul Scheerbart and Taut, and the crystalline cathedrals which litter the sketchbooks of Expressionists) come together in the form of the church.

This collective expression of the communal ideal as an architectural generator coincided with increasing interest in the Liturgical Movement in Germany, the aims of which were fundamentally in sympathy with the move towards architecture as an expression of unity. A slightly fuller examination of the Liturgical Movement is made later in this introduction; here it will suffice to say that it was a movement from within the Church towards a different kind of worship space; one which would increase the participation of the congregation in the Mass and decrease the alienation of the laity from the clergy. While this movement primarily came from within the Catholic Church, architects like Bartning, who was a Protestant, were coming to similar conclusions and a notion of 'unanimous space'. The Gothic was again the model (in idealistic and societal if not liturgical terms), as it seemed the result of a community working in harmony towards a common ideal (in contrast to the bitter fragmented contemporary German society which had been torn apart by war and poverty). But the architecture that sprang from the German debates was far from the historicism of the 19th century. It was a genuinely new expression created through a slowly emerging understanding of the capabilities of new materials, a sculptural and emotional approach to space, and the re-examination of the nature of worship and ritual.

Otto Bartning's churches developed from the same impulses that inspired Taut and the crystalline fantasies of Scheerbart. Taut's Glashaus pavilion for the Deutsche Werkbund in 1914 was illustrated in the accompanying pamphlet, captioned with the phrase 'The Gothic cathedral is the prelude to glass architecture'. The building was one of the first manifestations of the crystal mountain that appears in Taut's own drawings and those of his contemporaries. Until then, these fantasies had been confined to paper, more symbolic images than concrete proposals. Bartning was one of the first to develop them into three dimensions and to visualise them as buildings with functions: churches.

Whereas the Taut brothers, Wenzel Hablik, Wassili Luckhardt and the others had given these glass mountains spurious names, or simply labelled them 'monuments', Bartning saw that this vision could be translated into a functioning type, a church which would inspire and unite, achieving the lofty ideals of the Expressionists while steering clear of the rational, materialist, positivist approach of the Functionalists. His project for a stellar church (Sternkirche) in 1922 is a remarkable example to begin with. Constructed of a series of shells formed around a circular plan, this is one of the most visionary church designs of the century. Its conception can perhaps be seen in the prose of Bruno Taut. An article which appeared in the Expressionist magazine *Frühlicht* (edited by Taut himself, 1920–2),4 contains the following extract:

> The visitor will be filled with the joy of architecture, which will drain all human elements from his soul and make it a receptacle for the divine. Building is the reflection and the greeting of the stars: its plan is stelliform, the holy numbers 3 and 7 combine in it to form a unity … the illumination comes from between the interior and exterior glass shell … it shines from afar like a star. And it rings like a bell.

Bartning used the star shape with which Taut was also enamoured to create the structure for his church. Structural ribs, which support the shell, define the points on the plan; these could be described as resembling the articulated back of an armadillo with glazing between the joints. Steps push outwards from the form like ripples in water and elevate the building until its image becomes familiar as the embodiment of the crystal mountain from the sketches. The mystical obsession with the magic power of numbers referred to in the text is here applied to the building's structure; seven bays create the internal space while the sanctuary is supported by three piers in a bay which departs from that unit seen elsewhere. The design is the personification of Johannes van Ackern's vision: 'Now trigger the process off by adding Christ, which must be a clear and purposive liturgical awareness of Christ, and the whole will grow into the new and powerful crystal unity.'5

Although it is a beautiful and visionary structure, the true significance of the design lies at its heart: the altar. The plan is centralised and symmetrical and the altar is at its centre in a radical departure from the orthodoxy. From the *Cathedral of Socialism* is derived the socialist cathedral. This is a building in which the congregation surrounds the altar, the church is brought to the people; the crystal mountain has come to Mohammed.

The other revolutionary feature at the heart of the building is the pulpit. One of the long-standing problems of Protestant church architecture had been the positioning of the pulpit relative to the altar. Bartning's remarkable solution was to create two scenarios within the same building. In one variation the congregation would face the pulpit at its centre while the altar stood above. The move to an altar-centred space was achieved by the worshippers physically moving around so that the altar dominates while the pulpit is lowered away so as not to interfere and, thus, the crowd partakes in a symbolic journey or pilgrimage around the space. The floor dips towards the pulpit in a rake (the symbolic valley) and rises around the altar, a metaphor for the mountain: altar as extension of the earth while the canopy of the sky and the forest of vaults and columns form the covering. Some of these remarkable ideas were later realised at Bartning's Church of the Resurrection at Essen.

Although the Sternkirche remained a paper project its influence was felt strongly and some of the innovations inherent in the scheme were realised by the other towering figure of Expressionist and Modern church design in Germany, Dominikus Böhm. In the same year as Bartning's proposal, Böhm designed a scheme which was sadly also destined to remain a sketch; the Circumstantes. This was an elliptical church with the altar where you would expect the stage to be in a theatre. The structural piers all point towards the altar, as if defining some mystical energy emanating from the heart of the building. An arched baldachin surmounts and emphasises the altar in the midst of the cavernous space while in elevation the building is almost reminiscent of the Tower of Babel.

A number of other buildings that were executed display a remarkable Expressionism. Böhm's St John the Baptist, Neu-Ulm (1926), is executed in a brooding, powerful Gothic Expressionism with a wonderfully mystical cave of a baptistery. The interiors of his Church of Christ the King in Mainz-Bischofsheim (1925–6) and the Parish Church at Freilingsdorf (1926–7) are defined by curious triangular Gothic pointed arches that spring from floor level. These vaults are in fact of concrete on an iron-mesh framework, which is itself suspended from the steel structure; theatricality was a greater concern than Functionalism. Wolfgang Pehnt has compared the shape of these vaults to Lethaby's All Saints Church in Brockhampton and, while the structural integrity and honesty that obsessed Lethaby is wholly missing, there is no mistaking the shape or the concerns about mystical archetypes which the architects obviously shared. Böhm's sketch for Christ the King, Kuppersteig, of 1928, also presents a powerful vision of a great, single parabolic vault covering an undeniably impressive, cavernous space.

The parabolic vault which replaced the almost triangular vault in Böhm's work reached its apex in his design for the Church of St Engelbert, Riehl (1930). In one of the most influential buildings of its era, Böhm created a perfectly circular church; the first modern Catholic church freed from the tyranny of the rectangular plan. The points of Bartning's Sternkirche have evolved into great arches,

almost disappearing as thin piers on plan. The body of the church is left free for corporate worship; the ancillary functions including baptism and the campanile are banished to the side for the sake of clarity while other rooms are housed beneath the building (there is also a community centre beneath; this was a popular facility at the time in Germany and a reflection of the ideal of the church's role as *Volkshaus*). The uninterrupted space leaves the congregation free to concentrate on the service without distraction while the circular plan brings them into a closer and less hierarchical union with the altar. The altar, however, is set in a small sanctuary in a recess from the main circle and is reached by a series of steps; thus Böhm deliberately retains the directionality of the building, the idea of ritual procession and progression towards the altar while maintaining the unity of the congregation.

This is fundamentally a church belonging to the Modernist tradition but its form is so spectacular that it merits its place with the Expressionists, as do many of Böhm's other designs. Huge parabolic arches of reinforced concrete meet to form a structures that is as unusual as that of a perpendicular church. The structural ribs converge on the building's apex-like segments of an orange from the inside – where an unseen lantern spreads light around the roof, like the halo around the sun in an eclipse. The effects of the shadows and the remarkable natural lighting which models the curves and arches so boldly would have found its place on most Expressionist film sets. It is an extraordinary and powerful space, which achieves the effect of Gothic monumentality in an unsentimental manner. There is no question of historicism; this is a purely modern structure, using the latest technology and materials.

The form of the parabolic arch had been used in factories, hangars and engineering projects (as well as notably by Gaudí) and its effect remains almost shockingly modern. From without the building is a mass of bricks, almost unrelieved but for a few small details – the round windows beneath the apex of the arches and the ends of the concrete beams which support the choir and organ gallery protrude through the wall above the door and form a kind of visual canopy to attract attention to the main entrance. Again, approached up steps, the whole has the effect of a great mountain rising from the mud of the earth towards the heavens.

Böhm was also responsible for a series of monumental churches, which while not exactly Expressionist, speak a language of Monumentalism that belongs more to the *architecture parlante* of the Expressionists than to his later, profoundly modern work. Among these, the Church of St Joseph, Hindenburg (now Zabrze, Poland) of 1938 is a haunting composition of arches and brick bulk. It has the brash engineering power of a Roman aqueduct and a rational solidity that make it enigmatic. It can be seen as a forerunner of some of the curiously sterile monumental works constructed under Fascism in both Germany and Italy, particularly the EUR buildings and later the Rationalists.

The Church of St Adalbert, Berlin (1931–3), by C Holzmeister uses a similar archetypal architectonic language successfully in a tight urban setting, and Böhm's Church of St Elisabeth, Cologne (1932) and St Engelbert's Church, Essen (1935) also belong to the same genre (if rather more muted in ambition and reference to the vernacular), while his Church of the Holy Cross, Dulmen (1939), is a fine example of his later crisp Modernism, exquisitely articulated, beautifully lit and liturgically functional, a very high level of architecture indeed.

Other architects were also creating astonishing Expressionist designs through the 1920s. Max Taut's Marble Church of 1919 was a pioneering vision of the church as a pilgrimage way ascending into a crystalline paradise while Otto Kohtz's project for a cathedral as far back as 1905 (published in *Gedanken über Architektur*, 1909) seems to presage the Taut brothers' geological inspiration. The designs of the Czech Cubists may also be linked into Expressionism although their concerns were rather with the creation of a new national mode of expression and a geometric configuring of space as the tectonic answer to the revolution in the depiction of planes in Cubist painting. Jirví Kroha's design for a church at Vinohrady (1919) and the sketches of Bedrich Feuerstein and Josef Štepánek, however, create an interesting parallel over the common border.

Hubert Pinand's St Marien's Church in Limburg an der Lahn (1927) featured the altar in an apse of parabolic vaults and crescent-shaped windows in a surreal vision of what appears to be a melting morass of structure and light. Hans Poelzig himself, the great Expressionist master, made his contribution in model form with a striking design for a pilgrimage chapel reminiscent of a huge, ordered stalagmite formation, the form of the Gothic church lingering below the surface. Fritz Höger's Wilmersdorf Church in Berlin (1932) blends an almost Art-Deco Modernism with Expressionist devices and a triangular Gothic entrance to build a dramatic church with an attenuated belfry, constituting one of the most distinctive buildings to come out of the era.

By the end of the 1920s the focus had shifted towards a more rational response to an increasingly defined liturgical brief. Bartning and Böhm are the two key figures that stand astride both Expressionism and the next phase. Their pioneering work formed the foundation of a powerful new Modernism born not of aesthetic whim but of solid, underlying liturgical and theological reform. The centre of progress remained in Germany, but we need to move to France and back a few years to pick up the thread of the narrative.

VI. AUGUSTE PERRET
Prophet of the Modern Church

With the building of one particular church by Auguste Perret, the focus of innovation in ecclesiastical architecture shifts momentarily from Germany and back to France. The last mention of France came with Anatole de Baudot's St Jean de Montmartre of 1894. Pevsner names this church as the first non-industrial building to 'use reinforced concrete systematically'.[1] Equally importantly, the architect has abandoned the historicist vocabulary and the church's interior is light and simple, the structural ribs providing the form and definition of the space and the articulation of the structure itself; they are left exposed and proud of it.

By the time St Jean was finished in 1902, Auguste Perret, another structural innovator, had designed an apartment block in the Rue Franklin in Paris with a concrete skeleton, a staple building in books on the origins of modern architecture. It was to be Perret who would single-handedly shift the focus of innovation back to France 20 years later with the Church of Notre Dame du Raincy in Paris.

The Church of Notre Dame du Raincy was completed in 1923, the year which saw the publication of Le Corbusier's *Vers une Architecture*. The influence the church exerted and the effect it had on 20th-century church architecture is easily comparable to that of Le Corbusier's most famous book on secular building and planning. At a stroke, Perret demonstrated the worth of the liberation

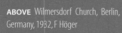

ABOVE Wilmersdorf Church, Berlin, Germany, 1932, F Höger

RIGHT, TOP AND BOTTOM Church of Notre Dame du Raincy, Paris, France, 1923, A Perret

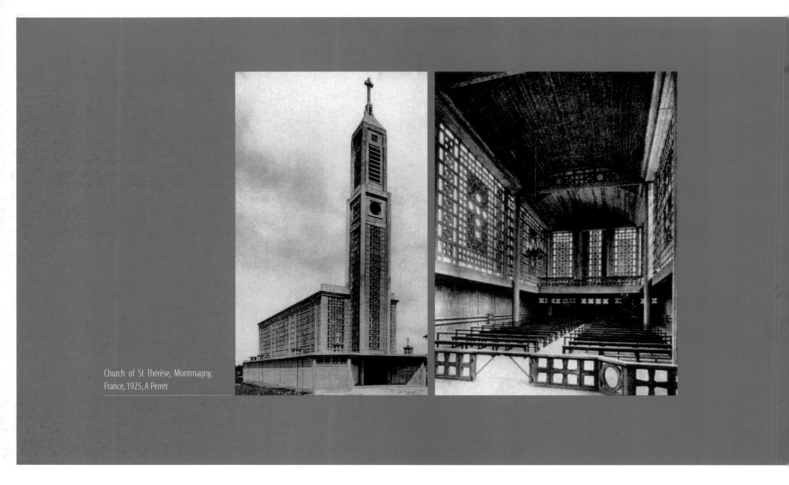

of church building from the straitjacket of historicism; as Gropius states in *Scope of Total Architecture* (1943) he 'succeeded in freeing architecture from its ponderous monumentalism'.[2]

Perret had been commissioned to design the church largely because other architects had submitted proposals that were far too expensive. He had never designed a church before, making it all the more remarkable that at Le Raincy he created such a visionary and insightful masterpiece. Using reinforced concrete, Perret was able to create a new type of space, a single great hall reminiscent of the basilica form where the early Christians worshipped and a space which presages the great 'single-space' (*Einraumkirche*) churches that German architects would later develop and which became common currency in the postwar period.

As well as freeing the internal space, the use of reinforced concrete negated the walls' structural function thereby allowing the expansive fenestration that gives the church its character and its intense quality of light. GE Kidder Smith compares the revelation of the liberating effects of structural concrete to the effects of Abbé Suger's order to 'open up' the walls of St Denis to allow the light to flood into the church[3] and there are indeed similarities with the Gothic. The invention of the flying buttress was a similar leap forward in Gothic structure, allowing a greater freedom of expression in the windows as a metaphor for the light of God in structural acrobatics that finally led to the perpendicular style, where the wall as solid element almost disappears.

Perret's church is also reminiscent of the Gothic in its massing, its form culminating in a slender, reeded spire tapering to open-work fins surmounted by a crucifix. But it would be superficial to dwell on these interpretations. The church is an important innovative structure, not only for its daring use of exposed concrete (the marks of the shuttering are left exposed and there is no effort expended to cover up the nature and texture of the concrete), but also for its plan.

Although there may seem nothing particularly innovative about the single long rectangle which constitutes the building's interior, on closer inspection it becomes apparent that Perret has done away with the choir and consequently with the marked separation of the altar and the congregation in a move that is the very antithesis of the Gothic plan. The relative strength of the concrete means that the arcades which broke the space of the Gothic interior into nave and side aisles have been reduced to spindly columns that barely demarcate a separation, so that the whole space melts into one and the congregation feels as one great body. In an extension of this breaking down of the demarcation of solid and void, interior and exterior, Perret replaces the walls with concrete lattices. These lattices seem to deny the weight of the structure and open it out to the

light so that the walls disappear into an abstract pattern of light and colour: the physical structure of the church is reduced so that the emphasis is on the single collective body of the congregation; the mass shifts from the building as the House of God to the worshippers as the Body of Christ.

The church is flooded with light; a wonderful spectrum of colour follows the ritual progression from entrance to altar. The glass nearest the entrance is yellow and, going east, it changes through orange, red and violet until the shallow curve of the apse wall bathes the altar in a mysterious deep-blue light. Other innovative touches in Perret's church include a floor which falls slightly towards the raised altar in an effort to achieve better visual contact in what is a large building, designed for a capacity of 2,000, and the placing of the vestry and sacristies beneath the raised chancel so that the purity and simplicity of the single space is retained from within and without.

It should also be noted that this was a design with economy in mind. The building elements were designed to be cast as simply as possible and with the minimum of forms. The columns are repetitive as are the lattices which make up the walls, so that the whole could be constructed with the minimum fuss and labour. Far from leading to a poor space, this repetition introduces a sublime simplicity: the use of the curtain wall adds to the metaphor of the church as 'God's tent', as if the walls have disappeared into a tarpaulin of exotically coloured fabric. It is a prophetic metaphor that recurs later in church design.

Soon after the completion of Notre Dame du Raincy, Perret executed another church commission, his Church of St Thérèse at Montmagny, near Paris (1925). The building is similar but less powerful than his earlier masterpiece and although it continues with the same concerns and devices it lacks the effortless elegance of his church at Raincy. He further developed and articulated his architectural language with a design for St Benedict's Church, Carmaux, in 1939, a design that shows a refinement of his vocabulary to a monumental classical language closely related to his work at the Musée des Travaux Publics of 1937. But the design he submitted for a competition in 1926 to build a cathedral to Joan of Arc was a reassertion of his genius. In the design, Perret developed his ecclesiastical architectural language one stage further. He proposed a huge tower which was to have been open much of its absurd height and would have flooded the interior with an extraordinary light.

This was a monumental proposal with less in common with the simple aims of the Liturgical Movement than his other churches; a building with perhaps too big an ego, but architecturally it would have been a *coup*. It had something of the New York skyscraper in its stepped forms and the monumental nature more like a ziggurat than a cathedral, but it was not chosen and lost out to a dull entry; a sad loss to the history of church building. The consolation is that Perret was given a chance to try out some of the ideas of the failed scheme in his capacity as architect and planner for the French town of Le Havre, which he helped to rebuild after the destruction it suffered in the Second World War.

At the Church of St Joseph, a square plan is surmounted by a huge tower that, like its predecessor on paper, is open throughout and lets a shaft of brilliant light down to illuminate the altar which is placed centrally beneath. The body of the church is simple and does not distract from the service which is conducted in a progressive fashion, with seating surrounding the altar on all sides. The effect of the light above the altar is almost mesmeric; the same use of colour is employed as at Le Raincy, noting the liturgical importance of the colours and relating this to their position in the architecture.

From without the church is a symbol, a great spiritual lighthouse, its tower a looming beacon for the harbour. In it can be felt an echo of St Andrew's, Roker, where Prior was also aware of the church's spiritual and physical significance in its dockside location. The similarity between two architects who were concerned to create powerful and simple forms as houses for worshippers and to abandon trivial aesthetic considerations is not a superficial comparison.

By the time St Joseph's was completed in 1959, Perret was dead. In the time that had elapsed between the genesis of the ideas which formed the basis of his submission for the Joan of Arc competition and their realisation at Le Havre, the momentum in the world of Modernism in church building had shifted back to Germany again after the brief flirtation with France due almost entirely to Perret's genius.

VII. MODERNISM AND LITURGICAL REFORM
A Brief Background
The word 'liturgy' is derived from the Greek words '*leiton*' (people, the same root as 'laity') and '*ergon*' (work). The Liturgical Movement was, in essence, a re-examination of the roots of the word.

To outline the situation at the turn of the century, it is necessary to go back to the Middle Ages, and before. There had been a gradual erosion of the participatory nature of the early Christian celebration so that by the Middle Ages, the laity was virtually excluded from the ritual. The Mass was celebrated in Latin, which was understood by few across Europe. Primitive and illiterate peoples and tribes had followed their leaders into Christianity and understood little about its nature; their exclusion from the Eucharist became almost inevitable. The priest celebrated Mass with his back to the congregation while he mumbled away in meaningless tones. The Church itself treasured and protected its privileged position as the sole guardian of knowledge, education, enlightenment and mystical powers.

Architecturally the effects of the change are embodied in the Gothic cathedral when seen against the early Christian church form, the basilica or the simple room in a domestic house. The chancel, originally an area for worshippers, came to exclusively house the clergy and grew in length as their self-importance and pride increased. The area became increasingly separated physically from the rest of the church with the advent of rood screens and other devices so that the laity became alienated from the clergy and the ritual. The Reformation had reacted to both these circumstances and an increasingly corrupt and powerful clergy, and in Protestant architecture the focus was generally shifted to the pulpit, as the sermon and the Bible itself (spoken in the vernacular) became the underpinning elements of the service, along with private prayer and a personal relationship with God, without the brokers.

The Counter Reformation followed with a massive effort to draw people back with gold and angels and a new, sumptuous plasticity in architecture (after the humanist experiments of the Renaissance which were seen as pagan-based and part of the reason for the decline in the Church's authority). The 19th century saw a return to a blind admiration of the medieval forms and the Latin Mass which affected many Protestant countries (a short account of which occurs in Part I). Thus, the situation at the beginning of the 20th century was comparable in many places to the Middle Ages. Architecture had ceased to be a living response to changes and developments in theology and had become a historicist exercise concerned with the minutiae of detailing and style; even within the Gothic camp there were debates about what period of Gothic to copy. Architecture had become fossilised and largely irrelevant.

Secular buildings had appropriated the historical styles that were the mainstay of church building. A Gothic building was as likely to have been a town hall or a station; domes and towers could be found on concert halls and pumping stations. The symbolic significance of building elements had been diluted and meaning became fuzzy around the edges. As well as this, the Church had been gradually losing its central position in an increasingly materialist and Rationalist society, its fundamental precepts being eaten away by theories of evolution, positivism and political ideology on the left and right but particularly by the rise of Marxism.

This situation led a handful of reformers from across the Church to reassess its role in society and its most important manifestation, the liturgy. The early moves towards this analysis and rethinking emanated from Belgium towards the end of the 19th century and spread through the Netherlands, Germany and France and beyond. The real boost came at the beginning of the 20th century from Pope Pius X who encouraged the reforms throughout his papacy (1903–14). The pope died at the beginning of a war which would change the political landscape of Europe and see a revolution in Russia. The war was devastating and left behind it a trail of disillusionment with the status quo that gave an added momentum to the urgency of the reforms if the Church was to retain its vitality as an institution.

The objectives of the reformers were succinctly described by Anton Henze in his book *Contemporary Church Art*:

> The aim of the liturgical movement was to transform the faithful from 'silent onlookers' (Pius XI) to active participators in the offering; the individual worshippers were to join with the priest to form one community united by sacrifice. It was the task of church architecture to conform to this developing community of the altar, confirming and strengthening it and providing it with an environment in which each person should be in contact with each, and all with the altar, participating visually and orally, unhindered, in the sacrifice of the mass.[1]

Henze begins to outline the implications of this fundamental reform on ecclesiastical architecture by stressing the central importance of the altar. This was a return to the conception of the altar as the table of the Last Supper, around which people gather; a very different notion to that of the high altar which is seen as exclusive and separate from the people, the preserve of the clergy. The Protestants had already experimented with moving the altar during the Reformation when the traditional stone altar was replaced by a table of wood. This had the effect of making the communion table moveable and it could be set up in a forward position in the chancel or actually among the congregation in the nave. The wooden table constituted a return to the symbolism of the supper, and of the participation in the meal of the congregation. It also meant that the celebrant could face the congregation across the table and not with his back to them. But as the focus in Protestant churches tended to be the pulpit and the 'Word', the significance of this move was sometimes lost. The change in priorities also led to the demand for all to be able to see and hear and, ultimately and inevitably, in the reduction of the size of churches.

For these reasons, the elemental shift in liturgical thinking that occurred during the 20th century can almost be seen as a new reformation and the effect that it had on architecture was as drastic as that of the Reformation itself. The architecture of the Reformation was a reaction to a group of Gothic buildings, which had become an anachronism, no longer relevant to the new situation, and generally adopted a stripped, austere classical vocabulary with light, simple spaces which were seen as the most modern architecture at the time.

Similarly, the Liturgical Movement in the 20th century responded to a debased historicist vocabulary and a set of buildings that had nothing to do with the new liturgical perception by using the most Modern architecture available to them. The aims of this were broadly in line with those of the Reformation: light, humane spaces. The idea was not to intimidate or instill with awe, but to facilitate communion, participation and a sense of the congregation itself as the House of God and the Body of Christ. The function of the building was not to be in itself a representation of some paradise, or a trailer for the forthcoming attraction of heaven (the spirit in which the Gothic was conceived). Instead, the aim of the architecture was to promote community and (here we return to the Expressionist vision of the submission of the will of the individual to the crowd), in the words of Otto Bartning, to encourage 'active contribution of the individual's emotion as expanded into and absorbed by the collective emotion of the foregathered community'.[2]

What made the period so fascinating from an architectural point of view was that it coincided exactly with the birth of Modernism and in many ways the objectives of both the Liturgical Movement and the Modernists coincided. Both were a rejection of the hypocrisy of a prevailing situation that was characterised in both fields by complacency and a lack of understanding of the brief or the fundamental roots of space and the liturgy. In *The Church Incarnate* (1938), Rudolf Schwarz, the great prophet of modern liturgical design, wrote:

> We cannot return to the early cathedrals and take up their interrupted discipline once more.
> This was the error of the Historicists. Even the tools, our 'technology' would fail us. It would of

course be possible to copy the deep doorways and the mighty pillars of the Romanesque or the pointed arches of the Gothic. But it would not be true. For us the wall is no longer heavy masonry but rather a taut membrane, we know the great tensile strength of steel and with it we have conquered the vault. For us the building materials are something different from what they were to the old masters. We know their inner structure, the positions of their atoms, the course of their inner tensions. And we build in the knowledge of all this – it is irrevocable. The old, heavy forms would turn into theatrical trappings in our hands and the people would see that they were an empty wrapping. They would draw premature conclusions about the matter which is served by these empty forms.[3]

That part of the Modern Movement which was concerned with Functionalism, the inheritors of Lethaby rather than the builders of white villas which adopted only the Functionalist aesthetic, was concerned principally with a rational examination of the brief. When this approach was applied to ecclesiastical architecture, architects did not have the clear brief that a factory, hospital or house could provide. They had to return to the fundamentals of worship, another move that ran parallel to the aims of the Liturgical Movement. Simply an application of modern technology and forms to the problem of ecclesiastical design was an inadequate solution and would have been a betrayal of Modernist ideals. Schwarz summed up:

> … it does not suffice to work honestly with the means and forms of our own time. It is only out of sacred reality that sacred building can grow. What begets sacred works is not the life of the world but the life of faith – the faith, however, of our own time … that sacred substance out of which churches can be built must be alive and real to us.[4]

VIII. THE CHURCH INCARNATE
Modernism and the Church

Perret's Notre Dame du Raincy constituted a fundamental turning point in ecclesiastical architecture. It illustrated that modern materials could be used in a modern idiom to create an architecture which was both sacred and relevant to an industrial age. It was a result of a change in liturgical thinking allied with a grasp of modern technology and construction; in effect, the first modern church. What Perret achieved in concrete, Otto Bartning was to achieve in steel.

Bartning (whose experiments in modern church architecture were referred to in Part V and were among the most advanced) dismissed the mysticism and sentimentality to which church architecture had been bound (and which, it has to be said, was not entirely absent in his own earlier expressionistic designs) to transcend stylistic arguments and create an architecture which was fundamentally of its time: an architecture which took the liturgy as its heart and which developed its expression from the inside out. Thus he was closer to the spirit of investigation associated with the Functionalism, that was developing in contemporary Germany. He wrote: 'It is wrong to believe that by using modern materials and building techniques we secularize church construction. There is a spiritual quality in any material. It is our task to find this spirit and put it into the service of religion.'[1] In so doing he freed church architecture from the constrictions to which it had been subjected and was able to undertake an experiment in steel which became one of the foundations of modern ecclesiastical architecture.

The Stahlkirche (steel church) was built for an exhibition at Cologne in 1928 and was later re-erected in 1929 in Essen. As Perret had done, Bartning used the structural strength of the material to free the walls from their load-bearing responsibility. This allowed him to break down the sense of enclosure through fully glazed walls which 'close us in and at the same time open up the inside to the outside and hold us in the magic spell of the changing light of day and night'.[2] The concrete grille framework of Perret's church has here given way to a butterfly-wing effect, the frame is like lace and the whole church is light itself. The columns of the structure stand out against the glass as expressions of the aspirationally vertical.

The plan of the church was also a departure from Perret's basilica form: it is roughly parabolic, its apex being the curved apse of the sanctuary. The seating fans out slightly to place the congregation closer to the centre of the celebration. As the walls melt into one continuous membrane, what is left of the hierarchical division is expressed through the floor. The altar and pulpit are granted equal emphasis by their position on the central axis although the altar sits on a raised dais giving it extra importance in the composition and a natural culmination to a plan that is focused entirely upon it. Just as the altar is raised to express its sacred nature, so the whole building sits above ground level and is entered via a ritual procession heavenward. Below the church are accommodated all the ancillary facilities so that the single worship space is kept pure and unhindered.

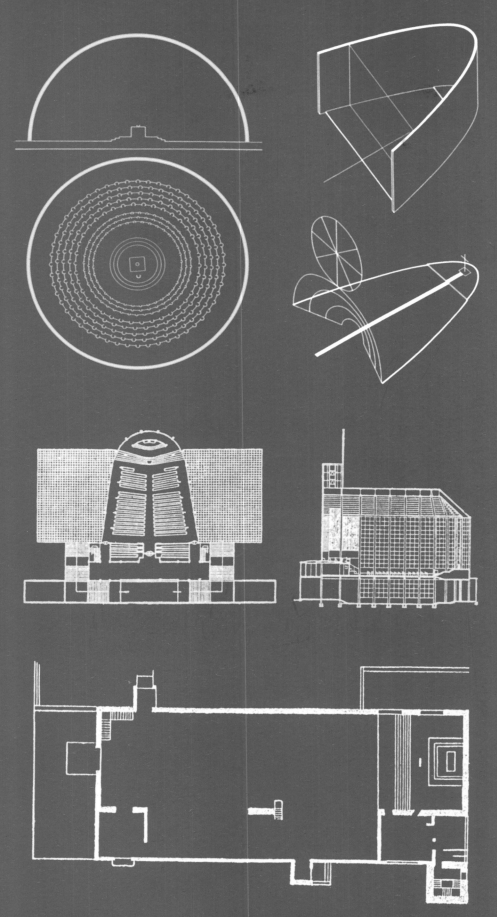

ABOVE L TO R 'The Ring' and 'The Sacred Cast' – illustrations from *The Church Incarnate* (1938), R Schwarz

CENTRE Stahlkirche, Cologne, Germany, 1928, O Bartning

BELOW Church of Corpus Christi, Aachen, Germany, R Schwarz, 1930

The church was erected using very simple constructional techniques so that it could be easily dismantled and rebuilt. The building presages prefabrication and is a model of the mass production ethic of the Bauhaus, genuinely cheap and mobile (in a dramatic nod to the metaphor of the church as tabernacle, 'God's tent'), utilising the standard elements of engineering construction, notably the humble I-beam which forms the basis of its construction. Bartning used a solid foundation, a plinth of reinforced concrete which contrasted with the delicacy of the glass, and the building was massed in such a way that it rose to the church above from the massive to the light. This also meant that at night, when lit within, the building appeared to be a floating crystal of light in what was both a reflection of the form of the Gothic cathedral with its broad, curved apse and the Expressionist obsession with transparency and light. Yet the picturesque preoccupations of Expressionism have been expelled and the Gothic sentimentality which survived in Perret's spires has been replaced by a rational response; the tower remains, but as a blocky mass to house the bells and signify the entrance. This is a tough church for an industrial age and an industrial area. It revels in the local technology of steel and sits comfortably in the industrial landscape of northern Germany. If Notre Dame du Raincy was the first modern church, the Stahlkirche was the first Modernist church.

Another of Bartning's highly original designs was the Gustav-Adolf Church, Berlin-Charlottenburg (1934), where he explored another plan form, that of the fan, which can be seen as a variation on the parabola plan of his Stahlkirche. The fan is a segment of the circle, thus the perfection of that form is implied but with a clear directionality which is lost in the often aimless circular plan, the focus of both space and structure (the concrete beams of the roof) being firmly fixed on the altar.

Bartning's earlier buildings appeared in the Expressionist section along with those of Dominikus Böhm, although the works of both men could simultaneously appear in the Modernist section as pioneering and experimental, but the buildings which I included in that section retain a whiff of the picturesque and the deliberately mystical. Böhm's great Church of St Engelbert, Riehl, was the first building to exploit the perfect circle as a plan for a democratic church, a body for truly corporate action, the circle being the traditional symbol of togetherness and wholeness, of God himself.

It was consequently one of the most influential of 20th-century church designs but Böhm was in fact preceded by his contemporary, Bartning, with a circular church which embodied a harder approach than his slightly self-consciously elegant parabolic forms. The Round Church, also at Essen (the final destination the Stahlkirche until the bombing), is an example of the 'gasometer' design propounded by Otto Wagner. Stacked circles form a subtle pagoda effect, executed in stark materials: brick, concrete, glass and metal. The interior is light and functional and highly centralised although, curiously, focused on the font rather than the altar.

Robert Maguire and Keith Murray in their book on modern churches (1965)[3] compare the form itself to the traditional form of the baptistery and specifically to a baptistery designed by Bartning in Berlin in 1927, where a simple circular space reminds us of Bruno Taut's pavilion at the Cologne Werkbund exhibition. There is an element of the courtroom about the church and the organisation is definitively democratic but it is a curious building and, although more modern in its language than Böhm's church at Riehl, it is perhaps a less successful church, though a highly influential scheme.

The other German church of the same period, which had a similar impact on Modern ecclesiastical architecture, was Rudolf Schwarz's Corpus Christi in Aachen (1930). Like Bartning's Stahlkirche this was Functionalist architecture but it was derived not from superficial aesthetic concerns and the 'white' architecture of the International Style but from a deep understanding of the liturgical renewal. It is a Modernism that has developed from the functional requirements of the changing liturgy and not imposed as a stylistic vocabulary. It is the embodiment of Walter Gropius' assertion in Scope of Total Architecture (1943) that 'Modern architecture is not a few branches of an old tree – it is new growth coming right from the roots' where those roots are the liturgy and a re-examination of the spirit and meaning of the Eucharist. The building is a starkly plain mass, unrelenting in its purity. At the time it was referred to in a derogatory fashion as 'the factory' due to its uncompromising functionality.

The church consists of a single cubic volume with another rectangle at right angles to it that contains the ancillary accommodation and is divorced from the worship space. A tall white campanile rises beside the building like the chimney of a great power station. The interior of the church culminates in a chancel raised seven steps above the floor. Below the eaves is set a series of small square windows. The black marble altar contrasts harshly with the dazzling white of the interior. The pulpit is wrapped around a long pier, also of black marble, which divides the Eucharistic space from the lower-ceilinged aisle to its side and which runs the length of the church. Thus the twin foci of the church are highlighted by material and elevation alone. The only other relief to the interior is that of light: both the simply punctured openings and the pendant light wires which fall like a shower of stars from the ceiling. These innovative fittings could be switched in such a way as to change the pattern and intensity of light; they serve to fill the austere emptiness which surrounds the congregation.

The idea of emptiness is considered and deliberate. Schwarz was at the heart of the Liturgical Movement and close to one of its key figures, the theologian Romano Guardini. When Guardini visited the Church of Corpus Christi he spoke of the 'silence' of its interior. This arose partly from Schwarz's studies of oriental thought and form and is close to the intense spiritual contemplation of Zen in many ways. Just as Japanese students were taught to contemplate the form of a jug by attempting to visualise the space contained within and without and ignoring the vessel itself, Schwarz compared the act of worship with God's act of creation 'out of nothing'. Consequently, in *The Church Incarnate*, he argues that:

> This creation [the corporate act of worship] should take place in living men, not in images and buildings – at the beginning the building should be simply the means of this creating and afterward the result of it.

Schwarz was perhaps the first architect to move on from the preoccupation with materials which informed Perret's concrete structures and Bartning's steel structure to a higher plane where the architecture is purely generated from the liturgy – from within – and is thus the clearest expression of the sacred.

Rudolf Schwarz had worked in the office of Dominikus Böhm, and the two architects – who, together, did perhaps more than anyone to revolutionise church architecture – were friends. In *Moderne Bauformen* (1927), Schwarz wrote of Böhm that he laid the 'path to the hard simplicity of the single, great interior' and while Schwarz was building his church at Aachen, his master was at work on a building which occupied a parallel plane to Corpus Christi.

Built at the same time as St Engelbert, Riehl, Böhm's church in Nordeney of 1930 is a complete departure from his Expressionist tendencies. Every bit as austere and rational as Schwarz's design, Böhm's church stands dazzling white against the surrounding houses. Its haunting open bell tower is engaged and casts great shadows on the white mass of the church, as does the spindly black cross that stands in front of the building. A stair rises up towards the single exposed bell in an emphatic gesture of ascent so that the entrance to the church becomes a symbolic pilgrimage. There is something of the purity of suprematism in the composition; the great sidewall of the church is relieved only by the single perforation of the stained–glass window which illuminates the altar.

As in Schwarz's church, the space is composed of a single long nave and a side aisle of lower height. The culmination is again a black marble altar, raised, but not aloof from the congregation. Columns are kept to a minimum and the space is kept pure and simple with no distractions. Böhm was also heavily involved with the Liturgical Movement and, like Schwarz, his plans arose from the liturgical impetus whence they gain their great spiritual power and boldness, while his architectural language was that of the finest European Modernists, a true ecclesiastical Functionalism.

Böhm and Schwarz continued to build fine churches including many important and influential designs, which there is no space to dwell on here. Their work became increasingly difficult owing to the rise of the Nazi party in the early 1930s and the subsequent return to anachronistic architecture. The impression should not be given, however, that the path of the liturgical reformers was ever easy or that the new architecture was universally accepted. It faced many obstacles among which simple conservatism was the greatest. Schwarz had written: 'Architecture is giving an example, but it shines on chaos; no-one understands it'.[4] Under the Nazis that conservatism became an even greater burden and although many architects continued pioneering work, the focus of innovation in ecclesiastical architecture shifted over the border to the more receptive territory of Switzerland.

IX. SWITZERLAND
The Consolidation of Modernism

The new architecture that was the fruit that grew from the union of liturgical reform and Modernism was largely attributable to the innovative work of Perret and France and the prolific German pioneers. The only other country that imposed its presence on innovative ecclesiastical architecture to a comparable extent was Switzerland. In 1927 Karl Moser built the Church of St Anthony at Basle. Leaning heavily on the achievements of Perret over the border in France, the church was not only a dramatic leap forward for ecclesiastical architecture in Switzerland but one of the first significant moments in the history of Swiss Modernism, representing one of the first truly modern constructions in the country.

The building exhibits greater clarity in the relationship of its elevations to its plan – it is a starker, more stripped construction, closer to the pared down, almost industrial aesthetic of the later German churches. The interior is perhaps more raw than Perret's, with chunkier, squarer columns and a great vaulted nave of rational, waffled concrete. The wall reappears here as a structural element as opposed to Perret's net curtain walls, although Moser too creates a space which is defined by the quality and quantity of light. The most notable presence of the wall is behind the altar where it serves to bring it down to the structure and the level of the congregation, whereas Perret exalted the altar at Le Raincy in a shroud of light. On the elevations the mass of the wall is emphasised by a cavernous entrance; like the gate to a tomb from a lost civilisation which casts ziggurat shadows on the raw concrete. Anton Henze has grouped together Moser's church and its ancestor, Perret's at Raincy, with Böhm's St Engelbert's at Riehl and Schwarz's Church of the Blessed Sacrament at Aachen, as the foundation stones on which all further development in modern ecclesiastical architecture would be built.

The rise to power of the Nazi party in Germany meant that the initiative in ecclesiastical design fell across the Alps to Switzerland and a creative surge was set in motion which presents the most homogenous vision of a developing church architecture intimately interconnected with liturgical renewal. In his book *Liturgy and Architecture* (1960), Peter Hammond states:

> Switzerland was the only country in western Christendom which, by the late thirties, had created a living tradition of church architecture. There is still no other country where modern churches of real quality take their place so naturally among the best secular buildings of their day … The Church has learned how to speak in the language of the living.[1]

As well as Moser, three other architects were adding to the country's stock of fine modern Catholic churches (Protestant churches were slower to take up Modernism but had begun to do so by the mid-1930s): Fritz Metzger and two former pupils of Moser himself, Hermann Baur and Otto Dreyer.

Metzger's Church of St Charles in Lucerne (1933–4) is one of the most exquisite buildings to come out of liturgical reform and a key monument. The church stands like a gleaming Modernist jewel on the banks of the River Reuss, the clean lines of its belfry a beacon of purity against the verdant hills. The plan is clear and simple, its single space wraps around the altar in a sweeping curve. A continuous band of window generously illuminates the space while the structure is supported on columns which define the aisles. The curve and the uniform treatment of the apse and the body of the church have the effect of drawing the space, the communion table and the congregation together. The elevations are clearly defined and elegant, the lower 'deck' containing ancillary functions while a terrace above the river is sheltered by an expansive overhang; the building is inviting and unambiguous.

Metzger's Church of Our Lady of Lourdes (1935) shares many characteristics of this earlier building including the clarity and the pared-down belfry with its clock (typically Swiss) and pure modern architectonic language. The same language defines Werner M Moser's church (the son of Karl) at Zurich-Altstetten (1941), which also incorporates a super-modern belfry and clock. What sets Werner Moser's church apart, however, is its unusual asymmetrical interior which aims to emphasise separately each aspect of the life of the church: font, pulpit and communion table. The building also contains a considerable amount of social facilities.

The original church was kept on the site as a chapel while Moser's building became the main church. The asymmetry which defines the scheme was part of the architect's solution to the retention of the old building, not wanting to smother it, and also led to a more self-effacing Modernism. Moser had worked for both Mies van der Rohe and Frank Lloyd Wright and this experience resulted in an effective grasp of spatial composition and a simple clarity of expression which led to this church, a highly influential structure. More than the other Modernist churches (which could often be seen as generic architectural solutions), this was a site-specific solution that took into account the old church and its vernacular surroundings. Moser writes:

To create a relation between the new and the old building without compromise for the new – just by careful proportions – was a special aim. It resulted in an asymmetrical shape, which was very individually fitted and just only to this solution.[2]

The open-work tower of St Johannes Church in the same city, by Burckhardt and Egender (1936), gives an idea of the building's almost high-tech interior, a celebration of the steel structure and glass wall in a simple and effective space: the first Modernist church in Switzerland built for a Protestant congregation. These few churches illustrate adequately both the varied architecture which emanated from Switzerland and the uniform high standard of so many of the works, all partaking in a living theological and spatial experiment at an almost unprecedented time of exploration.

X. EUROPE BETWEEN THE WARS

Germany provided the early impetus for the new architecture and Switzerland took over the mantle. France had not responded to Perret's genius and remained largely conservative. There were, however, notable exceptions: Paul Tournon's Church of St Thérèse de L'Enfant Jesu (1928) is an almost freakish experiment in plasticity, blending Perret's approach to structure and the dissolution of the wall into a geometric grille of light with a Gothic attitude to the stylised statuary that cloaks the west front. The interior is liturgically advanced; a single space focuses on the altar while a blocky pulpit protrudes into the nave from a column. Although individual and brilliant, the building belongs more to the modern, sculptural Expressionism of Gaudí than to the Modern Movement. The same architect's Church of the Holy Spirit (1928) in Paris is a monumental mass of concrete with an interior worthy of the power of Byzantine architecture, dramatic and theatrical in a positive and a negative sense but a stunning work nevertheless.

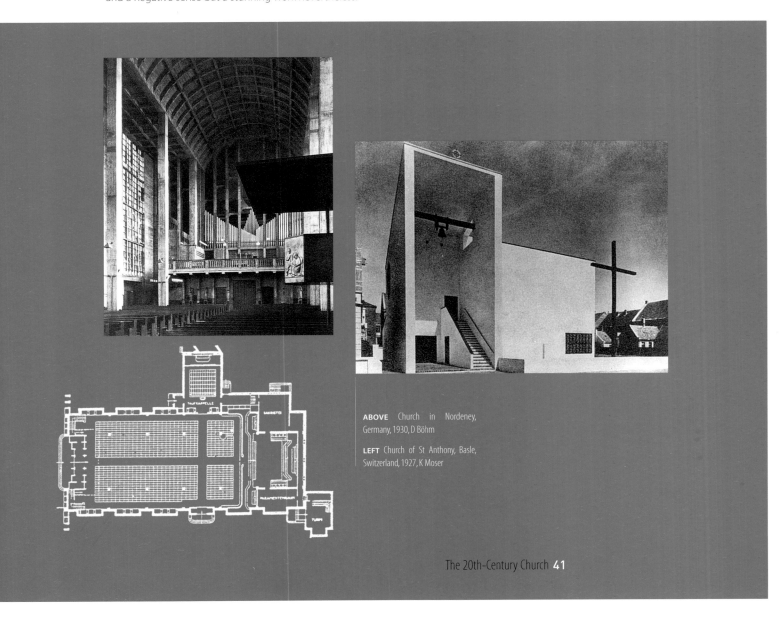

ABOVE Church in Nordeney, Germany, 1930, D Böhm

LEFT Church of St Anthony, Basle, Switzerland, 1927, K Moser

There were isolated incidents of innovation throughout Europe but nowhere was a momentum built up. Josef Gocvár's little Church of St Wenceslas at Hradec Králové (1927) is a remarkably advanced work of Functionalism within a Modernist urban setting and an early example of a trapezoid plan, illustrating the progressive search for new forms that grew out of one of the centres of European Modernism. The little church's interior is stunning in its simplicity, and its curved apse and converging walls bring the congregation into the heart of the liturgy. The sculptural stepped roof serves to illuminate the building brilliantly while the tall windows of the apse curve around above the altar to introduce an intense purity and brilliance. It is one of the few churches to match the clarity of the Swiss examples that followed a few years later but very different to Plečnik's great work of the same period.

Elsewhere in Central Europe there was entrenched conservatism. Two fine modern churches were built in Budapest: Városmajor Church (1933) by Aladár Árkay – a fine, elemental, blocky Modernism of a very white kind – and Pasarét (1934) by Gyula Rimanóczy, which has Italian-influenced Modernism. Neither advanced the cause of the functional re-analysis of the interior although both are wonderful works of art. Poland was yet more conservative; nevertheless, Jan Witkiewicz-Koszczyc's competition design for the Church of the Holy Providence (1930) is a fascinatingly bizarre mix of Expressionism and New York skyscraper, while Oskar Sosnowski's Church of St Roch, Bialystok (1927–46), is a strange modern Gothic creation, beautifully massed and utterly anachronistic.

In Italy, LG Daneri's Church of San Marcellino, Genoa (1931), provides us with an example of a circular plan, built a year later than Böhm's seminal St Engelbert, Riehl, although Peter Hammond reminds us that its precedent (with its apses containing side altars around its plan) could be baroque as easily as modern.

I Gardella's chapel in the Sanatorio di Alessandria is an early example of Italian Modernism applied to ecclesiastical design in a rational manner. There were other examples of Modern, Rationalist and Expressionist *oeuvres* in Italian church building although here, too, much of the action was dominated by historicism.

Britain was also stuck in the backwaters of conservatism. The few bright sparks had little effect but nevertheless created some interesting works. Eric Gill was one of the first to realise and utilise the consequences of liturgical reform; his Church of St Peter, Gorleston-on-Sea, presented a centralised worship space but little else. NF Cachemaille-Day was probably the most adventurous and consequently interesting architect on the British scene. His Church of St Michael and All Angels, Bemerton (1937), uses a plan of two intersecting squares, one rotated through 45 degrees to create a space capable of successfully involving the congregation in the celebration, which he combined with a clean modernly architectural style which is almost close to that of Baudot four decades earlier.

The same architect's St Saviour's Church, Eltham (1934), is another of the few good examples of interwar church architecture in Britain. With its rugged brick detailing and robust shell it appears a mix of the earthen solidity and curving forms of the Amsterdam school and the municipal style of the country's councils. Its close relative, St Barnabas, Tuffley (1939), displays similar, if perhaps more Gothic characteristics, while St Nicholas' Church, Burnage (1932), is a streamlined Art-Deco construction with a finely modelled and light interior.

Many architects were using the 'moderne' style without applying the investigation of the brief that characterised much continental building, the Modernism of the Odeon rather than the Bauhaus. Other architects were still working firmly within the historicist camp, including J Ninian Comper who, despite his anachronistic vocabulary, was among the first to respond to liturgical change in generous, light interiors which began to resemble the 'one room plan' advocated by Pope Pius X.

Architect A Randall Wells continued the line and symbolism of his master Lethaby, one of his most interesting achievements being the Church of St Wilfrid, Leeds (1938), an odd, eclectic blend of an eccentric nature. Another great eccentric was HS Goodhart-Rendel who created some of the most interesting British churches using an architectural language that was both monumental and highly individualistic and in which he continued working until the postwar years, his greatest achievement perhaps being the massive brick pile of the Church of the Most Holy Trinity, Southwark (1957–60), which is almost Roman in its sheer power and force.

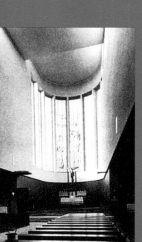

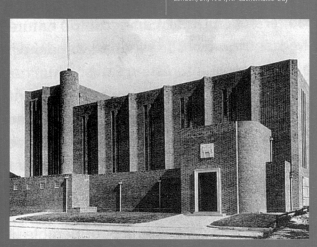

LEFT Interior of St Wenceslas

CENTRE Városmajor Church, Budapest, Hungary, 1933, A Árkay

RIGHT St Saviour's Church, Eltham, London, UK, 1934, NF Cachemaille-Day

One character who made a considerable impact on ecclesiastical architecture in Europe at this time was Dom Paul Bellot. A monk and an architect, Bellot was a central figure in the move towards the realisation of the architectural implications of liturgical renewal. His architecture was a fantastic cabaret of devices that could place him as easily among the Expressionists as it could among the historicists or the early Modern Movement. His work has something of the intensity of Plečnik and the remarkable organic conception of the sculptural qualities of brick, which defined the approach of the Amsterdam school and Expressionism, glued together with a passion for a modern Gothic idiom that stemmed directly from the tradition of Viollet-le-Duc. If this sounds an eclectic mix, then it has succeeded in giving an inkling of one of the most interesting of 20th-century architects.

Standing outside the formal language of Modernism, Bellot has, like Plečnik, only recently come to attract wider attention and it is impossible to outline his *oeuvre* in this short introduction. But for some of the best examples of his work one can look to the simple, beautiful brick-encased spaces of Saint-Paul d'Oosterhout (1906–20) in the Netherlands, Quarr Abbey, Isle of Wight (1907–14), the polychromatic Art Deco blue-burst of the Church of Saint-Chrysole, Commines, France (1922–33), the Expressionist structural lines of the Church of the Immaculate Conception, Audincourt, France (1928–33), and the remarkable, almost Deco Moderne of the interior of another Church of the Immaculate Conception, Porto (1938–47), among many other masterpieces.

All these interiors were liturgically advanced but never starkly modern like those of contemporary Swiss and German churches. They delight the eye and the spirit, a fine testament to a man who believed that to create good Christian art, a man must be a good Christian; the intensity of his faith and love for God are finely expressed in an incredible collection of works.

XI. POSTWAR DEVELOPMENTS
Theology and Architecture
The Liturgical Movement began in Belgium at the beginning of the 20th century, and was spurred on by the Benedictine Lambert Beauduin and the monks of the Abbey of Maria Laach in Germany. It slowly gained momentum over the course of the century and proved a living impetus for architectural innovation in Germany between the wars. Its effect was felt little elsewhere in Europe but in the last years of the Second World War and immediately afterwards it gained a powerful foothold in France, where architects could build on the foundations laid by Auguste Perret in the 1920s, but thereafter it was ignored.

In 1947 the Papal encyclical *Mediator Dei* was issued and constitutes a formal recognition of the advances made by the German Liturgical Movement. After this date liturgical renewal spread throughout the Catholic world at differing rates. Although the movement began in the Roman Church, the fundamental upheavals and changes in thinking had a profound effect on other churches; many began to move in similar directions, and this had the effect of drawing the churches closer together. A decade after, the *Mediator Dei* the bishop of the Roman Catholic Diocese of Superior, Wisconsin, set up a commission to issue a set of directives for church building, which contained far more detailed recommendations for church architecture. It begins with the words: 'The primary purpose of the church is to serve the sacred liturgy.'

The widespread acceptance of the imperatives of the Liturgical Movement, however, dates from the convening of the Second Vatican Council (Vatican II) in 1960 and the coming into force of its *Constitution on the Sacred Liturgy* in 1964. This embodied the principles of bringing the clergy closer to the laity through the celebration of Mass in the vernacular and a physical closeness brought about by a proximity of the altar to the congregation, whether physically within them, 'in the round' – to use a theatrical analogy – or at least to not separate the chancel from them by the use of physical or symbolic barriers.

The architectural implications were enormous and the expression of these ideals was highly varied. It allowed great experimentation with new plan forms and structures; some are merely architects playing at creating a building which 'looks like a church' or is supposed to instill some vague, abstract notion of sacredness, others are genuine expressions stemming from deep understanding of the liturgy and the role of the church in both spiritual and secular life.

The reforms coincided with a period of rebuilding in Europe and the Americas and led to a great deal of experimentation with forms, materials and space. Some are brilliant, others irrelevant, while some are irrelevant and yet still brilliant. Le Corbusier's church (see Part XIII) is one of the latter. There is not room here for a comprehensive overview of church architecture for the second half of the 20th century. I have attempted to select a few buildings to complement those in the latter half of the book to give a brief context for those works.

XII. POSTWAR GERMANY
A Church Meant for Our Own Time

The art of building … is the creation of living form, and the church … is not merely a walled shelter, but everything together; building and people, body and soul, the human beings and Christ, a whole spiritual universe – a universe, indeed, which must ever be brought into reality anew.

… This holy work is comparable to no other. It cannot be derived from contemporary art and its fashionable motifs or from the aesthetic doctrines or from social theories or from cosmic myths. Rather is church building a work in its own right, bound strictly to its own meaning and with it exhausted … a church must be developed wholly and in all its parts out of its own inner meaning, that is, out of prayer – this is to us the meaning of sacred objectivity.

Rudolf Schwarz, *The Church Incarnate*, 1938

The exterior of a church should not attempt to imitate contemporary secular buildings either in its proportions, its structure, or its decoration. Nor should it try to catch the attention of the passer-by with the architectural equivalent of the cries of the market place. The aim should rather be to announce in a manner which is both dignified and eloquent the totally different nature of what lies within the church – totally different because belonging to another world – and yet at the same time to allow the building to take its place harmoniously in its surroundings.

Point three of the *Guiding principles for the design of churches according to the spirit of the Roman liturgy*, issued by the German Liturgical Commission, 1947.

Less than a decade lies between these two quotations but it was a decade that saw Germany launch Europe into the most devastating war in its history. Schwarz was writing under the difficult conditions of the Nazi state, what Mies van der Rohe called 'Germany's darkest hour'. Mies wrote the foreword to the English language version of *The Church Incarnate*, published in 1958. He wrote:

Rudolf Schwarz, the great German church builder, is one of the most profound thinkers of our time … [The Church Incarnate] is not only a great book on architecture, indeed, it is one of the truly great books – one of those which have the power to transform our thinking.

National Socialism interrupted the advance of ecclesiastical architecture on its most fruitful territory and the mantle of progress passed to Switzerland. The war virtually stopped building throughout Europe in its later stages. In 1945 Germany found itself again in the wake of a terrible and devastating war and, again, this created a great impetus for rebuilding and rethinking. The war had destroyed many German cities and churches and there was an urgent need for rebuilding. More than any other nation except perhaps France, the Germans launched themselves into the task with a rare combination of thoughtfulness and enthusiasm.

The period saw a consolidation of the aims of the Liturgical Movement (set in stone by the work of the German Liturgical Commission and the publication of their report in 1947) and a reassessment and reinterpretation of the Expressionist vision that had followed the First World War. It once more proved a fertile blend of vision and function and the range of church buildings that rose from the ground in the postwar period was staggering. The weightiest presence was exerted by the old masters Rudolf Schwarz and Dominikus Böhm and by Böhm's son, Gottfried, who developed the Expressionist aesthetic to a higher plane and built on the notable achievements of his father's *oeuvre*.

Both Schwarz and Böhm senior moved from their Functionalist application of minimal design to the sole service of the liturgy to reintroduce elements of symbolism and monumentality. The Church of St Michael, Frankfurt (1954), is based on a frankly phallic plan (which is related to the ovoid shapes of the German baroque); a long ellipse forms the Eucharistic space and two apses serve as choir and chapel and a freestanding campanile. It is a realisation of Schwarz's concept of the 'open-ring', a restful space which does not confine but embraces and opens up to the infinite at its apex in the altar. This is expressed by the culmination in the apses and in the different articulation of the east wall, which is free of the strip window that otherwise runs around the church below the roof. The building achieved both weighty presence from the exterior and an austere and calm interior, an inner peace that was rarely equalled.

The Church of St Anna, built two years later (1956), is closer to Schwarz's notion of the 'sacred journey', based on a long rectangular space with an arm which branches off to create a more

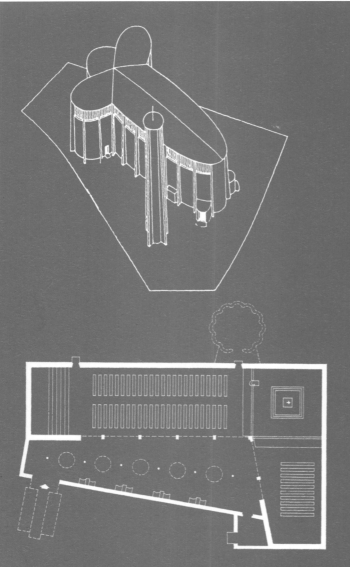

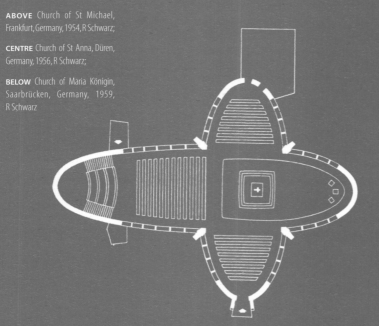

ABOVE Church of St Michael, Frankfurt, Germany, 1954, R Schwarz;

CENTRE Church of St Anna, Düren, Germany, 1956, R Schwarz;

BELOW Church of Maria Königin, Saarbrücken, Germany, 1959, R Schwarz

intimate worship space for the parish sharing the same square altar. The church rises like a phoenix from the flames that engulfed the city, and is built from the rubble which the urban fabric of Cologne was almost totally reduced to. Its walls are sheer cliffs of stone and it is a serious and imposing structure both inside and out. Entry is through an aisle or pilgrimage wing that runs the length of the church, linking the side chapel into the main space, then through arcades to a confrontation with the awesome bareness of the great stonewall.

The church is illuminated by massive windows which constitute the whole wall over the arcades, above which a pattern of diagonal beams relieves the elemental concrete ceiling. Behind the altar a 'Tree of Life' pattern emerges from the stone, rippling through the coursing and illuminated by fruit as little roundels (like Lethaby's 'Jewel Bearing Tree' in *Architecture, Mysticism and Myth*, a reference to a tradition of mythical burning trees, Moses' burning bush, for example, and the Jewish Menorah candle-holder). This is one of the boldest and most genuinely impressive works of sacred architecture in the 20th century: Expressionism without whimsicality.

The same architect's Holy Cross church at Bottrop (1957) is the embodiment of another of Schwarz's ideas, the 'Sacred Cast'. In *The Church Incarnate* of 1938 he writes:

> The structure is simply open roundedness; it is that roundedness which is end and shelter, the simple presence of joy, the awaiting light – that into which the people finally surrender themselves as if into an open hand.

The parabolic plan culminates in the blocky stone altar with its chunky legs that is very much a representation of the table of the Last Supper. The curved wall of brick effectively embraces the congregation without enclosing or constricting them. The light comes from the decidedly odd west wall and is filtered through a swirling pattern of coloured opaque glass (meant to represent infinity), which seems to presage the spirals of Friedensreich Hundertwasser a couple of decades later, while a positively disconcerting eye of God design in the window above the altar looks down on the congregation.

In 1959 Schwarz's attention returned to the plan explored in St Michael's, tempered with the parabola of the Holy Cross and the design of the Church of Maria Königin in Saarbrücken. Here a cruciform plan is united by the altar at its crossing and brilliant illumination emanates from four huge windows of translucent glass set in the mass of stone that forms the church's bastion-like walls. Schwarz skilfully manipulated the forms to eliminate glare so the altar is nearly always seen against a background of plain wall, yet the space is light and airy. The building stands like a great castle among the trees, an immensely powerful work which evokes the force and strength of medieval building while utilising the most liturgically advanced of plans and a modern architectonic language.

Schwarz's smaller works also spread their influence widely and were impeccably skilful examples of their genre. These include the Heilige Familie, Oberhausen (1956–8), which consists of a perfectly square plan in an urban setting with a peaceful forecourt and separate courtyard, its walls broken down by a repetitive and consistent pattern of glazing, and St Christphorus, Cologne-Riehl (1950), his last church: an interpretation of the small missionary church.

Dominikus Böhm's great contribution to German postwar church design is the Church of Maria Königin, Marianburg (1954), built a year before his death. It is an exquisite and intimate work of pure Modernism. The plain worship space focuses on an altar in a curved apse, illuminated by a wall of stained glass of the architect's design. This wall opens up between the seating and the chancel to a shrinking corridor of glass leading into a small, delicate baptistery, also highly glazed. There is a feeling of rebirth as one enters the space through the false perspective of the passage, a beautiful sanctuary among the trees – a subtle building to end a magnificent career. Böhm's son was at hand to continue the tradition of church building at its height of creativity and response to liturgical requirements.

Gottfried Böhm's Church of St Albert in Saarbrücken (1955) is reminiscent of a monstrous spider about to engulf its prey; but the Expressionist imagery of the exterior gives way to a more sensitive interior. Within the egg-shape of the church a ring of columns encloses the sanctuary . This is both an expression of Rudolf Schwarz's idea of the 'sacred ring' form of church plan and a clear demarcation of the altar and the most holy space from the church which is never, however, separated from it visually or physically. A symbolic demonstration of the transition – 'The altar is the border between time and eternity' ('Threshold' Rudolph Schwarz) – the altar is raised on a plinth at the epicentre. From the altar, set at the narrow end of the egg, the seating radiates outwards so that the altar is surrounded almost entirely by the congregation.

There is a curious lack of structural expression on the inside as these duties are undertaken by the external concrete framework (the spider's legs), which lends an ethereal feel to the space, enhanced by the ovoid opening in the roof that illuminates the altar. The altar itself seems a reversal of the building's structure; the mensa is supported on a sculptural form reminiscent of the fingers of an outstretched hand. If it were the form in microcosm then the mensa would represent the earth to which the structure is anchored, and the altar is seen as the earth reaching up towards heaven. The baptistery is related in form to that at his father's church, Maria Königin, a pure circle at the end of a glazed, reducing corridor.

The unusual Church of St Gertrude in Cologne (1964–5) illustrates a return to the sculptural approach of Expressionism with its craggy concrete roof simulating a hard, jagged landscape, a literal analogy of the rock of the church. The ideas which he began to explore at St Gertrude's reached their climax at Böhm junior's most complete and fulfilling ecclesiastical building, the pilgrimage Church of Neviges (1966–8).

Here he comes very close to a realisation of the early idealism of Expressionism, the notion of the sacred mountain. Böhm describes the pilgrimage as 'the expression of a living, continually moving church',[1] and his idea of the pilgrimage church as the culmination of a great route justifies a gesture which he might see as inappropriate for a parish church but wholly fitting as a climax of the great sacred way. A landscape of brick terraces builds up and climbs past the pilgrims' lodgings to the inevitable crest of a jagged mass of angular concrete forms which is the church. The interior is like a great cave carved out of the mountain; rugged and irregular prismatic planes of concrete build up into an interior landscape broken into light and shadow.

The structure is one of the very few among modern buildings which have the power and monumentality to answer Rudolf Steiner's Goetheanum. Its presence is immense and it dominates the town's skyline just as did the ancient cathedrals and, like the medieval cathedrals, its interior is as much an urban gesture as a sacred space; it embodies a town square, a centre for the community and the gathered pilgrims. It has been forgotten that the cathedral was at the heart of the town; that people ate and drank within its walls, conducted their business there and escaped from their tiny constricted dwellings. Böhm is one of the few architects to recapture the essence of the cathedral as the spiritual and physical centre, both the culmination of the sacred way and the focal point of urban life; the Expressionist dream of the sacred mountain and *Volkshaus* in one great, unified gesture.

Elsewhere Dieter Oesterlen's Christ Church, Bochum (1957), imposes a wonderful prismatically sculptured roof onto an angular plan, which avoids glare by its dogtooth arrangement. Windows are set into the blind side of the serrations in another building, which realises elements of the Expressionist vocabulary. Sep Ruf's Church of St Johan von Capistran, Munich (1960), presents a new slant on the early Expressionist round churches; a close counter to Schwarz's recommendations on the circular plan-form in an impressively sparse and nonmonumental modern style. Egon Eiermann's Kaiser Wilhelm Memorial Church rises next to the old bombed-out tower which was left as a symbol of the destruction wrought by the war. A simple refuge, bathed in the coloured light of its wholly perforated walls, it became a symbol of Berlin's resilience, an urban monument and the gesture of a new generation of architects. Paul Schneider-Esleben's St Rochus, Düsseldorf (1955), is defined by a parabolic dome rising like an absurd bishop's mitre but not competing with the neo-Romanesque tower that stands next to it, another fragment of the legacy of war.

Hans Schedel's Church of St Joseph, Hasloch-am-Main (1958), uses a spartan set of white walls which ingeniously interlock to embrace a calm interior expanding from the altar which is mysteriously lit from an unseen window formed at the junction of two wall elements – a building with some similarity to Richard England's Manikata Church of a few years later. The Paul Gerhardt Church, Mannheim (1961), by Gerhard Schlegel, and Reinhold Kargel, presages a kind of early high-tech, unusual in ecclesiastical work, with a wonderfully simple barn of an interior, characteristics also of Joachim Schürmann's St Pius, Cologne (1961).

Another architect of great ability was Emil Steffann. His intervention into the ruins of a Franciscan church in Cologne is a masterpiece of the re-use of a shell and the reconfiguration of space to modern liturgical demands, with the simplest altar and pulpit creating a very pure chancel area. The superb bell tower rises like a rationalised ghost of the Romanesque from its side. The same architect's Maria in den Benden, Düsseldorf (1956–8), is described by Peter Hammond as a 'house for the local church' where the spaces, secular and sacred, are arranged in a building like a Roman villa around the atrium which was prescribed by the German Liturgical Commission. Steffann's Church of St Lawrence, Munich (1955), presents a stripped, elemental interior and the same curved apse as at Düsseldorf.

TOP St Albert, Saarbrücken, Germany, 1955, G Böhm

CENTRE Church of Neviges, Germany, 1968, G Böhm

BOTTOM Christ Church, Bochum, Germany, 1957, D Oesterlen

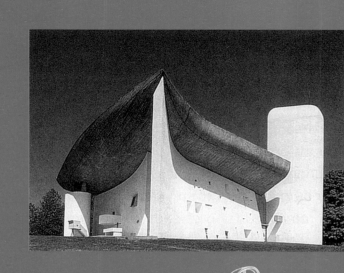

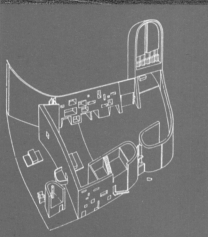

Taken as a whole (and including many other buildings for which there is not space here) the German contribution to church building after the war is as monumental as that of the prewar period; a final realisation of the experimentation and theorising of the earlier generation and a fruition of the pioneering work of Böhm and Schwarz, and certainly the most significant contribution of a single nation.

XIII. THE CHURCH BUILDING AS ART
Le Corbusier and the Mediterranean

When Le Corbusier was asked by a reporter from the *Chicago Tribune* whether he thought it necessary to be a Catholic to design his chapel at Ronchamp, he famously replied 'Foutez-moi le camp' (roughly translated as 'leave me alone'). The gulf between Schwarz and Le Corbusier could hardly have been greater even though they were both working within the same tradition of Modernism. Schwarz believed in an architecture that was solely generated from the liturgy, the requirements of the mass; what he termed 'Sacred Objectivity'. Ronchamp on the other hand is the fundamental turning point of the Modern Movement; the point at which something like Expressionism, a sculptural approach to architecture, found its way back into the fold, and like the prodigal son, was greeted with both mistrust and much rejoicing.

Some Modernists saw the Chapel of Notre Dame du Haut, Ronchamp (1952–5) as an affront to the Functionalism that its architect had been instrumental in creating; a wilful exercise in plastic massing and a lack of truthfulness to structure and material (the building is sculpted using concrete sprayed on to mesh). On the other hand it was greeted with a wild enthusiasm by those architects who felt they had been constrained by the rational logic of Functionalism; the master had moved on, the building had become a gesture of sculptural expression, and wilful symbolism was about to become acceptable again. Le Corbusier's chapel of Notre Dame du Haut is at once one of the greatest moments in 20th-century architecture and a virtual disaster for ecclesiastical design from the liturgical point of view: it led to a spate of idiotic 'gestures', buildings symbolising anything from praying hands to doves; buildings emanating from a single, bland idea, justified in the name of the new Modernism.

It may seem odd that Le Corbusier was chosen for such a commission. But he had the support of Father Coutourier, editor of the influential journal *L'Art Sacré*, who believed that the church should actively commission works from those artists who were the greatest in their field, only thus could a great sacred art emerge again. It is the precise opposite of the view of Dom Bellot who believed that good Christian art could come only from a good Christian. Coutourier's influence later led to great works being commissioned by the church from Matisse, Cocteau, Léger and others.

Le Corbusier himself saw the building's sacrality coming from a vague mysticism of the type that had been condemned by the German Modernists. He turned to the mythical sacredness of the hill on which the church was built, a tradition which stretched back beyond Christianity as a kind of universal expression of the sacred, and stated boldly that: 'The requirements of religion have had little effect on the design, the form was an answer to the psychophysiology of the feelings.'[1] He saw the chapel as a form of sanctuary at the culmination of an eternal pilgrimage. He explained in his dedication speech:

> In building this chapel I wanted to create a place of silence, of prayer, of peace and of internal joy. The feeling of the sacred animated us. Some things are sacred, others not, irrespective of whether or not they are religious.

The chapel is built on a pilgrimage site among rolling, verdant hills. Its brilliant whiteness stands out like a beacon against the landscape. The building is covered by the canopy of a huge roof which billows out like a reference to 'God's tent' and seems almost weightless as it is lifted from the structure, a gap being left between the walls and roof so that a crack of light can penetrate. It is entered via two bastions which curl inwards to invite the pilgrim who, on entry, is confronted with a huge battered wall perforated in an abstract composition of openings (Charles Jencks is prompted to ask, '"Swiss cheese" facade or "cotton candy"?'),[2] which has become an icon of modern architecture. The deep, coloured glass-filled holes illustrate the massive thickness of the wall and create an exquisite play of light and colour within the building. As well as the altar within, another altar sits outside under the shelter of the great sweeping roof and a pulpit is built on to the huge concrete column which supports the roof above at a single, tiny point. This is a place for commune with the landscape, a pantheistic celebration of the mystical presence of the object within the hills, close to the Greek temple in conception.

Christian Norberg-Schulz cites the church as a 'symptom of renewed interest in basic existential meanings' and continues to state that:

> Le Corbusier has succeeded in recovering the basic properties of the Christian sanctuary. His building is receptacle and giver, fortress and poetic vision of otherness. Above all he has managed to recreate the interiority of the early churches with means which are simultaneously new and old, making the interior … a space which simultaneously protects and liberates. It is a cave, open to the essential meanings of human existence, and supporting Heidegger's equation that 'on earth' means 'under the Heavens'.[3]

In his book *New Churches of Europe* (1964) GE Kidder Smith ends the Ronchamp entry by stating that it is 'to many the most impressive church of the last 500 years'. Maguire and Murray's comments in *Modern Churches of the World* (1965) are altogether different: 'seen as a folly it is outstanding; but in the development of church building, it is a blind alley.' These comments define the poles; that the building is still capable of arousing more comment than almost any other Modernist work is a testament to the power of Le Corbusier's art.

If Ronchamp was one of the critical moments in Modern architecture it was partly because of the intensity of the architect's conviction to a vision. It can be said that the vision of the artist has almost replaced religion in a secular age, that art galleries are the new temples, and the works of art treated like holy relics. The reverence for the artist (which comes out of the Renaissance humanist tradition) and his works provides us with one extreme attitude and the liturgically driven Functionalist provides the other; for him architecture can only be generated from within the faith. This polarisation remains as two threads that run through contemporary church architecture.

In his other famous scheme for the Church, the monastery at La Tourette (1957–60), Le Corbusier makes a return to the more humanist approach of his Unité d'Habitation. When working to a more specific brief, ie the housing of monks and a complete environment for their needs,

Le Corbusier seemed to return to the rational style which was more familiar in his work. He writes:

> I tried to make a place of meditation, research and prayer … The brief was to house monks while trying to give them what people of today need more than anything: silence and peace. Monks, in silence, find a place for God … It is the interior which lives. The essential goes on in the interior.[4]

The work is closer to that of an architect working for a functional sacred architecture and it evokes the interesting parallel of the artist himself as a monk in a cell creating true beauty from a mystical source; finding his God in contemplation of the darkness and the landscape.

The other great French architect who defined modern church building, Auguste Perret, made a reappearance when he was called in to supervise the building of a tiny chapel in Vence – its designer was Henri Matisse. The Chapel of the Rosary (1952) is a temple to colour, a *Gesamstkunstwerk* in which the artist created the whole vision, from the chasubles to the windows. The building itself is a simple canvas of white Mediterranean vernacular, and it is the art that is applied to it which makes it a pivotal work. Matisse wrote: 'My chief aim was to balance a surface of light and colour against a solid white wall covered with drawings.'[5]

The chapel was the apex of the concept of church as canvas, art itself as the expression of the sacred, pure, inner soul. Its influence was to be out of all proportion to its size. It was a notion which was reinforced by Jean Cocteau in his designs for the Chapel of St Pierre, Villefranche-sur-Mer. He explains: 'As an artist I wanted to create a chapel in which the poet, without losing any of his pre-rogatives, would become immediately accessible to fishermen and simple people'.[6] His surreal style created hypnotic and highly successful representations of biblical stories, a new interpretation of the symbolism of the bible as a link between the Freudian analyses of the subconscious in surrealism and the Catholic notion of the soul, two existential visions brought together.

Other artists were also brought in on a kind of crusade to reinstate the Church as a pivotal patron. Fernand Léger designed windows for the Church of the Sacred Heart, Audincourt, and the Church of Courfavre, Switzerland, while he also collaborated with almost all the most important French artists of the time on the Church of Notre Dame de Toute Grace in Assy (1950). This project was the ultimate result of Father Coutourier's efforts. Its architecture was merely a piece of Alpine vernacular interpreted in a modern manner, but its importance is as an art gallery. It brought together the talents of Léger, Chagall, Braque, Rouault, Lurcat, Matisse and others in a cornucopia of Modern art. It is an emotional achievement which attained the expressiveness of ancient religious art in a way that had been unprecedented in modern times, a final realisation of Father Coutourier's assertion that 'it was our duty to procure for God and our faith the best art of the present'.

The Church of St Thérèse in Hem by Hermann Baur is another fine example of the church as a total work of art and makes full use of the French technique of Betonglas – rough chunks of coloured glass set into a concrete frame – designed by Alfred Manessier as well as a tapestry by Georges Rouault.

There was an increasing consensus in France that the qualities of Modern art which sought to depict an other than figural world, to reveal a reality which is not physically visible, was 'more suited to the expression of what is sacred' (Father Coutourier, 1949), of which the surrealism of Cocteau born of the Freudian subconscious is the finest example. The Church in France had been generally conservative and had not followed up on the progress made by Perret in the 1920s but this began to change during the Second World War and the pace of reform dramatically increased in the postwar years until France took its place at the forefront of a radical new ecclesiastical architecture, an approach characterised by a deep understanding of both the structural possibilities of new materials and technologies, and of the demands of the changes in liturgy.

One of the most spectacular churches to appear was that of Notre Dame in Royan (1958) by Guillaume Gillet . In conjunction with engineer Bernard Laffaille, the architect created a spectacular church which is a reinterpretation of some of the concerns of the Expressionists; a building which evokes the heavenward thrust of the Gothic and imposes its monumental presence on the town as a kind of man-made mountain of concrete. A jagged canopy defines the entrance while exquisite spiral stairs rise to either side to give access to the galleries from which one enters the building's impressive concrete structural rib-cage, an expressive landscape of raw concrete prisms. The interior is less satisfactory despite its useful horse-shoe shape plan which focuses naturally on the altar. It is a cavernous space dominated by the bright light which emanates from the great east windows, dazzling the congregation and impairing a clear view of the altar; nevertheless a wonderful monument.

Another structural masterpiece built in the same year imposes a less monumental presence in the landscape at Lourdes. Pierre Vago's St Pius X Basilica – brilliantly engineered by Eugène

Freyssinet, virtual inventor of prestressed concrete – lies underground in an effort to limit the impact on the landscape of this vast arena that encloses a space approaching that of St Peter's in Rome. The building is designed to cope with the huge flow of people who flock to Lourdes (it is designed to shelter up to 22,000 pilgrims) and Vago came to the conclusion that the best and most practical solution to the plan would be the form of the ellipse in consideration of the vast structural spans involved.

A dished floor and a central altar raised on steps create the best possible proximity to, and view of, the celebration for the gathered masses. The interior is austere and plain, the concrete structure left bare. Vago specified a lack of decoration and the result is a brilliantly theatrical space which converges solely on the altar. The space is surrounded by the structure – a huge ring of braces – so that the feeling is almost of a great clearing in the woods, the archetypal temple. Vago had also been responsible for a very fine church in Arles-Trinquetaille (1950), an elegant response to liturgical reform in a crisp, clearly articulated Modernist shell, and later designed the Church at Salies-du-Salat (1962), a simple egg-shaped space with only the most minimal distractions from the altar, a pleasing and functional result of the Liturgical Movement.

As an antidote to the monumental scale of these buildings it is worth mentioning Rainer Senn's tiny Church of St André in Nice. The architect, himself from a small community, built this tiny elemental church out of logs. A square plan topped with a pyramidal roof and braces that emerge from under the eaves like tent poles, it is the personification of the mobility of the tabernacle. The church represents the notion that the building is a meeting place only, that the House of God is the congregation itself. An abject lesson in humility, and an influence which belies its tiny size.

Ecclesiastical architecture in Italy had not fully responded to Modernism in the years between the wars. The seeds of visionary Modernism sown by Antonio Sant'Elia, and later Giuseppe Terragni, did not seem to land on fertile ground. Terragni's remarkable plan for the Danteum could have been a blueprint for a new sacred architecture that stemmed from a source outside Christianity in the way in which Steiner's Goetheanum had done. Both were conceived as monuments to great humanist thinkers and interestingly it was to be Steiner's architecture which would seem to have created the deeper impression on the Italians.

ABOVE Church of Notre Dame, Royan, France, 1958, G Gillet and B Laffaille

LEFT Basilica of St Pius X, Lourdes, France, 1958, P Vago and E Freyssinet

ABOVE Baranzate Church, Milan, Italy, 1958, A Mangiarotti and A Morassutti

BELOW Church at Lungarone, Italy, 1975, G Michelucci

The architecture that emerged in the Italian church was often based on an Expressionism inspired by the malleable, plastic qualities of concrete. But there was another tradition in Italian design that remains familiar to us – the tradition of the beautifully designed object – an unmistakably Italian clarity and simplicity that shines through. Perhaps it can be seen most clearly in the exquisite Baranzate Church in the heartland of Italian design, Milan, designed by A Mangiarotti and A Morassutti (1958). If Abbé Suger's aim was to achieve a total dissolution of the walls into light, then this is the final realisation of his vision.

From without, the church appears as a harsh, almost industrial box of a building. The walls are articulated in rectangular panels crowned with a roof structure from which the ends of the beams are exposed, half a dozen X-sections emerging from the eaves. Steps lead up to the church (which is raised because of the high water table) and the simplest of wooden crosses defines the threshold from street to church. Once inside, the walls glow with a delicate translucence. The effect is achieved using a sheet of translucent plastic sandwiched between two sheets of glass while four sturdy columns that also subtly delineate aisles, chancel and nave fulfil the structural role. The usual criticism of dazzling glare is thus avoided and the evenness of the light across the whole interior is a brilliant solution to a perennial problem.

The effect is reminiscent of Japanese paper walls and the building's elegant and articulate minimalism would exert a significant influence across the world, from Ireland to Japan. Beneath the church a solid, dark crypt, lit only by a row of openings directly under the ceiling, makes another hauntingly simple space and creates a complete contrast of feel and spirit.

A harsher, more industrial aesthetic is exhibited at Luigi Figini and Gino Pollini's Church of the Madonna of the Poor (1952), also in Milan. These architects were some of the most advanced in Italy having developed their brand of Modernism during the interwar year. Here the chancel appears like a stage inside the church, separated from the nave by a geometrically perforated concrete beam like a proscenium arch. It is lit from an unseen source above, brilliant in comparison to the semi-darkness of the nave; a powerful, almost brutal design which captures something of the elemental nature of sacred space.

The other approach, the Expressionist way, is exemplified in a number of Italian churches including Nicola Mosso's SS Redentore (1957) in Turin. Apparently directly inspired by the dome of

Guarini's nearby baroque Sindone Chapel, the church is very much defined by its dramatic roof – a concrete vault of triangular coffers and diamond-shaped openings which sparkle in the bright light like gems. The elevations are treated in a similar crystalline stack of geometrics; the small hexagonal chapel is a mini version of the chancel itself. The composition seems a strong reference to the angular, geological forms of the Expressionists.

An exponent of the more sculptural side of an Italian neo-Expressionism appeared in Giovanni Michelucci. Le Corbusier had shown the way with the sculptural Expressionism of Ronchamp, and Michelucci took the forms in a more organic direction a decade later with his remarkable Church of San Giovanni (1960–3) on the Autostrada del Sole near Florence. There is something of the existential angst of 20th-century man in the design, a dramatic turnaround for an architect who had been a leading member of the Rationalist Movement in the 1930s, very much as Le Corbusier himself had reacted when his Functionalist approach was confronted with the notion of building a church.

Michelucci used an organic blend of materials and forms to create a highly plastic composition that has affinities with organicism in the US and with a kind of emergent Postmodernism – the billboard school of architecture, or an attempt to create new, dramatic forms for a car-based culture where everything is seen in glimpses which then have to encapsulate an idea or a specific vision. It also evokes the spirit of the roadside camp or tent. The interiors become theatrical sets, scenes of the heightened dramatic tension of the celebration.

His church at Lungarone (1966–75) embodies a womb-like sanctuary, in response to Vatican II, which encloses and hugs the congregation in an embrace of concrete. The sculptural organicism is reminiscent of Steiner's Goetheanum, particularly in the bold use of flowing concrete as an expression of both the structural and spiritual forces acting on the building. The roof is sculpted as an auditorium for services, a great amphitheatre with the background of the powerful, rocky hills; an answer to the pantheism of Greek architecture. The building is as close to modern theatre as the Mass has come; the idea of the Eucharist as catharsis, as the congregation becomes closely involved with the action unfolding on the theatrical altar on its stage at the centre of the galleried interior. The Chapel of Vergine della Consolazione in San Marino (1961–7) becomes an actual manifestation of an Expressionist set, a disturbing internal expression of an uncertain world.

Also worthy of mention here is Giuseppe Vaccaro's Church of St Anthony the Abbot (begun 1949) in Recoaro. His design embraces elements and characteristics of all the great architectures from early Christian to Renaissance and Modernism. The church features an archetypal and timeless vaulted space and a facade which is richly appreciative of Italy's urban tradition.

The competent weaving of references from the historical context into a thoroughly modern composition is one which has characterised much Italian architecture and is a thread which still runs through some of the fine churches being created, including the exquisite and thoughtful work of Burelli and Gennaro. Vaccaro has said:

> The Catholic Church, within its long history, has maintained within very different styles, some essential characteristics, both liturgical and psychological. I have tried to express these characteristics without, however, reproducing the building forms and systems of the past. Personally, and without reservation, I believe that religious architecture should be modern architecture. However, I feel that the Church would be wise to reject all formalized style, which is destined to lose its validity in a very short time. Rather than an anxious search after style, architecture should seek to be a sincere and lively expression of contemporary life and techniques of building. Such always were the greatest architectonic creations of past time.[7]

These are the beginnings of the questioning of a rigidly imposed Functionalism as the only acceptable way of working. They would be developed over the years into branches stemming from the broad trunk of Modernism. One of these branches has been termed Contemporary Regionalism and one of its earliest exponents was Richard England. England's master, Gio Ponti, had already questioned the tenets and the narrowness of Functionalism before the war. His own cathedral at Taranto (1964–71) is an impressive piece of sculptural design which echoes a rather late Gothic with its attenuated, pointed openings yet, like his exquisite little chapel at the convent in San Remo, its Modernism is never in doubt. However, England's church at Manikata in Malta was a more seminal work and an indicator of a new era that was increasingly conscious of the context and local tradition but which still carried with it the investigative exploration of Modernism. England's church takes the liturgical reforms as its kernel and pre-empts the changes of Vatican II in a subtle and sculptural design which also presages a move away from the formal language of Modernism while retaining its fundamental conceptions and, in some cases, a reassertion of the importance of the liturgy over the sculptural play of masses for the personal artistic expression of the architect. As Gio Ponti once told Richard England: 'Religious architecture is not a matter of architecture but a matter of religion.'[8]

XIV. UNITED STATES OF AMERICA
'For the Worship of God and the Service of Man'
The words that form the subheading here are inscribed above the entrance to the building that brought American ecclesiastical architecture into the modern age: the Unity Temple in Oak Park, Illinois. Its architect was Frank Lloyd Wright, one of the figures responsible for instigating and inspiring a new approach to architecture both in the US and in Europe, and here responsible for what can probably safely be called the world's first modern church.

Wright's approach to space and to the brief for the temple was prophetic and highly advanced. In a lecture given at the Art Institute of Chicago in 1931, he said of the Unity Temple that it represented:

An entirely new sense of architecture, a higher conception of architecture; architecture not alone as form following function, but conceived as space enclosed. The enclosed space itself might now be seen as the reality of the building. The sense of the 'within' or of the room itself, or the rooms themselves, I now saw as the great thing to be expressed as *architecture*.

The bold, angular forms of the building are not seen as style but as the expression of space and the building's function. Just as Gaudí's intense Catholic piety found expression in the ecstatic Sagrada Família, Wright's liberal Unitarian background found expression in the rational, democratic solidity of the Unity Temple. He abandoned the traditional symbols and elements of ecclesiastical architecture, the spire in particular. In his autobiography he wrote of Unity Temple:

Why not, then, build a temple, not to God in that way – more sentimental than sense – but build a temple to man, appropriate to his uses as a meeting place, in which to study man for himself for his God's sake? A modern meeting house and a good time place … What would such a building be like? They said they could imagine no such thing.

'That's what you came to me for,' I ventured

I can imagine it and I will help you create it.[1]

And lo, he did create it. Wright's rational approach led to a revolutionary new building: a solid mass of concrete. No effort was made to disguise the nature of a material which was widely regarded as only useful for a structure that would later be clad, and certainly not worthy of a church. Perret did the same in Europe nearly two decades later. The simplicity of the blocky exterior expresses the clarity of the interior. The building is entered through a space that connects the auditorium with the social hall; both elements are clearly and separately expressed in plan (it seems possible that Wright was influenced in the form of the building's plan by his experiences of Japanese temple architecture and their sublime and eternal simplicity of repose).

The auditorium is a galleried cubic space crowned by a coffered ceiling where the recesses are glazed to complement the light from the high windows and so make 'a creation of interior space in light'. The podium projects into the central space and is surrounded by and pushed into the congregation. It is an expression of the democracy of Wright's vision, both in the auditorium and the equal disposition of the building's sacred and secular parts. It carries a deep sympathy with the aims of the Liturgical Movement, although it is a coincidental affinity.

The Unity Temple has to be seen against a background of a United States architectural scene dominated by historicism. The building's austerity and plainness must have been a great surprise. As in much of Europe ecclesiastical building was particularly in the grip of the Gothic Revival. Grace Church (1843–6) and St Patrick's Cathedral in New York (1858–79), both by James Renwick Jr, helped to set the pace of the Gothic Revival in that city while even the Cathedral of St John the Divine (begun 1892) which had started life as Romanesque, metamorphosed over its construction into a Gothic structure. Others also operated in a Gothic vein, Ralph Adams Cram and HC Pelton and C Collens taking the Revivalism deep into the 20th century. Perhaps the most significant structure in terms of American architecture had been HH Richardson's Trinity Church in Boston (1872–7), which shows the architect's mastery of an original Romanesque solidity in carving out a modern idiom. It is a powerful building that exerted an effect on European as well as American architects, notably in Scandinavia.

Little had prepared the US for Wright's masterpiece and only Bernard Maybeck's First Church of Christ Scientist, Berkeley, California (1910–12) caused a comparable wave in the conservative church scene. He created (with Greene and Greene and others) a modern idiom using the reference of West

Coast vernacular and some of the same Japanese influences that had affected Wright, armed with a similar enthusiasm for modern materials. Maybeck remained attached umbilically to his Beaux-Arts training which shows in the axial planning of the church, and although the building is one of the earliest encapsulations of the 'California Style' it does not possess the revolutionary qualities of Wright's work.

Other churches would also emanate from Wright's office over his mighty career. Among these was the Unitarian Church in Shorewood Hills, Wisconsin (1947). This expressive triangular structure is often compared with that of a ship or an ark ploughing its way through the landscape, an analogy that would have the pastor placed at the building's helm. It is a slightly freakish building from a stage in the architect's career where he seems to have forgotten the lessons that he taught with the sublime clarity of the Unity Temple. The plan is unsatisfactory, with much of the seating facing away from the pastor due to the awkward triangular form. Yet the image is undeniably powerful and this rather extravagant symbolism (at the expense of functionality) became common throughout the world in the years following this scheme. Interestingly the Beth Shalom synagogue in Pennsylvania (1954), which uses a similarly expressionistic form, encases a more successful space.

Wright's Wayfarers' Chapel of 1951, built for the Swedenborgians in Palos Verdes, California, is a beautiful little structure with an organic relationship to the landscape and the sea. Delicate and intimate, it is a fine continuation of the mantle of organic architecture and is a precursor of Fay Jones' Thorncrown Chapel.

Wright's final building and legacy was another church, the Annunciation Greek Orthodox Church, Wisconsin (1956). It is a great UFO of a building that attempts to evoke the architectural language of the Byzantine Church in an effort to encapsulate the spirit of the Orthodox Church in something like a successor to *architecture parlante*. Wright created a huge, shallow, gilded dome to crown the building, possibly influenced by his love for the Hagia Sophia. The building inside is more Las Vegas than Istanbul, focusing a curiously tacky sanctuary of souvenir icons, gold and lightbulbs.

LEFT First Church of Christ Scientist, Berkeley, California, US, 1912, B Maybeck

RIGHT Unity Temple, Oak Park, Illinois, US, 1907, F Lloyd Wright

Chapel at the Illinois Institute of
Technology, Chicago, Illinois, US, 1952,
Mies van der Rohe

Wright made a terrific impact on the US architectural scene and his followers began to develop individual approaches that led to some of the country's most eccentric but most original buildings: Charles Warren Callister designed the First Church of Christ Scientist, Belvedere, California (1954) in an extension of the style which Maybeck started. Callister's opinion was that 'Architecture evolves from faith'.[2] His approach was more unified than was Maybeck's, and the result was a fine little build-ing of timber with a delicate spiky spire and walls subtly broken down to admit light through slots of leaded windows.

The building echoes the prow metaphor of Wright's Unitarian Church but the interior here is far more thoughtful and successful; its intimate scale and layout brings the congregation close to the altar. The feel is deliberately that of a log cabin – the structure this church replaced but which the congregation had become sentimentally attached to – so the architect used that most archetypal American form as a point of reference in this friendly structure.

Another architect from the same background, Bruce Goff, was creating some of the most inter-esting designs. His 1927 plan for a cathedral was remarkably similar to Bartning's Sternkirche while the sketch elevations bear a marked German Expressionist influence. His Methodist-Episcopal Church in Tulsa, Oklahoma (1926) was a fascinating design that reflected both his Expressionist interests and contemporary Art Deco styling. The stepped, ziggurat form of the skyscraper had usurped the role of the church spire as urban marker, and Goff's church is an acknowledgement of this, an exercise in spire scraping. It is a soaring design capped in copper and glass fins to reflect the light. The church consists of a round auditorium and numerous social facilities reflecting the con-cerns of the Expressionist ideal of the palace of the people. Goff came even closer to a realisation of the dreams of Taut and Scheerbart with his Crystal Chapel design (1949), a dramatic vision of the crystal mountain sheltering a non-denominational chapel.

Goff's interest in transposing Expressionism to an American idiom was shared by Barry Byrne. Byrne, who started off in the Prairie School and travelled to Germany to meet the Expressionist masters (Böhm, Poelzig, Feininger and the others), went on to create some of the most interesting and advanced church designs anywhere. His writings echo closely those of the Liturgical Movement architects in Europe. In *The Western Architect* (October, 1929) Byrne stated his principles:

The way of architecture is from the ground up; from the general to the particular.

Function is first; Building second.

In a Catholic church, then, what are the functions?

First, the altar. It is primary. The church building exists to house it, the celebrants at it and the people who come before it.

The building structure surrounds these with walls, covers them with the span of a roof. This is a church.

The people come to worship and to participate in worship. The liturgy of the mass is not for the few, it is for all to follow, as intimately as they can. The altar and the worshippers then must be as one, or as much so as space and a large number of worshippers permits.

The modern church is for the people who build it and of the day that produces it. It fulfils the functions and its use of its structure, it is a church in the truest sense of that word.

This text appeared with the designs for the Church of Christ King, Cork, Ireland, a scheme which closely reflects Expressionist experiments in its stepped plan and its ziggurat form; a very powerful design which blends the aspirational climb of the Gothic with the populist Modernism of Art Deco, yet transcends easy classification. The seating begins to curl around the sanctuary in a presentiment of liturgical reform, and the shape of the plan brings the whole congregation together very much as a single unit. The church was finally built in 1937, as Ireland's first modern church – a notable achievement in a conservative country.

Byrne went on to design a number of churches in a less dramatic but nevertheless highly modern style. The Church of St Columba, St Paul, Minnesota, is a sleek, streamlined piece of Modernism that nevertheless retains a resemblance to Gothic massing. Its less fortunate aspect is that the plan is apparently based on the shape of the fish as a reference to the symbol of Christ; these gestures are at best spurious and usually futile, no matter how well intentioned. Among Byrne's other churches is the innovative Church of Saints Peter and Paul in Pierre, South Dakota, with a fine plan based on two converging rectangles that meet at the focus of the altar.

Frank Lloyd Wright had spent his life trying to create an American architecture and he greatly resented the awe in which European expatriates (Tom Wolfe's 'White Gods') were held and the way in which they had dominated the US architectural scene. But despite Wright's influence on their

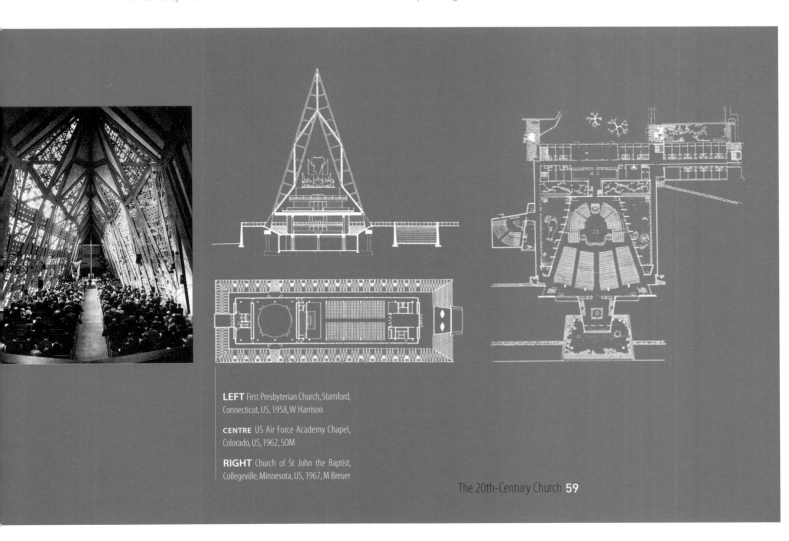

LEFT First Presbyterian Church, Stamford, Connecticut, US, 1958, W Harrison

CENTRE US Air Force Academy Chapel, Colorado, US, 1962, SOM

RIGHT Church of St John the Baptist, Collegeville, Minnesota, US, 1967, M Breuer own early work, it was these European Modernists who set the agenda for American architecture over the next decades.

While Wright was experimenting with increasingly eccentric forms, Mies van der Rohe was paring down the elements of architecture to a minimum, and out of this impetus came the chapel at the Illinois Institute of Technology in Chicago (1952). It was a wonderfully simple building: if less was more, then this was the most. A load-bearing brick structure, a glass wall at the front, a single, solid block of travertine for the altar and a silk hanging to separate the sacred space from the utility rooms at the back, there is little innovation, but a striking clarity. Philip Johnson once said that 'What makes Mies such a great influence.... is that he is so easy to copy.' Mies' buildings may have been masterpieces traceable back to Schinkel's universal classicism but in the hands of others, the vocabulary was used too often to cover up a lack of skill and thoughtful design.

Mies' minimalism did not stem from the same spirit which drove Schwarz or Böhm. Theirs was a Modernism which combined with a zealous passion and a heartfelt connection with liturgy to create a purity which came from the soul, even when their forms hinted at an odd mysticism or Expressionism. Mies was interested not in the specific solution for the church or the forms that would facilitate changes in liturgical practice, but in the universal form; an architecture which could accommodate any function which would have been anathema to his contemporaries in the German Liturgical Movement despite their often common roots in early Expressionism.

Yet Mies' minimalism gave rise also to positive trends. The architecture of the Kaija and Heikki Sirens in Finland can be deeply connected to Mies's minimalism and his architecture did have the benefit of stripping away the superfluous paraphernalia that had accumulated around ecclesiastical architecture, to make a fresh start.

Another recent European immigrant from the Bauhaus created one of the most important US schemes of the century. Marcel Breuer was a Hungarian who had come to prominence at the Bauhaus largely as a furniture designer (he designed the famous tubular chair). In the US he was given the chance to practise architecture on a huge scale as the partner of Walter Gropius.

In the 1950s the monks of the Benedictine Abbey of St John the Baptist in Collegeville, Minnesota, commissioned him to design a new church. It was an unusually enlightened community and one that was keen to promote the ideals of the Liturgical Movement, one of the first to do so in the US. Breuer's architectural place is exactly between Mies and Wright. He clearly rejected the notion of an organic architecture but he was also wary of the over-rationalisation of Mies.

The church was to be the focus of a large community, as well as being a parish church and a scene of great procession during holy events. As such it was decided that the church needed a certain monumental presence and, as he had recently designed the Paris Headquarters for UNESCO, Breuer was felt to be an appropriate choice. He carried his large-scale civic vision through to St John's where the church was placed at the entrance to the community with its great bell tower forming a physical gate to the internalised world of the monastery.

The sound of the bells and the striking of hours is an essential part of the lives of the monks while the towers used to guard the monastery from intruders became a symbol of the insulated monastic world, so it is entirely appropriate that this becomes the building's visual identity. The entrance sequence shows an acute awareness of symbolism and the history of the Church as well as its regard for the Liturgical Movement, of which this church was possibly the most complete expression.

A baptistery is placed as the first element in the progression after passing under the bell tower. It serves to fulfil the function of the atrium recommended by the German Liturgical Commission, a preparatory space for the church, and it makes manifest the importance of baptism as the entrance rite to the faith; the font is on axis with the altar and accorded due significance in plan and not shoved into a corner. The plan of the baptistery is derived from the trapezoid and is a microcosm of the space of the church itself, a shape that is expressed first in the form of the stone slab that surmounts the bell tower. The plan form allows for smaller services in the horseshoe-shaped enclosure at the rear of the plan, and larger services for the whole parish and on holidays to be accommodated in the seating that fans out from the sanctuary.

A simple altar with a separate slab mensa forms the focus for whatever arrangement is adopted. It is raised on four steps and emphasised in the vast interior space by a canopy suspended by wires that appear like rays emanating from the centre. The huge space is uninterrupted by columns or structure, thus the architect achieved the great unity and oneness which was such a critical aim of liturgical reform. It is one of the most successful churches of its era both as symbolic gesture and as a practical response to a complicated brief.

Another Central European immigrant was responsible for two influential churches. The Viennese architect Richard Neutra was in the vanguard of a pure modern architecture and his chapel at Miramar, La Jolla, California (1957) is an exquisite exposition of his art. The building is perched by an artificial lake in which the slender cross that defines it as a chapel is reflected next to the delicate stair which rises in a symbolic gesture of ascent into the light of the interior. Its purity marks it out as a predecessor of Tadao Ando's little Church on the Water. The interior is a simple, single space with elegant curved fins supporting the walls; well lit and clear, a simple and impressive statement.

His later church at Garden Grove, California, is another building of great clarity. Here a glazed stair tower on the skyscraper belfry culminating in the imposing cross that surmounts the tower fulfills the symbolic ascent. The church is light and clear: a simple long hall. Again there is the relationship with the water, the implications of baptism, the reflection of another world and a return to the waters. It also includes the innovation of a drive-in church arranged in a fan shape inspired by drive-in movies.

While these Functionalist monuments to light and clarity were being erected, the form of the swooping triangle, the pyramid and the teepee as already seen in Wright's work was becoming a very widespread symbol for ecclesiastical architects often unsure of how to achieve a monumental presence using modern forms. Skidmore, Owings and Merrill's US Air Force Academy Chapel in Colorado Springs (1962) is a good example of the genre and an undoubtedly impressive structure against the mountains which form its backdrop; the church evokes the spectre of spiky visions of Expressionism, but it is a single, simplistic statement based on a dramatic form.

The same could be said of the swooping form of Victor A Lundy's First Unitarian Church at Westport, Connecticut (1960), and his Church of St Paul, Sarasota, Florida, with its swept-up curved front. Eero Saarinen's North Christian Church, Columbus, Indiana (1959–63), also features a penetrating needle of a spire directly over a central altar, while a sweeping roof encompasses all the building's functions under its generous eaves, creating a fine building based around the octagonal form of the church at its heart.

Perhaps most impressive of all in the tent/triangle category was the church designed by Wallace K Harrison. Not an architect much associated with church buildings, his First Presbyterian Church in Stamford, Connecticut (1958), is a remarkable crystalline structure. Harrison asked his biographer, Victoria Newhouse: 'Have you ever thought what it would be like to live inside a giant sapphire?' At this church he did his best to supply the answer to his own question with an interior that glows with a crystal sparkle that Taut and Scheerbart would have undoubtedly approved of.

From without, the church's exterior is simple and rugged with only the fractal formations of the glazing giving any inkling of the luminous quality of the interior. From within, the interior truly resembles a great tent with walls of jewels. It is not a groundbreaking building and is liturgically rather backward, but it is a stunning evocation of the tent of God.

Pietro Belluschi practised an altogether more restrained architecture; a simple and homely effect in which he used laminated timber to create sympathetic and human churches. His Church of St Thomas More, Portland, Oregon (1938), and the Zion Lutheran Church (also Portland, 1949–50) show off the effect, while the Church of the Redeemer, Baltimore, Maryland (1958), is church as barn, the simplest vernacular space given a Gothic feel by the pointed arches of the structure while remaining simple and modern. His First Presbyterian Church, Cottage Grove, Oregon, is an example of a return to the Japanese influences of Wright and Maybeck, a beautifully clear and elegant space articulated in simple, refined forms.

A similar simplicity, but expressed in brick, can be seen at Eliel and Eero Saarinen's Christ Evangelical Church, Minneapolis (1949), where architects usually associated with expressive forms and extravagant structures created a church of unusual clarity. Its tall, elegant belfry with its grid perforation and slender cross, allied with the light airy space contained within, evoke the calm simplicity achieved in the Swiss churches. Its older brother, the First Christian Church, Columbus, Indiana (1942) designed by the same architects, is a similarly exemplary modern church of great clarity and one of the first such structures to be erected in the US and indeed, the first modern building in the city.

Despite the quantity and quality of some of the churches in the US, many of the most impressive achievements in postwar American church building came from below the borders, from the Latin cultures and lyrical sensibilities of South America.

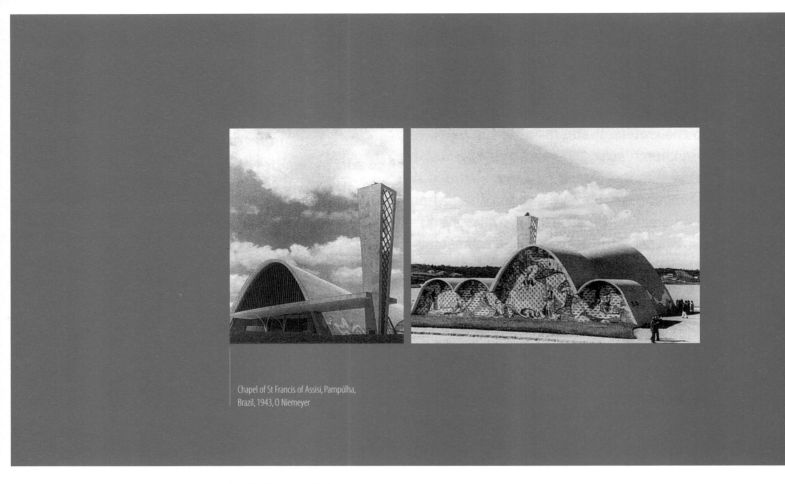

Chapel of St Francis of Assisi, Pampúlha,
Brazil, 1943, O Niemeyer

XV. SOUTH AMERICA

If there are many equally varied technical solutions to a problem, the one which offers the
user a message of beauty and emotion, that one is architecture.

Luis Barragán

Ecclesiastical architecture in South America grew from a combination of a poetic Borgesian world
of fantastic forms and fantasy, and an application of structural innovation and a rational approach
to the practical problems of building. The result was some of the most fascinating church architecture of the century which sprang from the deep well of a faithful people.

Perhaps the first manifestation of a new church architecture was seen at Oscar Niemeyer's
church in Pampúlha (1943). Here, the architect took a slab of concrete and folded it into parabolic
forms to create a sheltering, wavy roof which defines the building. The walls are decorated with a
bright mural in *azulejo* tiles reflecting the colonial influence of the Portuguese. A simple, flared
belfry stands by the church, its angularity emphasised by the curves of the church, and the whole
composition is distorted even further in the image it creates in the artificial lake on the banks of
which it stands. The curves are Niemeyer's homage to the undulating Brazilian landscape which he
loved: 'The whole universe is made of curves.'

It was a powerful reaction to the rigidity of orthodox Modernism and it is a building that pre-
figures Le Corbusier's plastic treatment of concrete and canopy at Ronchamp in the next decade
(rather than the landscape, Le Corbusier used a crab's shell as the inspiration for his roof). Yet
Niemeyer's building has not adopted the Expressionism which defined Corbusier's dramatic
departure from the Functionalist aesthetic. Gaudí had used the parabolic arch not because of its
expressive qualities but because it was a superior structural solution; it negated the need for
ungainly flying buttresses. But its very perfection made it for him a symbol of God and it became a
manifestation of his faith. The adoption of curved structures was a rational rather than an expressive decision, just as it was with Niemeyer.

But just as a powerful neo-Expressionism had affected church architecture in Germany and Italy
during the postwar period, so it struck many of the architects in South America. Less constricted by
history and tradition than the Europeans, many South American architects approached
problems of church building with a freshness and originality that was often stunning.

Eladio Dieste used brick at his Church at Atlanida in Uruguay (1958) in a way in which perhaps
only Gaudí could have prophesied; as a rational solution creating a wild expressivity as its

Church of La Virgen Milagrosa, Mexico
City, Mexico, 1955, F Candela

by-product. A fantastic wavy wall undulates like clay collapsing on a potter's wheel. The vaults of the roof are similarly wavy. Dieste was enamoured with the skill of the bricklayer and determined that it should not be lost to an invasion of industrial building techniques merely for the sake of the modern. The church is the apex of his search for forms that were revolutionary, structurally logical and expressively beautiful.

In Mexico, Felix Candela was also exploiting a language of forms which seemed to owe something to Gaudí. The Church of La Virgen Milagrosa in Mexico City (1954–5) seems to be a development of the dramatic, organic forms of the later phases of the Sagrada Família. As with Gaudí, the forms are guided by a sharp appreciation of the lines of force and stress and the inherent qualities of the materials, and are not the purely visual Expressionism that they might seem.

Candela was an engineer and mathematician as well as architect and, in a way, his structures reflect the engineering genius of his forebear Perret and his contemporary Pier Luigi Nervi, both of whom took the art of reinforced concrete to new peaks of creativity. His great feat at the church is his unification of structure and enclosing membrane. The whole fabric is working in unity to create an effect that sends the building soaring skyward in a single, angelic thrust. It is a true realisation of the verticality and vaulting as the earthly representation of the heavens to which the Gothic cathedral builders aspired.

The structure is light and ingenious and yet at the same time the shadows cast by the hyperbolic paraboloids and the spiky, angular form of some of the elements recalls a Cubist approach to space, leaving mystical patches of darkness and an ambiguity of planes. Both the extreme thinness of the concrete structure and its triangular form conspire to evoke the image of the tent, a canopy seemingly held aloft on faith alone.

Candela's other masterpiece was carried out in conjunction with architect Enrique de la Mora y Palomar. Although the Chapel of Nuestra Señora de la Soledad in Coyoacán, Mexico (also 1955) does not feature the structural bravado of his other church, it does embody one of the most liturgically advanced and innovative plans of the period. The seating is arranged on three sides of the altar in the church's triangular plan. The seats in front of the altar are on a slight curve to begin to surround the celebrant. This allows a versatility of use including the seating of a large choir around the altar. The swooping roof is based on a hyperbolic paraboloid which sweeps up at the sides, and the whole roof lifts towards the welcoming entrance.

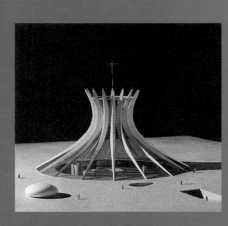  

The most influential design to come out of South America was, however, undoubtedly Oscar Niemeyer's new cathedral for Brasilia (1970). After Le Corbusier's Ronchamp this was perhaps the most iconic church of the 20th century, full of the optimism and hope of the modern spirit. The cathedral as a type was made almost anachronistic by liturgical reform. Although it has a clear function, the idea of a church to house a city full of people does not seem compatible with the increasingly accepted notions of the intimacy of the Eucharist and the desirability of the closeness of the celebrant and congregation. The great cathedral poses a serious barrier to these theological aims. Niemeyer used the circular plan to achieve optimum closeness to and involvement in the celebration.

The cathedral seems to be the continuation of the great urban plaza, swept up to an apex and flowering out at its crown. It is entered via a ramp from the square which descends into the subterranean darkness so that the emergence into the expansive and light world of the cathedral's interior is symbolic of the passage of birth and rebirth into the Christian Church, a metaphor which is made more explicit in the adjacent baptistery which is wholly unlit by windows, like a stalkless mushroom in the plaza.

The structure of the church could barely be simpler. Huge reinforced concrete struts rise to form the framework that is filled by coloured glass to reduce the glare. The building works like a cooling tower so that the hot air from within rises and is released at the top. The struts continue once they have fulfilled their functional role and blossom out in a symbolic gesture of metamorphosis. They cast a spiky shadow on the ground which moves around and dominates the great urban space like a huge crown of thorns.

The altar, pulpit and seating within the cathedral are grouped together around the centre so that there is close proximity of worshippers and celebrant, and even when the church is full there is good visual and aural contact. The cathedral's transparency opens it up to the city while its soaring presence is a symbol of hope and a grand urban gesture; a new conception in design, monumentality superimposed on the city at a human scale recalling the cathedral's organic presence in the heart of the medieval city.

The cathedral's antithesis in scale, but not beauty, is the chapel at the president's palace in Brasilia

(1958). The form is based around an unfolding shell, a sketch of a spiral brought into solid and void. It is one of the simplest sacred spaces with an intimacy and intensity that remain almost unparalleled. The cathedral was designed as part of a built dialogue with the palace; its enclosing concrete wall a private, meditative answer to the open glass structure of the public nature of the palace.

This essay started with Luis Barragán's definition of architecture. What this means in physical terms can be seen at his chapel in Colonia Tlalpan in Mexico City (1952–5). It is a small space, an intervention into an existing convent, but one that sparkles like a gem and illuminates the complex from its centre. There is little innovative about the chapel other than its beauty and simplicity. A golden altar shines against a glowing sunset background of pink and orange. One of the walls is replaced by a looming cross which acts as space divider between the sacred and the profane areas while the motif is echoed on the outside wall that is divided into quarters by a sculpted cross in relief casting its great, distorted shadow across the building.

It is the equatorial answer to the Nordic purity of Erik Gunnar Asplund's Stockholm Cemetery. God is expressed in its clarity and simplicity; it is, like so much South American church architecture, the solution which offers the message of beauty and emotion.

XVI. SCANDINAVIA
Modernism – The Organic and the Rational

The Scandinavian countries accepted Modernism far more comprehensively than most other European countries. The design that emanated from the area exerted a growing influence throughout Europe in the years following the Second World War. Two distinct streams emerged in architecture that largely defined the Scandinavian contribution to 20th-century ecclesiastical architecture.

The first of these is a Nordic classicism which treads the fine line between a traditional architectonic language and Modernism exemplified by Asplund, the second is an organic approach which softened the dogmatic harshness of Bauhaus-type Modernism and which responded more closely to the landscape and the body, a form embodied by Alvar Aalto. Both have had a lasting effect and, although less revolutionary than the developments in Germany, have continued to influence the architecture coming out of Scandinavia and elsewhere, largely for the better.

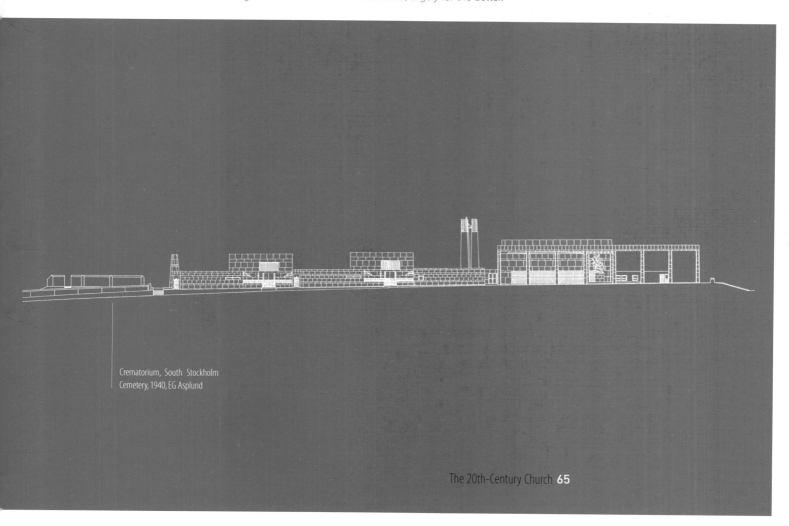

Crematorium, South Stockholm Cemetery, 1940, EG Asplund

In Scandinavia, as in much of Europe, the Arts and Crafts influenced National Romanticism, which defined the desire for independence after the turn of the century and gave way to conservative neoclassicism in the years before and after the First World War. The Swedish architect Asplund was one of the few architects who were able to impart a touch of genius to the genre through a blend of spatial manipulation, materials and reference to tradition in a modern manner.

His Woodland Chapel in the South Stockholm Cemetery (1918–20) was a reinterpretation of the Abbé Laugier's primitive hut, the archetypal shelter of columns and roof executed in a self-effacing vernacular. However, his triumph is the crematorium chapel in the South Stockholm Cemetery, 1935–40. Franco Borsi writes lyrically about it:

> Asplund succeeded in combining the blood-curdling yet romantic howl of the wind in the virgin forest and over the great meadows, a rarefied classicism with marble cross and open portico, and the aggressive functionality of the crematorium, where even the mouths of the furnaces are exactly shaped to fit a coffin. Thus he succeeds in giving to each part, each functional element, not only its own shape, but also its own essential symbolic form, so that nature is nature, the cross is cross without a base or any other architecture but itself, meadow is meadow, the wood is wood, and everything in the austere solemnity of the place exudes an impression of finality and proclaims indeed a final symbolic message.[1]

The austere portico stands in relationship to the wooded landscape like a Greek temple, rigid and eternal as is the simple, self-referential stone cross that stands in front of it. The vision recalls again the tradition of Caspar David Friedrich and a northern Romanticism, an almost pantheistic position, in nature and with it, yet outlined against it. The interior of the chapel sees the cold perfection of the elevation give way to a more humane enclosure. Gently curved walls embrace the mourners, and murals and rounded columns with capitals replace the stripped modern vocabulary. Outside a suspended clock acts as *memento mori*. It should be seen as a seminal influence on the work of Kaija and Heikki Siren who were to refine a minimal version of a similar language which is able to embrace pantheism, a classic Modernism and a minimal, archetypal architectonic language.

A similar softened classicism can be found in a building of the same period, the Resurrection Funerary Chapel in Turku, Finland (1938–41). Its architect, Erik Bryggman, had departed from his harsher, rational Modernism (seen in the Parainen Cemetery Chapel of 1930) to produce a humane synthesis of pure Modernism and elements of a formal, archetypal classical language tinged with an elegant Romanticism. The altar takes its place in a bright arched apse while the chapel is entered through an arcade of columns that gives on to extensive views of the greenery. In early photos ivy intrudes on to the wall of the chancel as if nature had not yet given up its claim on the space. His Mortuary Chapel, Pargas, is an even purer paragon of simplicity; a single space lit by one tall window that sheds light on the funeral bier. Light, airy and exquisite.

These words could also be used for much of the architecture of Alvar Aalto, who in the 1920s had worked with Bryggman. Aalto's church at Vuoksenniska (1956–9) is an odd but intriguing building and encloses a magnificent space. It consists of three segments designed to be used separately or as one; each can be divided by a screen to form a complete room for secular use. It is perhaps more auditorium than church in feel, but this is partly because of its Protestant lineage and partly due to its practical use. The church seems to waft away from the altar like a cloud, the soft curves of the walls billowing outwards. The metal roof allows the building to settle quietly into the landscape and the low eaves give it an eminently human scale while a slender belfry denotes its presence. It is by no means a revolutionary church, indeed its liturgical form does not respond to the new ideas, yet it is a seminal building with a decency and humanity that is rare, and an adaptability that is almost unprecedented.

Aalto's church at Riola in Italy (1966–8) is another highly influential scheme: a wavy roofscape of north lights rests on a series of ribs which look like the bent plywood of his furniture, giving an airy, irregular interior. His concept sketch recalls the expressionistic curves of Erich Mendelsohn while the plan has a jagged irregularity that is visibly modern, a deconstructed version of his earlier church at Seinajoki (1958–60), which also possesses an impeccably elegant Modernist campanile. Aalto's work continues to exert an inestimable influence on the benign Modernism of Reima Pietilä and many others practising today.

Elsewhere in Scandinavia a mini fashion for pointed and pyramidal forms was perhaps partly inspired by the local stave churches and partly by the experiments of Frank Lloyd Wright, as well as a penchant for their expressionistic forms in a mountainous landscape. Magnus Poulsson's church at Gravberget (1956) is an example of a reinterpretation of the vernacular belfry while Aarno Ruusuvuori's church at Hyvinkää (1961) is a modern tent of God, a dynamic prism containing an impressive space.

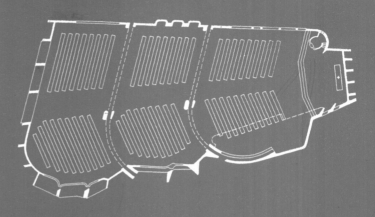

TOP Vuoksenniska Church, Imatra, Finland, 1959, A Aalto

CENTRE Church at Riola di Vergato, Bologna, Italy, 1978, A Aalto

BOTTOM Church at Hyvinkää, Finland, 1961, A Ruusuvuori

Scandinavian design, otherwise, was often sober and functional: Peter Celsing's St Thomas, Vallingby (1960) constitutes a serious urban gesture as well as a fine church and Sigurd Lewerentz's Markus Church in Malmovag (also 1960) is a timeless and understated work of great skill in handling the brick and containing the magically simple space. That Lewerentz had worked with Asplund on the nearby Woodland Crematorium is no surprise seeing the elemental clarity of this little structure. Lewerentz continued to produce some fine ecclesiastical work over the following years.

There is a consistency that runs throughout Scandinavian church architecture that was rarely equalled, an inherent humanising of the language of Modernism which continues in some of the finest of today's designs.

XVII. ELSEWHERE IN EUROPE

Britain was among the slowest European countries to react to liturgical change and for much of the 20th century ecclesiastical architecture was stuck in a vaguely historicist mode with minor concessions to Modernism. After the Second World War a tremendous amount of church building took place to cope with swelling populations, new suburbs and damage inflicted during the war. However, unlike France and Germany the architecture was not related to a living liturgy and was thus itself largely anachronistic.

Many schemes adopted the modern aesthetic without its reasoning. Churches began to look modern but not to be modern. The architect used unusual shapes for their own sake or as experiments in personal expression. By the 1960s, however, some of the ideas of the Liturgical Movement began to be accepted by the Church and a handful of architects. Maguire and Murray were among the first to create a thoughtful church that responded to the changes. Other great opportunities were lost. Alison and Peter Smithson's fine design for the Coventry Cathedral competition (1951) was ignored in favour of Basil Spence's scheme; a powerful design and one which recognised new liturgical thinking was usurped by one which had progressed in little else but structure from the Gothic.

The Smithsons wrote in the report that accompanied their entry that they hoped that:
the building of this cathedral will finally explode the fallacy that Modern Architecture is capable of expressing abstract ideas and will prove that *only* Modern Architecture is capable of creating a symbol of the dogmatic truths of the Christian faith.[1]
The scheme was based on a square plan on the diagonal, covered by a dramatic roof rising to the altar, a conception of space which did not enclose the church but allowed the space and the elements within to speak. Spence's church is elegant (particularly in its concrete structure) but uninspiring despite the wealth of artistic talent which contributed to it. It proved, nevertheless, an influential scheme.

Of all the ecclesiastical work to come out of Britain, that of Gillespie, Kidd and Coia was probably the most coherent and interesting even if it fell below the standards of much European work. Their St Paul's Church at Glenrothes New Town (1956–7) is a simple and subtle insertion into the landscape, its whiteness and clarity a response to Böhm's church at Nordeney, but features an interesting and innovative wedge-shaped plan and a plain tower over the altar which illuminates the sacred space below with an unseen and wonderful light filtered from the cold Scottish skies. The Church of St Bride's in East Kilbride (1963–4) is a robust brick construction, a heavily internalised building, which confronts the world with an almost medieval, forbidding harshness. Its plan is fairly traditional but there are good touches; in a dramatic gesture the font is placed a few steps below the level of the church in a channel of light from above, and the principal wall is something like a reference to Le Corbusier's Ronchamp with its randomly carved out niches and windows.

Frederick Gibberd's Catholic Cathedral in Liverpool (1960–7) was a dramatic utilisation of a round plan, part of a tide of churches inspired by Niemeyer's masterpiece at Brasilia. Ireland, which saw its first modern church designed by the American Barry Byrne, was the venue for a number of good churches in the postwar period. Among these, perhaps the finest is Michael Scott's Church of Corpus Christi at Knockanure (1964).

This brilliantly simple church is of Miesian clarity, but a far more successful building than Mies' own chapel in Illinois. It stands on a podium like a Greek temple and its wholly transparent facade is made a huge picture frame for a large stone relief that gives the facade a face. It is without doubt one of the purest pieces of Modernism to come out of ecclesiastical architecture and one of the finest pieces outside Germany. The other Irish church of great interest is Corr and McCormick's St

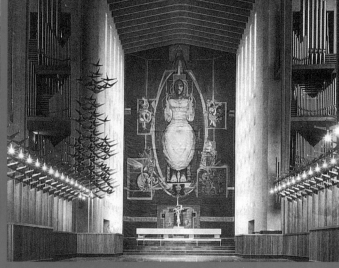

TOP Coventry Cathedral, Coventry, UK, 1962, B Spence

CENTRE St Paul's Church, Glenrothes New Town, Glenrothes, Fife, UK, 1957, GKC

BOTTOM Church of St Bride's, East Kilbride, Lanarkshire, UK, 1964, GKC

Aengus, Burt (1967), one of the best examples of a round church, with a roof that is dramatically swept up over the altar in a gesture that sits strongly against the powerful rural landscape.

Central Europe has more recently seen some fascinating developments. Wojciech Pietrzyk and Jan Grabacki's church in Nowa Huta-Bienczyce (1974) is a masterful piece of sculptural Expressionism in the vein of Le Corbusier's Ronchamp and within a bright modern worship space, while Tadeusz Gawtowski and Jan Grabacki's Church of the Good Shepherd (1965–76) is a jagged geometric assortment almost reminiscent of the fragmented forms of Frank Gehry. In Austria, the artist Friedensreich Hundertwasser transformed the Church of St Barbara in Bärnbach (1988) from a dull building into a splash of colour using tiles and ceramics and a golden onion dome in a heady blend of Gaudí and Klimt. The churches of Imre Makovecz in Hungary have attracted worldwide attention for their stunning creativity and an organicism, which has struck a chord as an antidote to a dulled Modernism, while György Csete's Church of St Elisabeth at Halásztelek (1976) is one of the few fine examples of a round church. It weaves archetypal imagery and clarity of form into an impressively simple work.

NOTES

I. A Matter of Morality

1. Nikolaus Pevsner, *An Outline of European Architecture*, Pelican Books (London), 1943, p 381.
2. Robert Furneaux-Jordan, *Victorian Architecture*, Pelican Books (London), 1966, p 174.
3. Augustus WN Pugin, *Contrasts; or a Parallel between the Noble Edifices of the Fourteenth and Fifteenth Centuries and Similar Buildings of the Present Day; Shewing the Present Decay of Taste*, Salisbury, 1836.
4. Johann Wolfgang von Goethe, *Baukunst*, essay, 1795.
5. Arthur Schopenhauer, *Erganzungen zum dritten Büch*, 1844.
6. Jean Gimpel, *The Cathedral Builders*, Michael Russell (London), 1983, English translation; *The Medieval Machine*, Victor Gollancz (London), 1976, English translation.

II. Arts and Crafts

1. William R Lethaby, *Architecture*, Thornton Butterworth Ltd (London), 1911, p 248.
2. Edward S Prior, 'The New Cathedral for Liverpool', *The Architectural Review*, Vol 10 (London), p 143.
3. William R Lethaby, *Architecture*, op cit, p 145.
4. WR Lethaby: *Architecture, Design and Education*, exhibition catalogue, Lund Humphries (London), 1984, p 40.
5. William R Lethaby, *Architecture, Mysticism and Myth*, London, 1891, p 16.

III. Secession: Rationalism and Nationalism

1. Diary of Otto Wagner, quoted in H Geretsegger and M Peinter, *Otto Wagner 1814–1918*, Academy Editions (London), 1979. Original version 1964: Residenz Verlag (Salzburg).
2. Otto Wagner, *Moderne Architecktur*, Verlag von Anton Schroll and Co (Vienna), 1895.
3. JA Lux, *Otto Wagner*, Vienna, 1914; quoted in H Geretsegger and M Peinter, *Otto Wagner, 1814–1918*, op cit.

V. German Expressionism: The Star and the Sacred Mountain

1. William R Lethaby, *Architecture*, op cit, p 245.
2. Bruno Taut, *Alpine Architecture*, Hagen, 1919.
3. Otto Bartning, *Vom Neuen Kirchenbau*, Bruno Cassirer Verlag (Berlin), 1919.
4. Bruno Taut, *Frühlicht*, Verlag Ullstein GmbH (Berlin), 1963.
5. Johannes van Acken, *Christozentrische Kirchenkunst, Ein Entwurf zum Liturgischen Gesamthkunstwerk* (Christocentric Church Art: Towards the Total Work of Liturgical Art), pamphlet 1922.

VI. Auguste Perret: Prophet of the Modern Church

1. Nikolaus Pevsner, *The Sources of Modern Architecture and Design*, Thames and Hudson (London), 1968.
2. Walter Gropius, *Scope of Total Architecture*, New York, 1943, p 61.
3. GE Kidder Smith, *New Churches of Europe*, The Architectural Press (London), 1964, p 9.

VII. Modernism and Liturgical Reform: A Brief Background

1. Anton Henze, *Contemporary Church Art*, Sheed and Ward, (US), 1956.
2. Otto Bartning, *Vom Neuen Kirchenbau*, op cit.

3. Rudolf Schwarz, *Vom Bau der Kirche*, Verlag Lambert Schneider. (Heidelberg), 1938; translated as *The Church Incarnate*, Henry Regnery and Co, (US), 1958, pp 8–9.
4. Ibid.

VIII. The Church Incarnate: Modernism and the Church

1. Otto Bartning, *Vom Neuen Kirchenbau*, op cit.
2. Extract from Otto Bartning's dedication speech, 1928.
3. Robert Maguire and Keith Murray, *Modern Churches of the World*, Studio Vista Ltd (London), 1965.
4. Quoted in Hugo Schnell, *Twentieth Century Church Architecture in Germany*, Verlag Schnell and Steiner (Munich), 1975, p 48.

IX. Switzerland: The Consolidation of Modernism

1. Peter Hammond, *Liturgy and Architecture*, Barrie and Rockliffe (London), 1960, p 62.
2. Quoted in Albert Christ-Janer and Mary Foley, *Modern Church Architecture*, McGraw Hill (New York), 1962, p 222.

XII. Postwar Germany: A Church Meant for Our Own Time

1. Quoted in R Gieselmann, *Contemporary Church Architecture*, Thames and Hudson (London), 1972, p 160.

XIII. The Church Building as Art: Le Corbusier and the Mediterranean

1. Quoted in Willy Boesiger (ed), *Le Corbusier, Oeuvre Complète*, Vol V (8 vols), Zurich, 1929–70.
2. Charles Jencks, *Le Corbusier and the Tragic View of Architecture*, Allen Lane (London), 1973.
3. Christian Norberg-Schulz, *Meaning in Western Architecture*, Electa (Milan), 1974, p 213. English translation: Praeger Publishers, 1975.
4. F Boit and F Perrot, *Le Corbusier et L'Art Sacré*, Le Manufacture (Lyons), 1985.
5. Quoted in Albert Christ-Janer and Mary Foley, *Modern Church Architecture*, op cit, p 88.
6. Ibid, p 98.
7. Giuseppe Vaccaro, quoted in *Spazio* no 7.
8. Quoted in Charles Knevitt, *Connections: The Architecture of Richard England, 1964–84*, Lund Humphries (London), 1983.

XIV. United States of America: 'For the Worship of God and the Service of Man'

1. Frank Lloyd Wright, *An Autobiography*, 1932, pp 153–4.
2. Quoted in Albert Christ-Janer and Mary Foley, *Modern Church Architecture*, op cit, p 259.

XVI Scandinavia: Modernism – The Organic and the Rational

1. Franco Borsi, *The Monumental Era*, English translation, Lund Humphries (London), 1987, p 137.

XVII. Elsewhere in Europe

1. Quoted in *Churchbuilding*, no 8 (London), 1963.

Naked Churches
The Northern Tradition

Edwin Heathcote

The harsh strictures of fundamentalist Modernism chimed in sympathy not only with the self-denial and innate minimalism of the traditional Catholic orders but with the sparse self-denial of the senses of Calvinist and Lutheran worship and the eschewing of decoration which led to the Catholic adoption of the Baroque as a method of architectural seduction. Thus the rigorous, often harsh language of Modernism was slowly adopted by both Catholic and Protestant traditions. But it was in a Northern Europe dominated by harsh Protestantism that a particular brand of architecture would emerge and remain hugely influential far beyond the small world of ecclesiastical architecture itself.

What is common to both Protestant and monastic demands is the idea of prayer as a part of the daily routine and of worship as something integrated into ordinary life. Although this sounds obvious it is in fact the opposite of the Catholic notion of Baroque theatricality, of pomp and grandeur, Mass as performance. The latter makes the building special while the former emphasises the sacred in the ordinary. To use a contemporary vernacular, one is about iconic buildings, the other is not. Our starchitect-designed art galleries, stops on the city-break cultural tours of the world and urban regenerators have surpassed the cathedrals that formerly stood at the key cultural, urban and architectural crossroads of our great cities. The Protestant northern tradition is something entirely different but nevertheless a strand which is becoming increasingly influential partly as a counterbalance to the relentless rise of the self-conscious architectural icon.

Arguably the churches of St Peter in Klippan (1966), St Mark in suburban Stockholm (1960), both in Sweden, by Sigurd Lewerentz, and the monastic buildings of Dom Hans van der Laan have become the most influential church buildings of the mature phase of Modernism, their influence spreading far beyond the limited world of ecclesia. The growing appreciation of their forms, spaces, materials and tectonics stems not from their sacrality but from their exquisite attention to the details of the everyday. While the most dramatic and freakish of contemporary church architecture tends to have little effect on other genres, these solid, beautifully executed and self-effacing buildings have grown in stature and influence because of their attention to the ordinary these are buildings from which we can extract inspiration whether designing a house, a school or a tool shed. They are buildings which see God in the ordinary, in the details. They are buildings in which making and meaning are bonded in the same way as the Cistercian Abbey of Le Thoronet, the influence of which was projected across the history of Modernism by Lucien Hervé's sublime photos. Lewerentz made Semperian walls, almost woven in the richness and hand-wrought qualities of the brick. Although far more classical, Hans van der Laan's work is also notable for its attention to the quotidian, indeed his work seems to somehow blend Renaissance proportional perfection with a mundane, municipal aesthetic, yet his buildings continue to exert a growing pull on contemporary designers. The works of Paul Felix in Belgium, particularly the nunnery in Ostend (1957), display a similar Modernist asceticism, the enduring influence of which can still be seen in the harsh, considered brickwork of some of the best contemporary Belgian work.

In the same year in Finland, Heikki and Keija Siren built their extraordinary students chapel in Espoo, another brick structure but one in which the east wall has been removed to make way for a plate-glass void which gives onto the lush forests in which the building sits, and a ghostly white cross embedded in the landscape. The influence of this pantheistically striking building remains powerful, Ando's wedding chapel being the most obvious, as well as the finest, example.

Ando's architecture also raises the fascinating spectre of the drift of religious traditions across continents. If Ando's architecture is inspired by Mies and the Sirens, then it provides a counterbalance to the pervading influence of Japanese architecture on Modernism, in particular the sparsity of contemplative Zen traditions. This cultural exchange is increasingly informing and occasionally confusing the architecture of the contemporary church. Christianity has little in common with the contemplative focus of Zen yet the lazy cliches of such easily embraced concepts lead, in their own way, to buildings as alien and illiterate as the grand icons of contemporary Mannerism.

Yet there are also achievements. There is terrific irony in the anecdote related by John Pawson himself that the monks who were later to commission him to build their new monastery at Nový Dvůr, were initially seduced by his store for Calvin Klein, and then one monk, while looking around his house after approaching him about the commission, was overheard whispering 'don't you think it's a bit austere for us?'

Pawson travelled seamlessly from temples of consumption to the monastery proving that minimalism, the term so derided and denied by contemporary architects, still has something to say about the contemporary space for worship.

There has also been a noticeable, slow but sure rediscovery of the architecture of the everyday, of the value of the found object and a recognition of the sacred in the ordinary. While this is not true of the broad mass of churches constructed today, in which the extraordinary and the clumsy vie for the attention of parishes and architects, the work of a generation active in the 1950s and 1960s has sparked a renewed interest in subtlety and thoughtful carelessness. It is possible that it is this rediscovery of the quiet architecture of Dom Hans van der Laan, of Lewerentz and of the German, Swiss and Austrian architects who instigated the great changes in modern church design, that will lead to a reappraisal of the typology, an approach based not on expression but on restraint, not on the special but on the ordinary. 'God' is, as Mies said, 'in the details', and nowhere is this lumbering architectural cliche more important than in the church.

EXPRESSION AND REPRESSION
Gesture and Function

Edwin Heathcote

The state of contemporary church architecture could easily be summarised in the wonderfully succinct (and extremely contemporary) term 'option anxiety'. Architecture has become, like everything else, an arm of consumption, it is full of choices. It would be naive to suggest that it was not always like this. From the Gothic cathedrals with their competing spires to the churches of the Renaissance and their exquisitely sacred proportions and altarpieces by superstar artists, one-upmanship has always played a serious role in the architecture of the church. But pride and continuity had, for centuries, induced a gradual progression in language, symbol, form and meaning. Whether it was to be a bible in stone set forth for the illiterate, a trailer for the forthcoming attraction of heaven or merely a place intended to concentrate meditation, prayer and gathering, the church had always been readable in its intentions and its ideas through archetypes and familiar models. Just as we have broadly lost the ability to read art (and art increasingly loses its ability and ambition to engage with the intellect), so we are losing the skill of reading meaning in buildings, and the two building types which suffer most are the house, and the house of God.

Domestic architecture for the masses has descended into an intellectually debased kit of parts so that the most formative and meaningful spaces of our lives are stripped of symbol and intelligence, of the archetypes of threshold, entrance, light, dwelling and shelter: the house has become a (badly) decorated box. If we are unable or unwilling to seek and see meaning in our dwellings, how can the church building develop? Does it become a bland, themed approximation of images we have become familiar with as church-like? Or does it become the architectural equivalent of the big-box retail shed? Or, is it just possible that it could become the last repository of meaning and symbol in an architecture which signally fails to address issues beyond the purely functional, the expressionistically simplistic and the blatantly commercial?

The signs are not good. Arguably the most thoughtful and meaningful contemporary international architecture is devoted to art – to value and to tourism. Our equivalents of the great pilgrimages are the obligatory trips to the big cathedrals of art. Where is there a modern cathedral with the intensity of Tate Modern or the sculptural ambition of Bilbao's Guggenheim? The Millennium forced a major bout of soul-searching in the Church with new buildings commissioned around the world in celebration of the endurance of Christianity. In Italy in particular the drive for the Jubilee churches provoked argument and debate but, by the time the buildings had been completed (well into the third millennium) the momentum had been lost; the church had signally failed to reclaim its status as the pumping heart of architectural innovation.

The real growth in ecclesiastical structures has left architecture far behind. The out-of-town megachurch has to contend with the mega-mart, the big shed retailers for the Sunday audience. For the builders of the big evangelical churches, architecture is all but irrelevant. Tin sheds with epic forecourts full of cars, they could have been the ideal vehicles for Venturian experimentation, but their patrons remain profoundly cynical about the importance of space, preferring instead to rely on the crowd, on the effect of the congregation on itself. It is an entirely valid angle, arguably as faithful to the spirit of the gospels as any other, if not more so. But it fails to enrich the culture of worship, or of the city; indeed it fails to return anything to the community and, ironically fails to exploit the evangelicising possibilities of powerful building. Interestingly, their one success has been to reinvent defunct urban archetypes, often cinemas, theatres or public halls, which had been stuck in limbo as historic, often valuable structures and spaces for which permission to radically change use would have been inconceivable.

In the ultimate of ironies, ecclesiastical architecture has actually suffered due to its popularity and status with architects. Most architects, regardless of their religious beliefs, foster a powerful desire to build a church at least once in their careers. Ronchamp has inspired so many that all would attempt to create their own pilgrimage chapel. The church becomes the repository for all their forbidden dreams and impractical desires. This tends to lead to a situation in which the church building becomes a vehicle for repressed self-expression, a one-off ejaculation of architectural fantasy. While this may lead to one or two inspirational designs, it leads to far more self-indulgent whimsies. The hangover from Ronchamp has been long and painful.

There are indications, however, that architects are turning their attentions to churches by others far more engaged in the language of liturgical form and far more interested in the expression of worship as a ritual of the everyday rather than the overblown expression of the numinous. Increasingly the buildings of Sigurd Lewerentz, Dom Hans van der Laan and Rudolf Schwarz are being seen as exemplars, as the most meaningful contributions of ecclesiastical design to the modern story. Just as the severe and austere monasteries of the Cistercians have been influencing the development of Modernism (from Le Corbusier to John Pawson), it is often the non-ritual spaces in church buildings that have emerged from the orders which have become most influential. Perhaps this is because these spaces have always retained and required a clear brief and Modernism is (still) functionally driven. Le Corbusier's most successful religious building is not the pilgrimage church of Ronchamp but the monastery of La Tourette, a machine for monks. The completion of the severely gestural cooling tower of Firminy looks set to confirm La Tourette's position at the apex of the Swiss architects' ecclesiastical works.

Modern architects, very often non-believers, have encountered great problems seeing a church commission in terms of a functional brief. It is an irony as the liturgy effectively provides the perfect narrative, hierarchy and aspiration, as well as a far more defined backstory and symbolic language than a house or public building. The knee-jerk desire to overawe with space continues to damage the prospects for the development of a defined and thoughtful ecclesiastical architecture.

THE CHAPEL AND THE RECONCILIATION

The seduction of the banal creation of the icon has led to the chapel, often private, usually extremely modest, as the driving force behind new ideas in the architecture of the sacred. Whereas the chapel used to be a kind of architectural miniaturisation, a junior version of ideas already seen in bigger churches, the seeming inability of architects to grapple with architectural problems on the larger scale and the relative flexibility engendered in the small chapel (where the brief is usually extremely uncomplicated and unencumbered with the functional issues of accessibility, congregation, secondary spaces and secondary functions) have led to a series of extremely interesting experiments.

The new ideas embodied in these small structures illustrate the diversity of contemporary architecture, the extremely powerful after-effects of Postmodernism combined, occasionally paradoxically, with the broad survival of largely Modernist ideals and formal and material languages.

The archetypal forms of the small dwelling, the tectonic vocabulary of the house, have proved a powerful and durable metaphor for a place where God dwells. In Christian Kerez's wayside mountain chapel we see these ideas stripped naked, the chapel presented as shelter, as shrine. The stark concrete ur-house embodies ideas of shelter, the primitive hut, Adam's House in Paradise and of the notion of the House of God in the simplest and most direct manner possible. It has been criticised for its relentlessly single reading yet it is among the richest of recent buildings, precisely because it is so proto-domestic in its imagery and so effortlessly overawed by its dramatic Alpine setting.

In Siza's family chapel, similar devices reappear, the basic concrete of structure, a material extruded from the earth and left unadorned, the simple but meaningful openings appearing like stars in its dark canopy. In Peter Zumthor's Saint Bruder Klaus Field Chapel in Mechernich the architect revives deep archetypes which seem to have disappeared from contemporary church architecture in a small building which promises to be one of the most intense of recent years, binding together the four elements: earth in the poured concrete structure; air in the open light at the top and the replacement of a conventional door with a metal gate; water in the rain that will fall through the oculus, pantheon-like; and fire in the floor of cast lead upon which the rain will puddle and in the burning away of the logs which make up the internal formwork once the concrete has set. By moving away from conventional Christian iconography, Zumthor reinvents the chapel as an almost pagan temple to the elements and the land and sky. Although in formal language Zumthor could hardly be more different, the kind of mythical pantheism he evokes in this chapel and the earlier building at Sogn Benedetg, there is a kinship in the poetry and symbolism with Hungarian architect Imre Makovecz whose churches remain among the most astonishing buildings of recent years. Although unbuilt, his plans for a church emerging from the rocks in the heavily forested Pilis Hills outside Budapest evoke the same kind of earthy symbolism, even in their form, although there is always a more literal symbolism with Makovecz and his followers.

That both Makovecz and Zumthor have emerged from central European Catholic traditions and in small countries is perhaps more than pure coincidence. Both remain dedicated to the respective rural landscapes of their countries and both remain reluctant to succumb to the lure of international commissions, in which they are also linked to Siza, who also emerges from an intensely Catholic tradition. But also, all three architects built on the traditions and strengths as well as on the deeply engrained symbolism and language of the local vernacular which is in turn tinged with the Modernist tradition with which they all matured. Whereas elsewhere ecclesiastical architecture is in danger of being swallowed up by the ubiquitous slide towards the universal domination of the commercial aesthetic, it seems in these cases architects are able to revivify it using the basic tools of symbol and local technique tempered by the language of Modernism and without resorting to a pastiche of either tradition. It is in these small, intense, often rural buildings that the twin traditions which had formed the fissure in 20th-century church architecture are beginning finally to meld together, and it may be that any advances in church architecture emerge from private chapels rather than lavishly funded public commissions. It is perhaps a reflection of a societal change which is seeing church attendance drop throughout the developed world and a Europewide population slump which ensures that new churches are rarely needed to serve shrinking and increasingly secular (or at least non-Christian) communities. While parishes continue in their efforts to create 'open and welcoming' buildings, which end up as bland, sub-corporate glazed boxes, church architecture remains unlikely to regain its position as the power behind advances of art and design, and intensity and meaning may have to be concentrated into smaller packages from private chapels to contemporary shrines.

LIGHT AND MASS

More than with any other building type, architects approaching a church design become obsessed with light. As the most abstract cipher for the ethereal and for the presence of the heavenly, light has become both the greatest cliche and the most powerful resource of architects often unfamiliar with the rituals and formal language of the contemporary church. Light is uncontroversial, unlike say art or even form. It is universally understood and taken to be ideal for the purpose of expressing God. It appeals to atheists as much, if not more than to Christians and it has become one of the motifs of modern architecture, somehow self-sufficient, as if light itself was able to express everything an architect is not able to believe: the other, the beyond.

In the hands of some architects it has produced wonders, in others blunders of a Brobdingnagian scale. In Northern Europe where light, in its virtual absence or near-permanent presence is the most radical indicator of the seasons it is celebrated like nowhere else. In the buildings of Juha Leiviska, most notably the Myyrmäki church (1984) the planes become a De Stijl disappearing act, ethereally fading into the blinding winter light reflected off the dazzling whiteness of the snow or the softer brilliance of the summer sunshine. In Jorn Utzon's wonderful church at Bagsvaerd (1976) in Denmark (the building with which he followed up the Sydney Opera House), the light floods in in waves through a roof which reflects and directs the glow in an extraordinary undulating serpentine section.

In Kaija and Heikki Siren's Otaniemi Chapel in Finland (1957) it is the factory-section of the monopitch roof dragging light in from behind the congregation while the celebrant fades into the forest background like an actor on a set. In Philip Johnson's extraordinary Crystal Cathedral and its skyscraper campanile (1980 and 1990 respectively) in California's Garden Grove it is the bright light and air-con of the desert mall or the airport, a final realisation of the Expressionist dream of the crystal mountain executed in the brutally commercial language of US boomtime rather than the socialist utopianism of Taut or Mendelssohn.

Meinhard von Gerkan, like Johnson a commercial architect, does something similar in a less epic way, the joy in his Christus pavilion coming from the even glow of the thin-veined marble cladding, an old trick well-revived and one that was used before him by Angelo Mangiarotti at the Mater Misericordia in 1957 and before that by Otto Bartning in his Stahlkirche in 1928. The opposite of this effect is supplied by the deep, thick walls, the fortified aesthetic of everything from Ronchamp to Siza's Santa Ovidio chapel, but even here it is the light that gives emphasis and form to the mass, to the physical weight of the structure. It is ironic, but perhaps also predictable that perhaps the most powerful tool that architects have at their disposal can be debased into one of the greatest and dullest cliches, the easy trope. It has been the good luck of the museum and the gallery that their functional requirements are far more clearly and formally established and the breaking of the rules is seen as a step out of line and one that is both carefully thought about and much discussed. Issues of view and contamination, of letting the outside in and allowing the sacred space of art to be polluted by the realm of the everyday outside are ironically far greater architectural and artistic issues than they are in the genuine field of what has come to be known as sacred space. It is a mark of the relative position of art and religion in contemporary culture that while art's status grows, boosted by its cultural and financial value, its place on the new pilgrimage trail, the church, the model for the great new cathedrals of art, is left behind as an anachronism. In fact there are many ways in which the two typologies could beneficially cross-germinate, yet it seems that the intellectual and artistic discourse will, for the moment, always come down on the side of art while the church languishes among the vague sentiments of well-meaning architects.

THE PRESENT AND THE FUTURE

The inexorable strength and painful weakness of contemporary church architecture are paradoxically both due to its outsider status. Architects from Schwarz to Zumthor have managed to create buildings of breathtaking emotional impact and visceral power while ignoring fashion. That the church stands apart from the commercial demands of contemporary building, that it is expected to be something else and provide something more has enabled these architects and countless others to create thoughtful, powerful and important buildings which have seeped into the general architectural and public consciousness rather than exploding over the pages of the colour magazines. But other architects have failed for the same reasons, because they have tried too hard.

The church, alongside the architect's own house, remains the dream commission, one which every architect secretly desires but one which suffers from the over-literal interpretations of a lifetime's rejected plans. Churches are not able to contain the imagery, the desire and the intensity architects often attempt to inject into their overwrought forms; they are, after all, only buildings.

There is now none of the desire to re-examine ecclesiastical form. Little of the sophisticated cultural, philosophical, urban or formal thought which has become commonplace in the creation of a new museum or gallery filters down to the church. There is, probably thankfully, no discernible trend, no specific philosophical, theological or liturgical direction, no undercurrent of coherent or rigorous direction or rebellion. Christianity finds itself in decline and where it is most strong, in the developing world, architecture has yet to take on the importance it has held in the Western tradition. There are moral issues in many historic communities about the building of new churches at all, the preservation of existing buildings is something which exercises minds and budgets throughout the old world and beyond and many of the architects who think most deeply about the future of the institution and who are involved most closely personally are employed on the adaptation of historic buildings to contemporary demands, with wildly differing success.

Few churches make the news beyond their local communities and the attempt by the Vatican to inject new life into the architectural genre at the turn of the millennium produced profoundly mixed results and an eloquent cross-section of contemporary problems. Designs by Santiago Calatrava, Tadao Ando and Gunther Behnisch displayed wildly differing approaches, none of which entirely convinced, yet perhaps least convincing of all was Richard Meier's victorious entry, a tired regurgitation of the old turkey of hands in prayer. Of the few buildings which do make the headlines Renzo Piano's San Giovanni Rotondo in the dusty, plastic shrine-scattered wastes of a Puglian hillside made it more for scale than innovation. A new type of building, it responds to the almost fanatical devotion to the beatific monk who has become the patron, almost saint, of the region, and is the upmarket version of the stadium used by US evangelists. Indeed it is those evangelical sheds which have become the dominant typology; quick to erect and cheap to run, they are no more than a roof over the heads of the often huge congregations, a reiteration of the notion of the mass of the people as the metaphorical House of God.

Other new typologies would seem to be available but have yet to attract any serious intention. Airport and hospital chapels spring to mind while the private chapel is enjoying a renaissance, perhaps unfortunately, as a lifestyle choice for clients who want an extra luxurious and intense room but have difficulty ascribing a function to it beyond the dozens of redundant bedrooms now de rigeur in the houses of the wealthy.

The future of the church as an architectural type is not in doubt it is precarious but it is assured. The balance to be struck between the careful conservation and adaptation of an awesome stock of historic buildings and the creation of new buildings remains delicate and frequently controversial. Churches are working buildings, more than symbols or monuments, they are excluded from art because they have a function, and because they have a function they lose meaning when that function becomes debased or inhibited.

It is almost impossible to look back on the last few years of church building and come to any solid conclusions. The changes made by the responses to Vatican II have taken two generations to disseminate and to be absorbed into the culture, and it is by no means certain that the process is complete. At the same time Christianity itself is struggling with the conflict between traditionalism and the urge to modernise. Arguably church architecture has advanced beyond the position of the church itself, easily assimilating and absorbing contemporary trends and ideologies and radically transforming its tectonic and functional language over a period of maybe half a century in a way which a huge institution may find it difficult to follow. The differences between Protestant and Catholic architecture have melded so that they are virtually indistinguishable and, if anything, it is a Lutheran/Calvinist simplicity and self-effacement which has emerged triumphant combined with the monastic asceticism so popular with architects. As faith, strength of faith and the number of faithful all wane, the role of the church needs again to be reassessed. But it remains a pivotal building in the community, the place where birth, marriage, death and the rites of passage continue to be celebrated, mourned and marked. It is still an accessible public space amid an increasingly, and occasionally frighteningly commercial and privatised world, and it remains a sanctuary. Its role is perhaps more important than ever as a space of quiet contemplation and concentration, of escape. It is therefore essential to all of us that the church as a type remains vital and that architects continue to apply themselves with rigour and intelligence to the most enigmatic and historically rich and nuanced of our contemporary architectural seams.

SANTO OVIDIO ESTATE CHAPEL

Álvaro Siza

Location: Douro, Portugal
Completion date: 2001

RIGHT The three walls, each with an aperture – cross, half-circle and door – hold a rather Trinitarian metaphor in tension. The altar, appropriately in the midst of this and illuminated by the dome of natural light and a bare bulb, meets all intersections of the chapel's underlying grid.

In the 1990s the Portuguese architect Álvaro Siza enriched his prolific and distinguished portfolio with a church complex at Marco de Canavezes (see p 178), a building whose large fluted sides have lodged themselves in the minds of architects and Christians alike. The church's intervention in an urban landscape is typically tightly controlled and balanced, an uncompromising exercise in simplicity. It is no surprise, then, that another ecclesiastical commission was quick to follow, albeit it for a much smaller private chapel on the estate of Santo Ovidio in Douro, northern Portugal.

The same restraint is evident here, a restraint which completely belies the accuracy and attention paid to the context and topography. Framed by a driveway wall, a small baroque gatehouse and well-established trees the chapel's outward features are, at first glance, almost so innocuous they could be mistaken for those of a water tower or another simple gatehouse. But elevated approximately two-thirds of the way up the facade is a small half-circle window. Like a sun setting on the horizon, or the perfect dome of more 'ambitious' buildings, it is an unusual form for a solitary east window but, nonetheless, a very positive signal that the building is more than functional.

A protruding block that contains the tiny sacristy also disrupts the whitewashed cuboid form. Flush with the front wall, it overhangs the pathway lending dimensions on a human scale and alleviating any sense of imperiousness. The path leads up some stone steps to a small courtyard that almost mirrors the footprint of the chapel itself and shares the same level as the entrance to the chapel. There is continuity between the courtyard and the chapel in the stone cladding of the entrance wall, as if the chapel has been lifted up from the courtyard floor bearing the imprint of earthliness and solidity. The courtyard is also a deft way of slowing down and building up the experience of entering the chapel, something that subsequently enhances and enlarges the very small space within.

Passing under a broad stone lintel and a single Moorish arch cut into the stones above, the interior volume is tall and cast in bare concrete. The half-circle window now becomes a theatrical porthole for natural light above the altar, and a cross, similarly carved out of concrete, has a backdrop of densely glazed golden marble. A bare bulb brightens the third wall over the sacristy door. Such detailing is reminiscent of Le Corbusier's treatment of his concrete monastery at La Tourette where, deep in the crypt, 'light cannons' direct generous shafts of light onto the monks' private altar. Despite our post-Brutalist view of concrete, which has aged and mellowed (not unlike the buildings themselves), the visual resonance of the material is arguably as poignant as ever. In 1965 Robert Maguire and Keith Murray wrote of La Tourette: 'it is silent and empty with the silence and emptiness of the tomb, but transfigured by light' (p 52). Such words could be aptly used in reference to the chapel at Santo Ovidio.

The blocks of cast concrete also serve to form a grid by which everything else takes its cue and falls into place. Again, the human dimension seems implicit in the proportions of each block so that the effects of a domestic dwelling (or monastic cell) are subliminally felt. Furniture is equally consonant with the chapel's proportions: low and chunky pine benches rest on the same wood used in strips for the flooring. These in turn line up with the edge of a platform of granite, like a well-fitting rug or indeed a nave. The altar itself is hewn from a solid

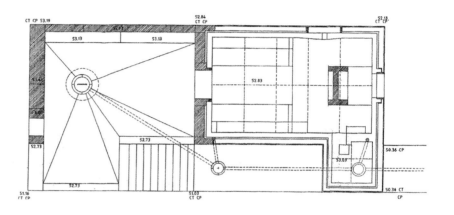

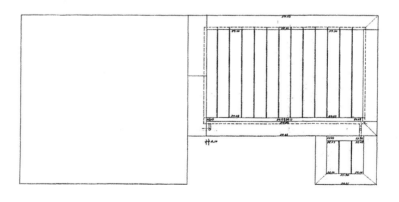

FAR LEFT At the entrance to the Santo Ovidio Estate the chapel looks almost perfunctory in its restraint. The small half-circle window is an allusive symbol, and the detailing of the stone cornice is one example of Siza's typical attentiveness.

LEFT The almost T-shaped cross is an echo of the cross in Siza's acclaimed church of Marco de Canavezes. Golden marble is set behind it, one of a few warmer elements in the chapel that contrast and relieve the grey concrete walls and granite furniture.

ABOVE Siza's response to the site is understated but virtually immaculate when one considers its relation to the small original gatehouse, its size in comparison with the existing trees and driveway, and its positioning with respect to the sight lines from the road.

NIGHT PILGRIMAGE CHAPEL

Places of pilgrimage are often in far-flung rural locations where the remoteness from civilisation or proximity to nature seem to contribute to the journeying, the arrival and the genius loci of the place in question. The site at Locherboden, in the Tyrolean Upper Inn Valley, owes its pilgrimage status to a miracle of the Virgin Mary of 1871, said to have taken place at the already existing Chapel of Grace. Another chapel was built just after the miracle, since when the numbers of pilgrims attending has reached over 2,000 at a time. The pilgrimage is special in that it is walked by night (happening six times a year). The apex at which pilgrims would remain for a candlelit service was once simply a clearing between trees and a rugged cave in the rocks. Now, at the end of the path leading up from the valley, a low open chapel sits at the foot of the caves, luminescent at night, deliberate and poised in its form.

Gerold Wiederin, whose design was chosen from a countrywide competition run by the Catholic church of the site's nearest village at Mötz, did not seek to glorify or enhance the natural environment of this site but, rather, to provide 'the framework for a religious observance in the midst of unformed nature' (Gerold Wiederin, 2001). Equally, the chapel does not shy away from a strong architectural statement, borrowing heavily from Modernist themes and incorporating a vivid piece of glasswork as its central motif.

Wiederin also follows a traditional cross formation as a structural element in the rectangular roof, so two intersecting tramlines of poured concrete beams reach across the length and breadth of the ceiling, visible from within the chapel and from above it. One central bar of the cross is missing, which relieves the

Gerold Wiederin
Location: Locherboden, Austria
Completion date: 1997

OPPOSITE On the six nights of the year when pilgrims meet at Mötz, the floor-to-ceiling glass feature, set behind bars of branching ironwork, is lit from behind.

BELOW The openness of Wiederin's design is faultless and yet the space still evokes an intimacy and seclusion.

LEFT Helmut Federle's glasswork is a brilliant slice of colour and irregularity bringing the natural forms around the chapel into sharper focus and contrasting the otherwise organised geometry of Wiederin's structure.

RIGHT Wiederin uses the simplest support frame for this rectangular Modernist box, its boundary defined by the intersection of pillars, roof and platform. The ironwork on the gates to the adjacent cave replicates that over the glass centrepiece.

symbol of an over-obviousness (the beams can look merely functional) and means that on the underside, where fluorescent strip lighting is set into the beams beneath semi-transparent glass, one light is omitted and light from the coloured glasswork is given priority.

Four square pillars, the floor, the furniture, the sacristy and the ceiling are all cast in exposed concrete, which connects visually with the grey rocks and increases the sense of functionality and determination. The pillars' corners fall flush with those of the ceiling so there is an unarguable purity in the structure, like that of a Greek temple, or to another extreme, a 1950s American garage.

One step up raises the chapel from its grassy foundations and defines its boundary, and Wiederin centres the altar in front of the centred back wall (that of the sacristy behind). Only the lectern set to one side disrupts the perfect symmetry of its other components. Perhaps this is why the central glasswork by the artist Helmut Federle is so successful. Out of the clarity of Wiederin's geometry is an explosion of fragmented glass, falling (or rising) in a riotous river of colour. Welded branches of iron withhold the lumps of glass in green, blue, red and yellow (looking like factory leftovers but attractive nonetheless), so that the effect mimics a traditional stained-glass window but with added dimensions. On pilgrimage nights alone the glass is backlit, and is as opulent for the distant gaze of gathered pilgrims as it is at close quarters.

With the cross set into the ceiling like an overseeing and protecting sign, Wiederin has room to incorporate the symbol for the Virgin Mary and the papal cross on the front of the altar. Deeply inscribed into the concrete they are handled with a sense of abstraction, which is surely the way symbols ought to be treated, rather than as the kind of club emblem that many church architects resort to.

The small sacristy, with doors at either side, is an essential adjunct where the priest(s) can gather and prepare. A simple bench is provided along the sacristy wall and the baldachin effect of the chapel ensures that the priests at least are sheltered from the elements. The chapel is then set, not unlike a theatre stage, for a nocturnal Mass in front of the pilgrims and among the woods, mountains, neighbouring churches and the aura of past miracles and saints.

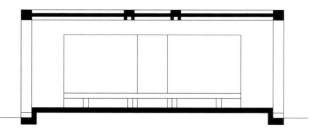

LEFT The chapel remains hidden from nocturnal pilgrims until they reach the clearing where once they gathered without the physical focus this small building provides.

BOTTOM LEFT A well-proportioned symmetry lies behind the fundamental layout.

RIGHT The chapel bears its Christian witness with a clever use of ceiling braces to depict a cross.

BELOW This plan shows how the elements within the chapel fall under the divisions of the ceiling's cross beams.

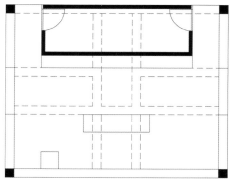

Los Nogales School Chapel

Daniel Bonilla Arquitectos
Location: Bogotá, Colombia
Completion date: 2002

Schools will always need large arenas for occasions when parents and the wider community are invited to join the pupils. A Colombian school in the capital, Bogotá, commissioned designs for a new chapel, that would be an intimate haven for the pupils and priest alone while having the option of adapting to a much bigger scale. Architect Daniel Bonilla's solution does that twenty-fold. Within an essentially rectangular box Bonilla creates a striking interior with only small channels of light breaking into its realm. The wall of the northeastern side, already set in like a backdrop to an exterior stage, breaks into two portals that swing open and, like outstretched arms, draw attention from the attendant crowds that can gather on its front lawn. Up to 2,000 can be seated in this area as opposed to 100 in the chapel itself, and the chapel's axis can be turned about 90 degrees so that the priest positioned on the raised side dais is facing outwards through the open portals.

Aside from this great advantage of enlarging its capacity, the chapel is, when its doors are closed, an exciting complex to move in and around. Formed of interlocking blocks of either creamy-grey concrete or caramel-coloured local hardwood its southern side tapers out from the perpendicular, and other planes follow its example, which understatedly opens up the facade and signals entrances and pathways. The high skeletal bell tower also marks the chapel out among the trees and the lower profiles of surrounding school buildings. As the northeast wall is that which can be opened up to the wider congregation, the small adjoining rooms including office and sacristy are tucked behind the soutwest wall. A moat-like pool of water touches the edge of these rooms, and in order to cross one traverses duckboards and so enters into the sacristy directly.

The main entrance at the south side opens into an interim space with a simple water stoup; plain concrete sidewalls and a glazed wall in front through which the pool and a hefty human-scale cross are visible. Turning about fully under a small doorway brings one in at the back of the chapel and into a much darker environment punctuated by boxy shafts of light. The wood-panelled ceiling is set with short narrow slits at right angles to each other so that illuminated crosses are spread over its surface. Some small panels of fenestration in the main doors and walls are stained in ecstatic bursts of blues and yellows and are scattered in irregular spaces, a referencing of the glass in Le Corbusier's chapel at Ronchamp, or of Mondrian's late abstractions. The blues, an indigo together with a turquoise, are the only colours within the chapel that veer off the red/yellow spectrum and as such sit a little awkwardly within the colour range. It seems unlikely that they are quite what the architect ordered, as their patterning does not sit well with Bonilla's overall scheme.

A short flight of interior stone stairs up the southwest side projects a gallery/balcony level overlooking the chapel nave. It is halfway up this staircase that the alternative altar can be used, facing out to the lawn; its wooden board is slim enough to be half handrail, half altar. The altar, for smaller congregations, sits on the raised sanctuary platform along with the lectern, priest's chair, wall-mounted cross and the largest of the chapel's downward-reaching light shafts, combining in a neat but relaxed composition. The light shaft resembles a refined extraction flue, boxed in wood and throwing a strong white light onto the altar. Bonilla repeats a device he uses on the south face of the building, which is

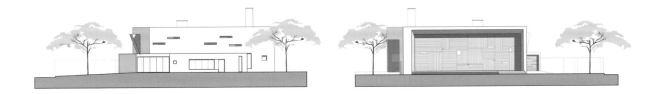

ABOVE A jigsaw of panels make a handsome facade to the chapel's west elevation and small horizontal bars of fenestration are staggered across the east side.

RIGHT TOP The two large chimneys funnel daylight into the chapel over the two altars. Faintly slanting roofs allow water drainage as well as a stage-like view when the main doors are open.

ABOVE A Marian sculpture stands in the sloping niche and is bathed in natural light from a protruding exterior duct. The seats, separable and-movable, are a fitting addition structurally and in both tone and texture.

RIGHT Uncomplicated windows and doorways overlook the water and a bare section of walling. Traversing the water over a simple bridge leads to the sacristy and office.

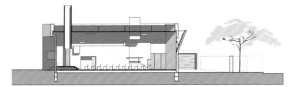
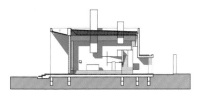

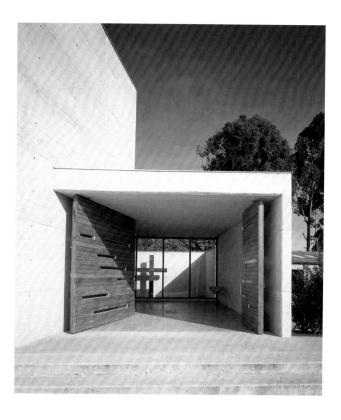

LEFT When the main doors are opened the immediate arena of the chapel is doubly expanded onto the concrete paving around its front. But further crowds can be seated on the lawn while the chapel becomes a kind of open-air stage.

RIGHT This steady oblong porch permits a view of the more private rear of the chapel and a primitive wooden cross, seen through the glass, contrasts with the shallow pool of water it emerges from.

BELOW A gentle broadening of the chapel's sidewalls opens it up to the arena in front.

to cut away concrete at an angle so that (an instance of this is behind the altar), a yellow light from one side seeps into the space gradually and graciously. Other details include the criss-cross of the wood boards that make up the main doors, the small round holes that perforate the concrete walls and the intriguing modular pews; all contribute to a keen impression of a place that is specially marked out for worship. It is exuberant enough to appeal to young people while retaining a maturity and sophistication that does not patronise their sensibilities and spiritual needs.

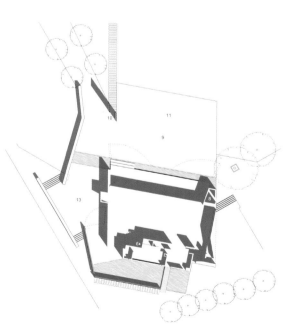

1. Altar
2. Main nave
3. Tabernacle
4. Statue of Nuestra Señora de Los Nogales
5. Main entrance
6. Choir
7. Reflecting pond
8. Storage room
9. Square
10. Bell tower
11. Outdoor sitting area
12. Priest's office
13. Patio of silence
14. Opening façade (doors)
15. Porch

CARMELITE MONASTERY CHAPEL AND SACRISTY

Níall McLaughlin Architects
Location: Kensington, London, UK
Completion date: 1996

Níall McLaughlin Architects has been engaged in some 10 years of repairs and improvements to the Carmelite Monastery in Kensington, London. From the road the church (mid-20th century) looks a little unwelcoming, but an adjoining passage leads to a Victorian complex wherein the welcome from the Carmelite Brothers is warm. McLaughlin's commission from this community included a new sacristy and private chapel for daily prayer and worship. Given two spaces to work with – one a more-or-less square room for the chapel, the other a smaller left-over space off the corridor between the church and the priory buildings – the two have been worked as autonomous rooms, but with a definite sense of connection between them.

The sacristy space required an unusual solution to bring in natural light while shielding the room from the overlooking residential sight lines. Ideas derived from Fra Filippo Lippi's *c.*1440 painting *The Annunciation*, in which the pictorial space is bisected by architectural elements as well as being framed by its arched format and the curve of the angel's wing, led McLaughlin to transpose this into a functional but evocative funnel. Unfolding from the northern aspect of the well in which the sacristy is sited, light is reflected between two curved white panels that run across the centre of the room. Daylight is thus delivered consistently and, at times, dramatically. A narrow window onto the garden also allows some southern light in without detriment to privacy.

To accommodate vestments, together with the communion ware and a relic, the sacristy is lined with white cupboard- and drawer doors of varying dimensions. Other surfaces and panelling are in oak. Given its functional nature the sacristy could be said to be almost workmanlike, but it serves well as a transitional room, a place to focus and prepare before moving on to the chapel.

A short walk down the corridors of the monastery leads to the heavy wooden door of the chapel. The entrance is placed at the back of the room, and to one side of it the tabernacle behind the door is in line with the centrally placed altar table. Two symmetrical rows of oak chairs – 12 in all to allude to the disciples – are ranged along the two facing sidewalls and make an immediate aesthetic impression. Together with a long peg set into a panel above each chair, they recall straight-backed Shaker furniture, or chairs by Charles Rennie Mackintosh. This is perhaps the strongest historical reference in a taut combin-ation of highly crafted fittings and deliberate gestures, both symbolic and metaphorical.

The Victorian room, which has original stone mantels, elegant leaded windows and a panelled ceiling leads out into the monastery's garden. The garden brims with well-tended plants and is as much a part of the composition of the chapel as the bricks and mortar. McLaughlin borrows from the idea of medieval cloister gardens to set up dichotomies of interior and exterior, refuge and wilderness, God and nature, prayerfulness and manual labour. The architect has also spoken of the influence of WB Yeats's poetic imagery in the poem 'Sailing to Byzantium' which sets the green nascent state of Ireland against the gold artifice of Byzantium. The materials – Spanish stone, Nuremberg amber glass, beeswax stucco, oak and leather – combine to give a golden effect which, illuminated by the light bouncing off the green of the garden, produces a 'retinal experience' (BBC radio3) derived from Yeats's vision.

Amber glass 'hats' hover over each monk's chair, as well as casting circular golden rings on the floor from the four larger room lights. Simple accessories such as the peg in the panelling behind each chair and leather kneelers are impressively thought through.

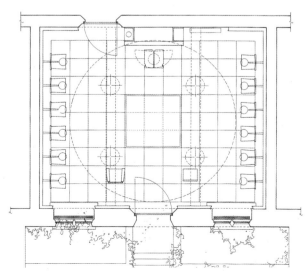

LEFT The curvature of the ceiling, which funnels northern light into the sacristy, is dictated by both function and McLaughlin's more esoteric references to angels' wings. Generous, variously sized storage spaces are provided along with niches for framing the monks' precious objects and a bench seat.

RIGHT The symbolically loaded form of the tabernacle with its references to the body of Christ, and thus to temples and tombs, is given large though human proportions and is constructed from a cube of oak and a perfect cylinder in which the sacrament is placed.

BOTTOM LEFT The plan shows two doors into the chapel. The north door is the main entry point from the corridor of the priory, and the southern door passes out into the garden, enclosed and sheltered by tall residential buildings. A symmetrical layout is used and forms are derived from pure Platonic geometries.

BOTTOM CENTRE Entering behind the tabernacle and to one side of the square-plan chapel highlights the otherwise symmetrical layout. The conversion from a fairly nondescript Victorian room to a space of rigorous aestheticism and sanctity has been achieved through precise choices of materials, proportions and forms.

BOTTOM RIGHT This axonometric drawing shows the height from which light is redirected into the sacristy. The two folding ceiling layers also give the room an axis under which the furniture and niches are aligned.

Detailing throughout is a matter of function, quality and beauty. The tabernacle, which forms a kind of reredos, or backdrop, for the altar table, is a chunky cube of solid oak, hinged and handled so that it can be opened up, revealing a gold-lined cylindrical interior space in which the consecrated bread is held. Each monk's chair is overhung with a reading light, the shade for which is hand-blown in amber glass with faint references to Pentecostal tongues of fire or, for the more worldly minded, hairdressers' dryers! Backrests in the two window seats are again cylindrical, upholstered in white silk and slung from the window ledge with generous leather straps.

While the Carmelite community's life in Kensington is an outward-looking one McLaughlin has provided the interior physical sanctuary in which reflection, prayer and communion are conducted. The rarefied material elements retain earthy and comforting attributes in ways that complement the garden's contribution to the overall scheme; the combination raises the contemporary standard of the design of ecclesiastical fixtures and fittings as well as for interventionist architecture.

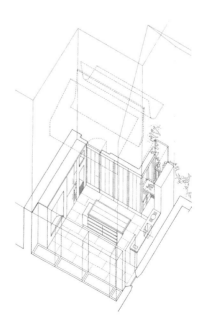

OBERREALTA CHAPEL

Christian Kerez with Fontana & Partner AG
Location: Oberrealta, Switzerland
Completion date: 1992–3

Designing a church is often seen as an architect's dream job, the icing on the cake of his or her oeuvre and an opportunity to explore metaphysical form. If the lessons of the 20th century's liturgical movement are to have any currency now, there will also be an expectation that the contemporary architect's foray into religious work will play a role in the very life of a Christian community, of their worship and mission and of their relevance to the society to which it responds, or as Peter Hammond put it in 1962 'the human activities from which the domus ecclesiae derives its true purpose' (p 25). Strange then to contemplate a new chapel with no attempt at symbolism save a small cross simply incised into concrete, and no functional features bar four walls, a roof, a door and a window slit to let in light. However, the Oberrealta Chapel's 'true purpose' is perhaps a little different from most. Situated high in the Swiss Alps the community it serves are sporadic attendees, often weary walkers, tourists immersing themselves in the awesome experience of mountains, so inevitably the parameters change. For Christian Kerez, a Venezuelan-born, Swiss-trained architect working at the time in the Zürich offices of Rudolf Fontana, the project became an exercise in reduction, a stripping down of expertise to find, at architecture's core, a few essential truths.

The chapel stands on the foundations of an older stone church next to a large deciduous tree, its back at the edge of the drop down into the valley. The approach is over an expanse of rough grass as the mountain path steers around a meadow to reach the chapel . A child's drawing of a house might suffice to describe the elevation of the front facade, except that this house has only a doorway and no windows. What matters is that from a distance the chapel has a straightforward appeal to passers-by signalling shelter and closeness. Solid concrete walls and roof were cast in situ and left uncoated and uncovered so that there can be no detraction from the elemental form. Two small steps up to the doorway (over which the cross is incised) are an abrupt transition, though not an alarming one, from nature to the man-made, from the vast scale of the mountains to the human proportions of this chapel.

Within the chapel, the stones of the original chapel's walls are left visible in the floor's border and a long vertical slit in the end wall lets in a bright streak of light. It is enough to see clearly for as long as the daylight lasts, but too narrow to permit any sight of the mountains. Instead the focus here is still and introverted, turned in on the landscape-saturated self, an antidote to travelling and touring, and although the design is derived from domestic architecture, the chapel provides less – there are no chairs, no altar table, no books, no sustenance – which forces the issue that this is a place to be in simply for prayer, for devotion requiring no material aid .

Conversely, we might question why there is a need for a building here at all. Why not pray underneath the tree or find some large boulders to shelter behind? The architect's role, rather than that of a provider of necessary buildings, becomes that of an intercessor, putting materials together to enact something of our physicality and our transience too. It is a very human and humane effort, the inverse of which is surely the unthinkable magnitude of the creative powers that Christians believe God holds. Man builds monuments and buildings to signify his presence in a place, sometimes overconfidently and unnaturally, or sometimes just to mark it out as especially beautiful.

All of these things could apply to Kerez's mountainside chapel. Whether it is a shrine to Christianity, existentialism or architecture, it carries with it the dignity of an inexpensive and yet poetic structure. Visitors can dwell, unjudged and unintimidated by the usual trappings of religious architecture.

ABOVE Winter colours warm the concrete of the chapel's sturdy frame and the open doorway allows a glimpse of the dark interior.

RIGHT Tapering outwards to increase the light through its interior aperture the slit window opposes the open doorway.

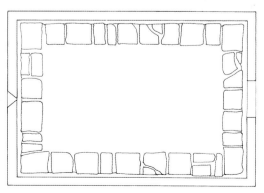

ABOVE The chapel, though high above most surrounding villages, is accessible to passing walkers and those who know the terrain. Its outward features replicate those of a small hut rather than a church, but its clean lines and attractive simplicity draw people to it.

LEFT One vertical slit in the end wall acts as meditative focus and a source of light. The stones of the original chapel's walls are left visible in the floor.

RIGHT It is hard to imagine a simpler design than this, overlaid on the foundations of the previous chapel.

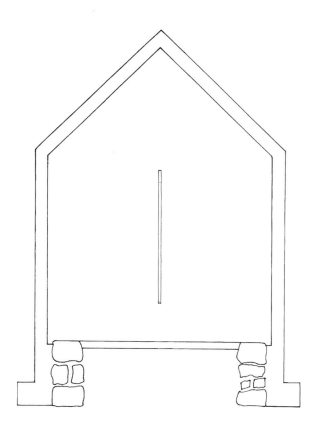

CHAPEL OF ST MARY OF THE ANGELS

Mecanoo Architecten

Location: Rotterdam, The Netherlands

Completion date: 2000

Discrete funerary buildings and cemetery monuments are something of a rarity when you consider the lineage of pyramids, Roman and Grecian mausoleums, Renaissance splendour, Gothic statuary, Communist excess and holocaust memorials – though the latter has, thankfully, adjusted to a sensibility more in keeping with the gravity of its cause. Apart from the self-promotional nature of many of these monuments' and buildings' sponsors, memorial chapels give good reason for architecture of levity, hopefulness and celebration as well as solemnity, piety and sorrow. And, as the passing from life to death is a universal experience, ritualised in all cultures, there is a good chance too that architects of little or no religious faith can conjure meaningful and responsive designs for this purpose.

Such a hypothesis is well evidenced by a new and startling chapel in the Roman Catholic cemetery of St Lawrence, in Rotterdam. Replete with modern urban architecture, Rotterdam is also one of the Netherlands' more multicultural cities and in many ways this chapel defies a traditional Christian aesthetic. The site has long been used for burial, but its first chapel, built in 1869 by HJ van den Brink, had to be demolished in the 1960s because of subsidence. The replacement chapel befell the same fate leaving only the footprint of the original chapel to rebuild upon in the late 1990s. A local priest commissioned the avant-garde Delft-based practice Mecanoo Architecten, and one of its lead personnel Francine Houben took on the job. Her vision of the project at the outset describes almost perfectly the fully realised building: 'I have a dream [that] it must be a jewel casket, with a big expressive roof, a golden canopy and a beam of light. I am thinking of a blue, continuous narrative wall. And the chapel will be part of a route, which is in turn part of a ceremony [...] I don't want a dead end chapel' (Church Building issue 72, p 7).

This emphasis on the 'passing-through' of the chapel is the crux of its form. Two doors line up with each other on the north–south axis and occur at the point where the almost symmetrical curves taper inwards, so that the gap between entering and exiting is a mere few steps, and the proximity to the surrounding graveyard more keenly felt. The curving perimeter, which follows a loose figure of eight, ensures that the interior is a fluid and sensuous space. The exterior, with its aluminium cladding, is an attracting surface that blurrily reflects the green of the trees, sky and grey stone graves. The form also embeds itself (on new firmer foundations) within the old chapel site and the expansion and contraction of the interior space makes a surprisingly large area for the congregation while maintaining an intimacy that the architect prioritised.

Light and visibility are also admitted through a strip of glazing at the top and bottom of the walls, allowing for plenty of transparency without breaking up the conterminous walls with fenestration. The doors, when shut, also continue the seamless curve. As if resting perilously on the undulating glass rim, the roof structure borrows its form from a piece of folded paper, perforated by three amorphous skylights. From the east and west elevations the roof sags graciously into the middle, giving the corners of the roof a jaunty lift and its underbelly a very minimal concavity.

One skylight encircles a simple steel frame on which a bell is hung above the roofline. Another is positioned directly above the sanctuary area whose white section of wall carries a grid of facial portraits by the artist Mark Deconinck. A striking

The curvaceous walls form a wide river of blue, trimmed with natural light. An amorphous plan is regularised by units of benches and floor stones.

LEFT With the two wide doors open a semi-open-air service can be conducted allowing a fluid passage into and through the chapel with two distinct areas, for the priests and for the people, dissected by the route.

BELOW The neat fit of the new chapel within the footprint of the old even follows the traditional east–west orientation. The roof is a plain rectangle with three apertures that increase its appearance of lightness.

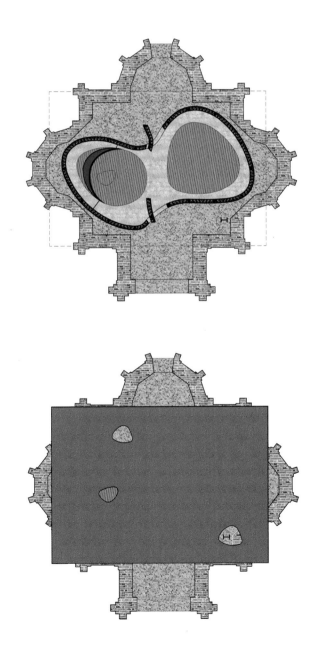

row of white candles on black stilts faces a more traditional devotional set of candles and above these is a small icon sculpture of Mary and the baby Jesus, while handwritten excerpts of the requiem Mass run along the walls . The lectern and small altar are cast in concrete T-shapes (the lectern also has a copper fall), and similarly simple constructions in wood make up bench seating for priests and the congregation. The floors for the sanctuary and seating areas are paved with shades of grey marble cut into the same amorphous – and yet precise – rounds that fill the space appropriately.

Perhaps the most defining and memorable aspect of Mecanoo's chapel, however, is the use of colour. A deep ultramarine unapologetically reigns over the enveloping interior walls (interrupted only by the section behind the sanctuary) while the underside of the roof is a golden mustard colour. The ultramarine is deeply suggestive of a Marian blue, traditionally the colour of the Virgin's robes or the heavenly skies that often, in Renaissance paintings, cover her world. But it is also a very fashionable blue, a colour on which the chapel's interior depends for impact, but one that may date the chapel more quickly than might have been anticipated. The building departs defiantly from the cool restraint of more Modernist projects and there is an optimism and rigour to the chapel that may engage visitors for longer than its previous incarnations.

LEFT The former foundations of the 19th-century chapel skirt the new perimeter. The sweep of roof to the south is punctured by a slim and simple bell frame and topped with a discrete cross.

RIGHT Firmer foundations support the squat though elegant chapel, which the architect wished to treat as a palimpsest of the former chapels.

ABOVE The consistent width of the metal cladding gives stability to otherwise undulating forms and is a contrast to the rich blue and gold painted surfaces.

Chapel of St Mary of the Angels **109**

PRIVATE CHAPEL

Estudio Sancho-Madridejos
Location: Valleacerón,
Almadenejos, Spain
Completion date: 2001

BELOW The site includes other residential buildings executed in Sancho-Madridejos' more trademark style. The chapel at the northeast corner overlooks the rest of the site maintaining some separation and solitude.

High in the arid southern Spanish planes stands a private chapel whose form, an artifice of severe angular planes, nonetheless looks remarkably congruous within its rugged landscape. It is part of a larger complex of a house, hunting pavilion and guard's residence. Situated slightly lower down the topography of the site the chapel, even from a distance, conveys a sense of separation and abstraction. From a distance you might also be able to recognise the planar motifs as those of the Madrid-based partnership between Juan Carlos Sancho Osinaga and Sol Madridejos Fernández working together under the altogether briefer practice name Estudio Sancho-Madridejos. Handling stone and concrete planes as if it were an exercise in origami, the design extrapolates undeniably good proportions from distinctly unusual and irregular shapes. And unlike so many ecclesiastical designs before it, this building eschews the symmetry and purity of forms that have long embodied and evoked the religious experience – a criterion demanded by worshipping communities. But neither does this chapel resort to the kind of organic and arguably almost pagan forms of some of its Modern predecessors – Le Corbusier's Notre-Dame-de-Haut has been criticised from a theological perspective in this way. The Spanish church of the Coronation of Our Lady of Vitória, built in 1960 and designed by Miguel Fisac, might be a more relevant reference in terms of its asymmetric but sharply defined configuration of walls and ceilings.

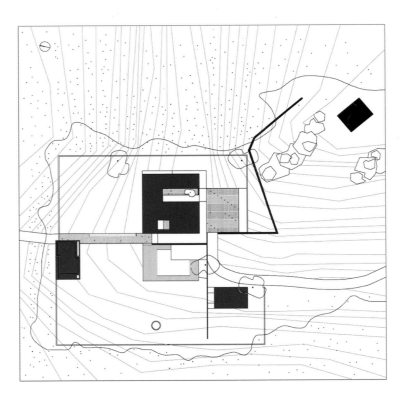

ABOVE Two receding angular planes at the front of the chapel are at first difficult for the eye to read, but its size and intimacy counter any sense of dislocation.

What Sancho-Madridejos manage to deliver is something that is exactingly contemporary, gorgeous and yet austere, sophisticated and complex but without pretension, self-consciousness or extravagance. The building's front, devoid of any particularly obvious pointers, sits at the corner of a sloping triangular plane, shaded a little from the strong sunlight. A cross is visible through a large trapezoid of glass next to the door; it serves as the chapel's only piece of iconography save for a minute square window to one side of it, revealing a handkerchief of blue sky. The cross itself is aligned to the right on the east wall. Other planes slip and slide into place around the one perpendicular corner in which the cross sits – a metaphor if ever there was for the ordering and calming presence of God. Shafts of light from unexpected corners of the chapel fall in equally dramatic patterns across the floor and walls, sometimes overlaying shadows of bars, 'T's and 'H's of the fenestration's framework on the top edges of units of cast concrete.

Sitting at an apex of land with almost 180-degree horizons in all directions there is plenty of light to play with. Many of the exterior and interior walls act as deflectors and the changing light is angled in such a way as to recede or come forward. The eye is frequently confused by the combination of irregular planes, but this is never without overall integrity to its composition. There is one notable ecclesiastical precedent for this fascination with irregular planes in the cathedral at Neviges, Germany (1972) by Gottfried Böhm (the son of the renown German church architect Dominikus Böhm). The architect said, quite simply: 'I was inspired by the possibility of uniting ceilings and walls into a whole' (Stock, 2002: p 144). His extraordinary composition is perhaps more Gothic than its newer Spanish counterpart, by virtue of its cathedral-sized proportions, but the ambition of both buildings is visibly a shared one. Equally, a comparison with the ideals of the prophetic and theologically attuned architect Rudolf Schwarz could translate into Sancho-Madridejos' contemporary architect-speak. Schwarz believed in an autonomous religious architecture that could operate without being slave to liturgical function, an artistic endeavour which through its own merits afforded worshippers an environment that could be called and felt to be holy (see Stock, 2002: p 159). Perhaps, with that in mind, it becomes self-evident that young architects like Estudio Sancho-Madridejos who have cut their teeth on establishing creative and autonomous forms (their 'fold-wrapper' technique would fall into this category) have been successful in tackling a religious brief so early in their careers.

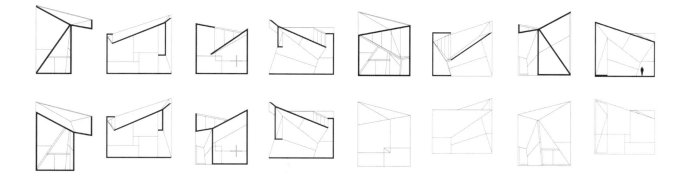

LEFT AND RIGHT This absorbing series of configurations reveals how exacting yet playful Sancho-Madridejos' architecture is at design stage.

ABOVE The confidence and austerity of the chapel's forms asserts its autonomy in the uncultivated landscape.

CHURCH OF ST THOMAS AQUINAS

**Sarah Hare and Thomas Höger
(formerly Höger Hare Architekten)
with Norbert Radermacher**
Location: Berlin, Germany
Completion date: 1999

Having decamped its headquarters to Bonn during Communist rule in East Germany, along with government and secular institutions, reunification has afforded the Catholic Church reacquisition of a site in the former East Berlin. A 1994 competition to build new facilities on the former garage and car park was won by the architectural partnership of Thomas Höger and Sarah Hare (developed with the artist Norbert Radermacher) and has evolved into a considered and well-articulated complex. Alongside various functional buildings that accommodate the public sphere of the Catholic Church's headquarters – auditorium, guesthouses, office space and restaurant – a new church dedicated to St Thomas Aquinas sits comfortably and contiguously on the site. Acknowledging strong ties to the architectural 'typologies of both the monastery and the traditional Berlin block', Höger Hare Architekten has used five courtyard spaces to delineate the composite parts, and the church sits in one of these, between the academy and guesthouse buildings and next to a small garden. Its front is dissected into a distinct top and bottom by a fenestrated ambulatory that encircles the whole church. The inner block rises above the restrained concrete pillars of the ambulatory, its thin horizontal bricks forming a landscape, or screen, of texture and light. Three tones are at play here: the courtyard in front of the church shares a stony grey with the church's granite slabs excavated from Santiago di Compostela; the fenestration and roofing mark out the well-proportioned units; and the lighting from within both the ambulatory and the church itself gives off a golden-yellow hue. The interior doors are also of this hue.

A unique and very contemporary play on the brickwork relies on this lighting. At random intervals, though more frequently towards the top of the church walls, a glass brick replaces the granite. These thin dashes of light produce, by night and day, an effect not dissimilar to a snowstorm on a television with bad reception. It is a compelling abstraction and one that alludes to a mysterious and metaphysical deity while being very much rooted in earthly symbols of light and dark. The interior walls are the exact reverse of the exterior giving a very straightforward sense of the building's construction. The ceiling is concealed by a Modernist baldachin, a white canopy held upon four concrete pillars in the far corners of the granite box. Lighting is added to the top of the baldachin, which emphasises the strata of glass bricks and provides a good indirect source of light to floor level.

The pillars are a clever concession to traditional ecclesiastical architecture, combining strength and agility as so many pillared churches have before, without contributing the usual problems of restricted sightlines and a disruptive metering of the space.

At eye level the glass bricks are few and far between and become emblematic peepholes onto the outside world. Small wall-mounted pedestals for candles, short vertical accents against the granite, measure the lengths of the sidewalls. There is a confidence here, perhaps aided by the collaboration with the artist Nobert Radermacher, in handling materials so that each element or detail commands attention while complementing and attuning to the others. The pews, for example, are made from a very dark stained wood and are quite bulky. And yet the legs of each pew taper gently, edges are left unstained and thus lighten the effect, and the contrast with the white ceiling makes plain architectural sense. The

The lighting above the baldachin gives the impression that it is the only thing separating the congregation from the sky. It also helps to illuminate the detailing of the glass bricks, their increasing numbers and the fluctuations in their colour and tone.

BELOW The site's courtyards break up the substantial non-sacred buildings. The Church of St Thomas Aquinas (to the left of this drawing) sits back from its taller neighbours framed by its ambulatory.

RIGHT Classical proportions are underscored by the use of carefully chosen materials and relate the church's forms to the rest of the complex, which borrow from monastic and Berliner architypes.

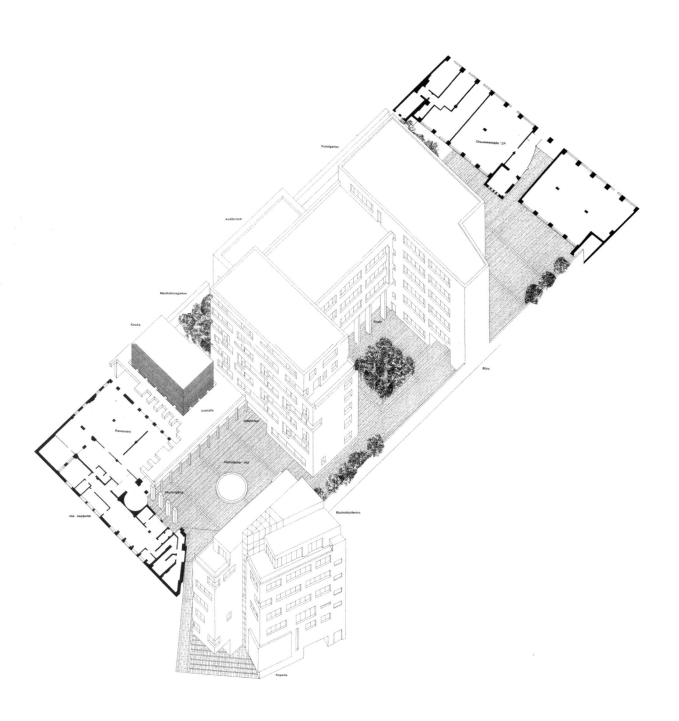

doors too have horizontal handles, the grain of the wood runs horizontally and they slide rather than open on hinges – tiny details but ones which play a role in the overall integrity and success of this church.

Traditional iconography is kept to a minimum and the exterior bears no obvious symbol of Christianity, but this is not a problem within the overall context of this Catholic plant. A processional cross is planted firmly to one side of the altar, which is punctuated by four large candles on slim iron candlesticks. The altar itself is a single tablet of granite resting on top of two piles of the same material (slabs the same height as the walls' granite bricks) whose intervening gap is no bigger than about 7 centimetres. On the back wall a tabernacle hovers above this slit in the altar, a simple visual continuity between the act of communion and the reserve sacrament. But the tabernacle – whose front is fabricated in yellow folded gold with one vertical fold making the upright bar of a cross – suggests more than its functional role as a possible cupboard or storage box. Its central position within the entire composition makes it a focus, a meditative unit allowing an open exchange between it and the viewer. Yet it is taut enough to suggest presence and to have integrity, like a good painting in a crowded gallery. As the Catholic theologian Jean-Luc Marion describes the rules by which an icon is an icon, the tabernacle at St Thomas', a haunting striped square, permits a 'gaze [which] can never rest or settle; it always must rebound upon the visible, in order to go back in it up the infinite stream of the invisible. In this sense, the icon makes visible only by giving rise to an infinite gaze' (God Without Being, 1991: 18).

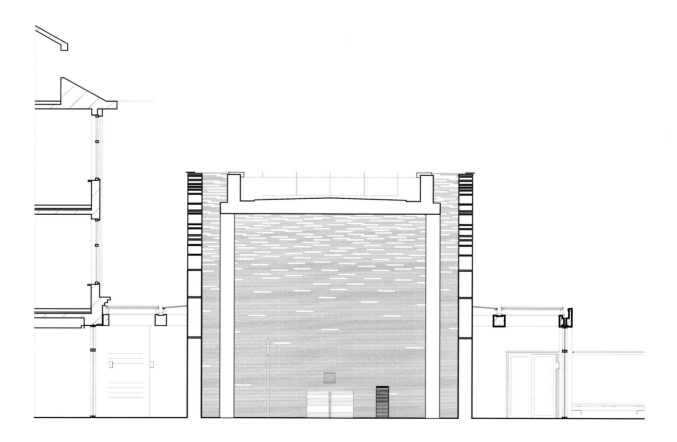

CHURCH OF ST JOHN THE BAPTIST

Mario Botta Architetto
Location: Mogno, Switzerland
Completion date: 1996

RIGHT The angle at which the glass ceiling cuts across the oval church makes a circular form in the vein of Gothic rose windows.

Amid the famous red-stone buildings of the medieval Italian city of Siena stands a vast cathedral, but its size is not the only thing to distinguish it. Its architects constructed it from striped black and white marble, a cavalier decision replicated in many other Italian churches of the period. It is hard to fathom why the fashion for this fabulous stonework died out, but Mario Botta, the Swiss architect born in Mendrisio in the Italian-speaking canton of Switzerland, and who trained at the Institute of Architecture in Venice, has revived it in forms not dissimilar to those in Tuscany. In particular, Botta's smallest ecclesiastical commission, the Church of St John the Baptist (or San Giovanni di Battista), stands out in the green swathes of Val Lavizzara in the Ticino region of Switzerland, much the way the cathedral stands out among the red brick of Siena. A massive avalanche in 1986 swept away the greater part of the village of Mogno including its 17th-century church, but undeterred a group formed to commission a new church in its place. Botta, being local but also an architect with a world-class reputation, was won over by the group's selfless determination to give future generations in Mogno a comparable building to that which they themselves had obviously cherished. Botta vowed to build them a church that would last a thousand years (see Teller: 2005).

Certainly, St John's has a solidity that suggests permanence and the type of protective, almost bastion-like structure that Botta believes humans seek out. Its oval plan belies a square floor plan within that, and corners and curves sit happily with one another in a stout cylindrical tower. But following the incline of the steep mountainside behind it, the church's circular roof cuts obliquely across the cylinder and is glazed in V-shaped striations. Facing up to the westerly skies it could be a large-scale solar panel, but the stonework on which it rests, and the crossover of interior stripes that are also visible through the glass, are too prominent to be deemed anything other than aesthetically enhancing features. Botta's preoccupation with this form – the obliquely cut cylinder – has since manifested itself in the new town cathedral at Evry in France, as well as in secular buildings such as the Museum of Modern Art in San Francisco (the latter also develops the use of the black and white stripes) and it is hard to deny that it is an ingenious take on the round church. Questions of how to roof a round church without it looking like an inert rocket or a tepee (as is all too clear to the infamously nicknamed Metropolitan Cathedral in Liverpool, 'paddy's wigwam'), are astutely sidestepped by enlarging and elevating the traditional rose window to a sloping ceiling, and a heavenward profile is maintained albeit without spires or flying buttresses. Botta also manages to find reasonable ways of integrating bells, an exterior fountain/font and a cross set high up without disturbing the purity of the oval form.

Perhaps the village's wish for this new church was in part a memorialising action, where the outward sign of a persisting Christian presence in the valley was as important as replacing the space where villagers would meet and worship. Indeed Botta only provides pews for a dozen people, although the space could be filled five times over if needed. Ranged along the church's broader north–south axis the pews face the altar in the east. The square floor plan is overlapped with extra inset corners at the east and west and with double-curved recesses (with small fitted benches) in the north and south. Resembling the style of a mosque's mihrab (the small niche that indicates the direction of Mecca), the

TOP LEFT Set on a small stone plaza the glass face follows the slope of the valley behind it making it seem at ease and in a good relation to the light.

BOTTOM LEFT AND CENTRE The inward tilt of the interior walls allows for the shifts from circular to square-edged forms.

BOTTOM RIGHT An oval plan overlaid with a rectangle and further recesses allows for a conjunction of traditional symmetry and geometry. The section shows the concentric archways behind the altar.

ABOVE Many different permutations of alternating black and white marble contribute to the focus at the altar, which is itself just two blocks of white marble.

corner set behind the altar is bricked over with arches of cubed marble stones alternating in a black and white chequerboard and above that a crucifix retrieved from the previous church hangs in fine proportion. The altar itself is carved of white marble and constructed in a wide T-shape. Two black candlesticks are its only adornment.

Across all of this the glass ceiling admits the day's continually shifting shadows in stripes that further elaborate the contrapuntal patterns of the marble. Two taut interior buttresses arch up to support the highest part of the wall with the central spine supporting the fenestration visible between them. For a rural village this is a sassy building and one might question how well a diminutive version of the buildings at Evry and San Francisco is suited to its congregation. However, with very precisely intuited dimensions, similar hues of rock formations apparent in the nearby mountains and a kind of earnestness that often accompanies church buildings for small communities, St John's looks far from being an impostor. For all Botta's replaying of familiar themes, of geometrical prowess and striking motifs, his practice is becoming honed to a masterly craft, and where better to 'give' this than to his own Ticinese brothers and sisters wishing to secure a building for perpetuity.

LEFT The bells maintain a simple rural feel bolted on their frame beneath the mid point of the glass roof's descent.

RIGHT A surprising feature in such a tiny village, the Church of St John the Baptist is both a sturdy monument to the past and a suitably impressive structure for future generations.

Jesuit Retreat Chapel

The advantages of fully separating ancillary elements from that of a church dedicated only to worship and prayer have ensured that, in the last half of the 20th century at least, Christian communities have become much more adept at defining what sacred space means to them, distinct from what function any ancillary buildings should perform. A Jesuit Retreat Centre in central Spain expressed this fully in a brief to build a new chapel in the grounds of a 1970s activity centre in which they had also been worshipping. The architects were briefed to improve the functionality of the existing building while adding to it, so the overall scheme had to relate one part to the other and at the same time differentiate church space from kitchen, dining, sleeping, shopping, storage and so on. The existing building is long and low, not much more elaborate than army lodgings or storage sheds, so the contrast of Ruíz Barbarín's circular appendage at one end is exacting. Like Mario Botta's church in Mogno (1996), and Heinz Tesar's church in Klostenburg, Austria (1995) the roof of the chapel slopes across a 45-degree angle (the same angle as the old building's roof) slicing the elliptical cylinder down to a height compatible with the old building. The same slate tiles of the old roof are used to swathe the chapel in a bricking layout with a Corten steel rim around its crown. The northern face of its ellipsis is highest and an upper section is glazed in vertical strips of U-glass in a wide opening just below the roof's rim. A centralised cross and a narrow vertical window complete this exterior marking of the chapel's main axis and its outward-looking stance.

The chapel can only be accessed through a small walkway, also fabricated in U-glass, joining the porch of the old building and opening into the back of the chapel just to one side of the ceiling's lowest drop. This entrance not only presents an increasing sweep of the curved walls but a range of oblong windows which direct the eye towards the north end and the focus of worship. The windows reveal the rural environment beyond the chapel in a sequence of slightly overlapping Corten frames, angled inward to maximise the southerly light.

The two converging ellipses of the floor and the ceiling are surfaced in materials of an equally dark tone: floorboards are of a sustainable hardwood called Merbau, a rich auburn brown that harmonises with the Corten windows and door; and the ceiling is cast in concrete, a dark grey (similar to the slate on the exterior) with an impression of wooden boards left visible – creating an imprint of the floor. The symbiosis of floor and ceiling is given further prominence by the uninterrupted expanse of the walls, painted in pure white with only a number of discrete white light fixtures metering its length. Where the glazing cuts into the north apse, intense reflections, particularly of the narrow vertical window, are produced in the shine of the wooden floor and light surges across the gathered congregation.

The curving of the apse wall is brought forward very slightly under a ledge at head height and makes a space in which the tabernacle is set. Double doors open up to form what resembles a triptych, a reredos lined in gold leaf; on its back wall the holy sacraments are placed in a box formed within a square steel cross and aligned underneath the central apse window, and small steel protrusions make room for a few books to be shelved and for a candle.

This cupboard device is simple and inviting and breaks out from the white walls in a manner that echoes the breaking of bread and the exposure of Christ's

Ruíz Barbarín Arquitectos
Location: Navas del Marqués, Ávila, Spain
Completion date: 2000

presence in the world. Though much of the liturgical action is restricted around this small area of the chapel, the flexibility of the empty elliptical volume (that has no other fixed furnishings) opens up new possibilities for other orientations, seating layouts, and non-religious activities as stipulated in the brief.

Precedents such as those mentioned earlier and older examples of oval churches such as Bernini's Santa Andrea Quirinale, Rome, and Rudolf Schwarz's Church of St Michael, Frankfurt (1954), show that Ruíz Barbarín's chapel stands in good company and states a strong case for the emotive impact of this elliptical form.

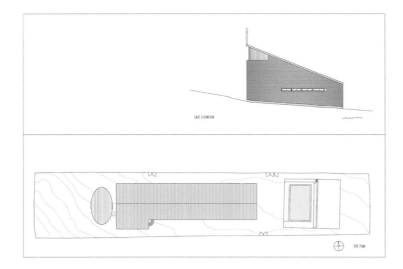

EAST ELEVATION

SITE PLAN

TOP LEFT Ruíz Barbarín's appendage to the existing buildings of the Jesuit Retreat is both charismatic and integrated. The muted exterior colours of the slate, glass and steel also help it to blend into the rural setting.

TOP CENTRE The mask-like visage of the chapel gives it both a defiant and friendly persona. The same vertical panes of glass that make the passageway adjoining the older building form its upper window.

TOP RIGHT Because of the scale of the chapel, Ruíz Barbarín's choice of materials was deliberate and tempered.

LEFT
The 45-degree slope of the chapel's roof aligns with the roof of the older building while the oval plan differentiates it from the other rectilinear forms.

RIGHT
Under the low pitch of the ceiling a surreptitious entrance provides a passage that climaxes in the clear oval volume.

CHURCH OF SAN GIOVANNI ROTONDO

Italy, a land of passionate religious belief and fervent secular obsessions (football, opera, art etc), demands architecture to accommodate this national enthusiasm. Renzo Piano, himself Genoese, has already significantly contributed to the Italian social realm with staggeringly beautiful, large-scale public buildings such as the stadium in Bari and music auditoriums in Parma and Rome. A commission to build a church was perhaps an obvious gap in Piano's work to date, so it may have surprised the monks of San Giovanni Rotondo, near Foggia on the southeast coast of Italy, when the architect initially turned down their invitation to design a new pilgrimage church to the 20th-century cult saint Padre Pio – whose life was played out on the very site allocated for the new church. A priest and a friar of the Order of Minor Capuchin, Pio is reputed to have received the stigmata in 1918 as well as founding a 'Home to Relieve Suffering'. Despite some criticism from within the Catholic Church he was canonised in 2002. Piano, who in retrospect gave some hints of his suspicion at the massive popularisation of this colourful Catholic icon, and whose cool modern buildings have a distinctly atheist air about them, certainly looked like an unlikely person to pursue. With fanatical persistence, however, including daily blessings faxed through to the Renzo Piano Building Workshop, the monks won their man. And it is doubtful they have ever regretted the choice: San Giovanni Rotondo now has the second highest number of pilgrims in the world outside of Guadalupe in Mexico, and squeezes in between St Peter's Basilica in Rome and St Paul's Cathedral in London to be the second largest church in the world.

While the monks' brief determined the vast 6,500 seating capacity and the parvis capacity of a further 30,000, it also stipulated the use of local stone. Never one to shy away from ambitious structures and armed with 21st-century technological aptitude, Piano's response involves 22 improbably long Bronzetto marble arches in a radial composition of an inner and an outer ring. Looking like elongated bridges, which should have supports or suspension, the tension held by these freestanding monochrome rainbows is in fact sufficient to support the expansive domed roof.

The spans of the arches decrease with the decreasing radius of the circle to form a spiral shell shape at whose centre the arches meet and the sanctuary is marked out. Seating is arranged in a semicircle around this epicentre, and the plastering between the groins above the altar is artist-painted* in Giotto-esque shades of blue and gold. One side forms a large arched facade on the exterior (not dissimilar to those of the great European railway stations), and one of these arches is set with a huge stained-glass window behind which is a painted screen depicting the apocalypse. Visitors enter and leave under this colossal mural-cum-window in time-honoured deference to this pictorial sermon.

The site, set into the side of a hill, is handled very much like that at Assisi, celebrated and well loved, about 320 kilometres northwest of Foggia. A gently sloping approach road flanks a stepped walkway and high wall, behind which Piano utilises the space underneath the church for halls, confessional chapels, a pilgrim's room, staff and support areas and so on. The vertical ribs of the wall poke above the horizontal level forming a subtle castellation and spaces in between where bells are hung. At the tallest end of the wall a stone cross soars up, its tapering parts magnifying its skyward tendencies.

Renzo Piano Building Workshop
Location: Foggia, Italy
Completion date: 2004

LEFT Overlapping stone arches meet at a central point in the site's spiral formation and form a concentration of mass and colour behind the main altar. To one side, the translucent painting on the arched window establishes a traditional narrative.

ABOVE The ceiling beams are sandwiched between sections of the stone arches whose tension supports the entire roof. The arches are much slimmer in the direction of the pews so that sight lines are only minimally restricted, and their mesmerising overlapping patterns are interspersed with a deluge of delicately strung lights.

RIGHT The repeating arch overrides all other forms both literally and metaphorically, a simple statement that echoes the form of God's covenant with man as expressed in the Old Testament rainbow. The chimney of light directed at the altar is visible here too.

A high flight of steps opens suddenly and broadly onto the parvis and continues the spiral form of the church in its paving stones. Old gnarled olive trees are planted haphazardly in holes in the paving alongside a raised bed carrying a shallow stream of running water. The rise of the church itself hardly interrupts the horizon, which is scattered with the local whitewashed and red-roofed houses, and its profile works hardest on a horizontal axis rather than a vertical one. This might be typified by the almost disconcerting asymmetry of the two most visible arches, their composite blocks of marble increasing in width at one end and creating a longer, straighter arm at the opposite end. It is hardly noticeable but does something to increase the sense of strength and agility. Above this the roof is layered in curling sections of prepatinated copper, startling verdigris in colour, in excitable contrast to the muted Bronzetto marble. Within the roof space a large chimney allows direct light to fall onto the sanctuary amid the criss-cross of overlapping arches and delicate wires on which the lights hang down. Piano's stone interior, true to local craftsmanship, restrains itself from grandiloquent architectural prowess by the apparent simplicity and almost brutal honesty of its construction.

If at first this church is a slightly unusual conflagration of architectural styles and ecclesiastical tradition – on the one hand reminiscent of aircraft hangars, on the other Gothic arches – it is as much a departure for Piano to work with the symbolic, the populist and the sanctified. Comparable with buildings such as his undulating Paul Klee Centre in Bern, or the stoic curves of the Rome music auditoria, the forms elicit an abstracted and cerebral connection to their functional and thematic roots. The Church of San Giovanni Rotondo, like the livelihood of Saint Pio, is attuned to the heady fervour of the faithful and delivers on their expectations.

*The interior was decorated by Italian artists Domenico Palladino, Giuliano Bangui and Arnaldo Pomodoro, who designed the bronze cross which hangs above the main altar.

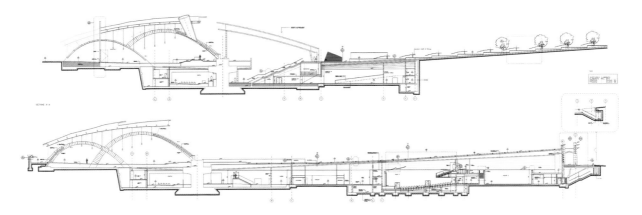

LEFT Fields of paving continue the concentric circles on which the church sits, leading underneath the great sweep of roof which is in turn supported by the wide leggy arches. Fittingly, the 40-metre high cross becomes the focal point on the horizon.

BELOW One half of the underlying spiral formation is given over to the main church space and the centrifugal focus is maintained throughout the site by elements of hard and soft landscaping.

ABOVE The relatively low rise of the church is a factor in the design and helps this vast building to feel approachable while still an impressive and lyrical expanse. Landscaping, staircases and walls punctuate varying routes across the long parvis.

BELOW RIGHT The monastic vernacular is adhered to in this cloister space running alongside the lower level of the parvis. Piano's use of local stone creates a cool and neutral passage.

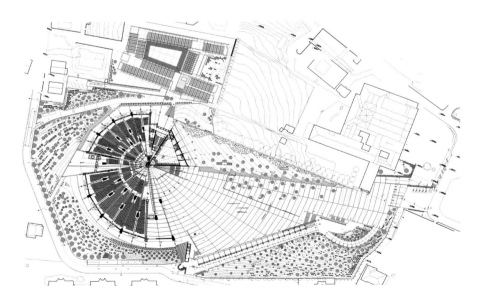

CHRIST CHURCH

Heinz Tesar

Location: Donau City, Vienna,
Austria

Completion date: 2000

RIGHT Shafts of light fall through the windows and skylight while the even covering of portholes on all four walls spreads a more diffuse light. The liturgical focus is made clear by darkgrey granite furniture and ironwork.

It is often said that the new gods to whom we build contemporary cathedrals are those of commerce and wealth. This truism could be used for the new satellite district of Donau City in Vienna where the 21st century speaks loud and clear through expensive skyscrapers, spaghetti-like transport links and landscaping that barely represents the terrain beneath it. By contrast, and in a deliberate move to respond to the working population of the vast United Nations buildings next door, Heinz Tesar has built an apparently restrained and low-slung church in the midst of all the architectural 'statements' of other discourses. That is not to say that Tesar's church does not make a statement of its own. Immediately recognisable by its dark steel shell – countering the gravity-defying glass buildings around it – and quirky round holes which pepper its exterior, this Roman Catholic church does not wish to express itself as simply a church but rather as a place which might draw in all peoples of variable religious persuasions. Certainly the polka-dot holes, which are either the size of a domestic clock face or smaller, are universally familiar almost to the point of being bland. But it is just this reluctance to deploy grand symbolic gestures that pulls Tesar's work away from the crowd and invokes an idiosyncrasy in the building that few architects achieve.

With a flat roof and essentially square plan, Christ Church sits sideways on to its neighbouring buildings but marks its approach on two sides with a triangular piece of green landscaping, a low steel bell frame, staircases to the entrance on the lower side and a broad expanse of red tarmac at its front. From an aerial view (which many in the surrounding buildings will have) a cross plan is visible as each corner inverts at roof level, and a slightly quiff-shaped skylight, which is situated directly above the altar, must attract curious onlookers.

The doors and fenestration are picked out in chrome, elegant diagrammatical lines that are sometimes curvaceous, sometimes perpendicular. One entrance to the church's south side brings you under a sloping tunnel structure. Fabricated in birch plywood its Eames-like curves are reassuring and the warmth of the wood in which the entire interior is decked is a welcoming and positive gesture. Pews are set in three tranches of concentric circles around a platform which demarcates the sanctuary – a composition of an altar and lectern-cum-pulpit in grey granite, a wide bench for the priests and a crucifix and candlesticks in slender iron. Behind the bench, off centre but at an eastern orientation, a large circle devoid of portholes is inlaid in the wall's panelling with a thin asymmetric cross in gold reaching to the circle's edges. Just centimetres from the cross's centre is one small porthole. It recalls the wound in the side of Christ, but without any real figuration it also alludes to a kind of Modernist sensibility, a belief in there being residual meaning in abstract forms and configurations. That said there is a definite Postmodern feel to Tesar's decentred motifs too. Humour and levity alleviate any assertion of Christian superiority over other faiths.

For architects, too, Tesar's vocabulary is a respectful if jovial take on Le Corbusier's at Ronchamp. Le Notre-Dame-du-Haut is riddled with small windows allowing illumination through apertures of varying size, shape and shades of stained glass. This manipulation of light becomes a key metaphor – the Virgin Mary is lit like the sun with a surrounding halo of stars – though in Tesar's treatment the regularity of the windows on their polka-dot grid express something much more grounded and earthly, perhaps artificial; a semblance of the potential

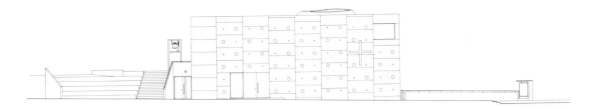

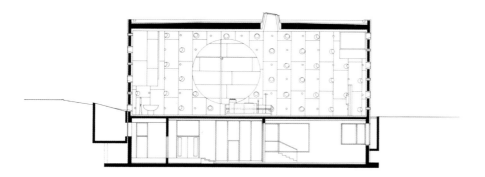

for human development and achievement not without God but as part of God's creation. Refreshingly, Tesar avoids the commonplace architectural misinterpretation of spiritual values into organic symbolism. From its exterior Christ Church is uncompromisingly urban without aping its commercial neighbours – even its wooden interior has a specificity and sophistication that is unapologetically man-made. Theologically, this is an important contribution to a more relevant church architecture – places of worship and contemplation that celebrate the developed world without pandering to other gods.

TOP Three sizes of holes are layered over each other in a polka-dot arrangement. Tesar's refusal to build anything that motions heavenward establishes an approachable environment for the non-Christian.

ABOVE This section shows the subtle change in the east wall's panelling which discloses a circle and a cross. The sanctuary furniture sits in close relation to it without disturbing the autonomy of the icon.

RIGHT Tesar's exterior plan for Christ Church makes a distinctive but discrete mark on the landscape. From an aerial view a cross-shaped plan is determined. The front and back are differentiated by the green and red landscaping.

LEFT The square and the circle are prevalent forms augmented by a few looser geometrical motifs such as the curved entrances.

TOP RIGHT A circular seating plan is often more efficient in a small church space like this one where acoustics and visibility are not hampered. Additional asymmetric elements of the site relieve the church of an overly boxy feel.

BOTTOM RIGHT Tesar's handling of the external steel shell betrays sensitivity to materials and texture as well as patterning and proportion. The nude steel frame that holds the bells is a satisfying contemporary adaptation.

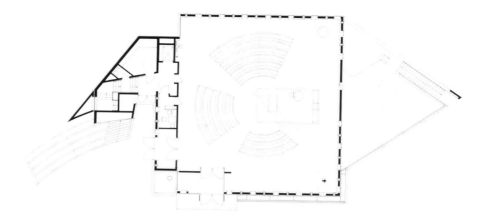

MORTENSRUD CHURCH

**Jensen & Skodvin
Arkitektkontor**

Location: Mortensrud, Oslo,
Norway
Completion date: 2002

The Scandinavian affinity with and respect for the natural environment has become imprinted on the international consciousness in recent times and its reality is a deeply held philosophy that manifests itself in social and physical spheres, not least architecture. Late Modernist examples of churches in Finland in particular demonstrate an earnest submission to the landscape: at Otaniemi (1957), Siren Architects developed a simple wood, glass and brick structure that reveals the surrounding woodland as a backdrop to the altar, and at Temppeliaukio Helsinki (1969), Suomalainen Architects' round subterranean church is lined with the rock face and drystone walls. Elements from both churches are in evidence at Mortensrud, just outside Oslo, in a complex where the site dictates dimension, materials and structural systems. Jensen & Skodvin approached with dexterity the challenge of least disturbance to the geology, mature pine forestry and other soft vegetation. Only the very top layer of soil was removed before building began and the trees were left in full glory, one a central feature of a glass atrium and others poking through the parvis that links the church with the community centre. A slim rectangular church rests on top of this rocky crest of a hill, and its glass facades reflect the trees and sky about it in an almost camouflage skin.

The form is not unusual in that it is based upon a standard steel frame supporting a regular pitched roof. The building blocks are local flat stones and no mortar has been used to cement the stone in place. Instead the steel frame carries the underside of the stonewall (which only begins at first-floor level) and flat steel plates are spaced intermittently to strengthen the stones' rigidity. Attached to the plates are twists of steel (looking like propellers) that fasten to the exterior glass shell.

So the interior drystone walls, though giving the appearance of a rustic agricultural building, are in fact, more sunscreen than weather shield, and more texture than load-bearing structure (though the roof does rest partially on the stone). Most natural light enters at ground-floor level – from the western side – through the aperture running along the edge of one side of pews, some through small windows in the stonewalls, and a minimal amount by a diffuse filter through the cracks between the stones. The brightness of the western flank encourages a kind of peripheral position within the church where the visitor can be both at a close proximity to the natural landscape and a participant in the worship.

Uninterrupted space within the nave allows for a wide aisle, asymmetric rows of pews and two places where the height of the underlying rock rises above the floor in natural outbreaks of heft and granite. It is hard not to imagine children clambering over these dignified humps in their own form of communion with the physical world.

A rise in contour from the road and car park to the west gradually merges the natural rocky surroundings with the informal parvis in front of the doors to the church. The primitively built wooden bell tower competes in height with the pine trees, and is something like a double-height version of that designed by the Sirens at Otaniemi; both are reminiscent of a forester's lookout. The entranceway is low, light and unfussy with two square atriums at either side of the walkway into the nave fully glazed but accessible for small acts of outdoor worship or

The interior stonewalling permits a naturally fragmented light, a device that might have hinted at the numinous without the additional symbolic artwork in the sanctuary.

ABOVE The outer side of the drystone walls are a jagged relief that increases the sense of the natural environment impinging on and influencing the architecture of this church.

RIGHT The altar's left leg falls underneath the central roof beam while a glass skin that insulates the drystone walls and makes light passageways and gallery spaces flanks the two sides of the church.

meetings. Extra spaces are also gained along the western flank of the church where a first-floor addition gives room for gallery seating.

Approaching the sanctuary, the off-centre pews on the left-hand side counter the glass reredos and the altar itself, which also do not align underneath the centre beam of the roof. This shifting around the main axis does not unsteady the balance; instead it invokes a nonhierarchical and relaxed arrangement. Colour is introduced at first in the blue pew cushions and then more emphatically in the semi-pictorial reredos designed by the artist Gunnar Torvund. Around a shimmering veil of golden orange glass – at the centre of which is the outstretched form of Christ crucified – dark-blue panels are embedded with traditional stained-glass patterning, as well as early Christian symbols like the fish. A golden dove hovers above this panel set against the stonewall and is repeated in the processional cross. As an assemblage of forms and colours this artwork fails to integrate itself with the rest of the church, although it does provide an imaginative focus and the sanctuary would be dull without it. This might be a case in point of an instance where the involvement of an artist is superfluous to that which the architects themselves are very well capable of designing. For instance, the kind of restrained detailing that the architects have used in the roof lighting – commercially available lamps suspended on horizontal forks of steel – might have been developed into a more intrinsic formula for the adornment of the sanctuary.

Mortensrud Church is not one to take the breath away with beauty and elegance, but Jensen & Skodvin have been undeniably true to the site, to the frugal budget and to environmental responsibility.

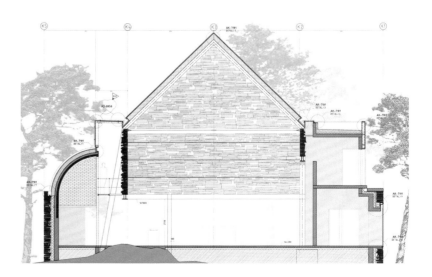

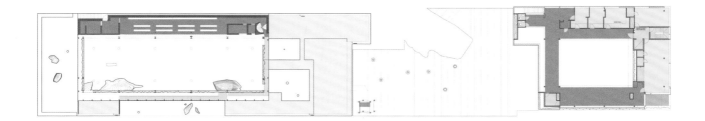

TOP LEFT The church's integration with the natural forestry around it extends to allowing mature pine trees to emerge from the platform of the parvis as well as the primitive wooden bell tower.

BELOW LEFT AND RIGHT Stretching along a suitable gap in the landscape, Mortensrud Church is fixed around a rectangular plan that can accommodate a number of natural features like rocks and trees.

ABOVE Sitting lightly on top of the unblemished earth, the church has generous entrance halls that lead past the trees left growing in an atrium.

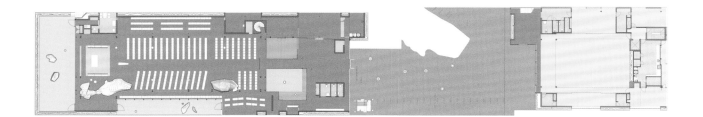

PAPER CHURCH

Shigeru Ban Architects

Location: Kobe, Japan

Completion date: 1995

OPPOSITE With all its doors open to the passing community, and plenty of visibility between the paper columns, numbers of congregants can expand informally. Ban's structure is about as undisguised as it can be.

BOTTOM The graceful proportions of Ban's ellipsis (formed by the paper tubes) allude to some of the grandeur of classical architecture. But with very simple devices such as the increasing gaps between the tubes, Ban services practical and economic concerns with a touch of Postmodern deftness.

It is a sorry fact of our commercially driven world that good architecture is typically the reserve of the rich, technology is by and large commandeered for the benefit of profit margins, and environmentally sensitive architecture is all too often a rural venture. It is refreshing, then, that Shigeru Ban, a Japanese architect with increasingly admired credentials – architecturally, technologically and environmentally – is being taken seriously, and perhaps more so that his buildings can be found in some of the world's worst afflicted areas of natural disaster. His route to such a distinction was arguably coincidental, though his approach to making buildings and his skills in envisioning them are well grounded. In the mid-1980s, as a result of budget constraints, Ban began using paper structures as an alternative material for an Alvar Aalto exhibition that he had been asked to design. Rediscovering paper's qualities of levity, availability, economy and sustainability he has racked up an impressive list of both extremely elegant private houses (with paper tubes as their main structural device) and affordable and quickly constructed shelters, both for temporary commissions and for areas hit by earthquakes in the 1990s such as India, Japan and Turkey.

The Vietnamese refugee community of the Japanese city of Kobe lost their homes and community buildings, including their church, in the 1995 earthquake that devastated the south-central region of Japan. Ban, having had his paper tube structure (PTS) approved by the Japanese government in 1993 as suitable material for permanent buildings, engaged a volunteer workforce and erected 30 paper log houses and a paper church.

Working with a relatively small site, Ban's well-established motifs of openness and transparency served the congregation well. Essentially an ellipse of paper tubes within a surrounding rectangle of polycarbonate doors, the gaps between the tubes widen and the doors can be left open, allowing for larger congregations to wander in and spill out. The tubes, though certainly a quirky material to use (children the world over must make their own constructions from the insides of loo-paper rolls), have an unquestionable elegance too. Five metres high and 33

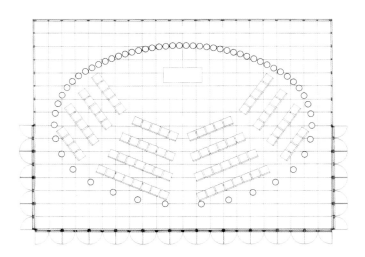

LEFT Other temporary buildings can also be found in this district of Kobe. The fabric of the Paper Church's roof is slightly transparent and becomes an understated beacon at night when the church lights are on.

RIGHT The long narrow doors forming the front half of the church's exterior shell are glazed with a translucent polycarbonate. There are definite echoes of traditional Japanese architecture but without sentimentality.

BELOW The roof of the church is, contradictorily, made from a PVC membrane, which is suspended like a marquee's structure from a central pole (though in this case the pole is not supported by the ground but by spokes attached to the rim of the ellipsis). The church's recent disassembly in order to move it to Taiwan is proof of Ban's commitment to genuinely transportable and practical buildings.

centimetres in diameter their proportions are not unlike cloister pillars, and their warm hue and smooth texture must be comfortingly domestic for a community so physically and emotionally shaken.

The roof is made from a thin white PVC fabric suspended from a central high-point that is in turn supported by a kind of upside-down skeleton of an umbrella. It leaves the main space free of supporting columns and a light and airy environment in which people worship. Behind the altar, which is positioned centrally along one of the broader sides of the ellipsis, the gaps between the paper tubes diminish to the extent that they form a wall, and behind that an area for storage. By night, among the other low and impermanent structures, the church's small pointed top glows with light from within. There is nothing about this church that is not welcoming, modest and entirely answerable to its cause. And in being that, it would seem a uniquely holy place that also recalls the Christian and pre-Christian protagonists who assumed nomadic existences, as well as Jesus's own promise that 'Where two or three are gathered together in my name, there am I in the midst of them' (Matthew 18:20).

In June 2005 the church was deconstructed and its materials shipped to and reassembled in Taiwan. The Paper Church, in the face of an entirely broken infrastructure, had served the community in Kobe for 10 years. It is contrary to most Western church-building instincts and theological reasoning to conceive of something that will not last for years to come' or 'endure generations of faithful worshippers'. But surely these notions, along with a great many expensive and burdensome buildings, though valid in some contexts, are too precious to be relevant for future global developments.

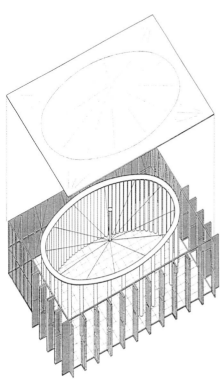

CHURCH OF THE SACRED HEART

Allman, Sattler, Wappner
Location: Munich, Germany
Completion date: 2000

RIGHT The woven metallic reredos dominates the north end although its flatness and permeability maintain the church's overall lightness. The stone flooring and furniture replicate the tone of the maple louvres so that there is continuity between all ground and wall planes.

The Church of the Sacred Heart has a number of important antecedents whose simple box-like structures have developed the language of ecclesiastical space beyond the need for arching vaults or heavenward trajectories. This template, often devoid of interior sight-restricting columns, depends on an invisible mastery of structural engineering in order to empty the cube. Italian architects Angelo Mangiarotti and Bruno Morassutti pioneered an exemplary cubical form in 1957 in their church at Bollate, Milan, dedicated to Mater Misericordiae, and Franz Füeg did the same at St Pius of Meggen, Lucerne, almost 10 years later. Both churches maximised the strength of the supporting framework of the cube to an aesthetic end in that the materials used between the supports were not load-bearing and could thus be made from a translucent fabric – a sandwich of glass and foam at Bollate, and slabs of marble at Meggen.

This system, which allows a ubiquitous diffuse light (by day at least) to blanket the church interior is a dominant concern at Sacred Heart where Allman, Sattler, Wappner have wrapped a glass exterior shell around another shell made of wooden vertical louvres. Entering through the double layer, there is an immediate feeling of privacy and enclosure. Yet this church can, on occasion, turn all that on its head by literally opening itself: its southern facade splits into two massive hinged doors that operate hydraulically. The courtyard then becomes an extension of the interior space or a large stage set for open-air liturgy.

For most of the time, however, the facade, designed by the glass artist Alexander Beleschenko, remains closed with just a small pair of doors at the centre for everyday access. This approach is nonetheless impressive, with the square panes of blue glass reflecting a continually shifting sky over traces of the structure within. A black steel frame is pinned together with chunky staples, a distinctive grid that from a distance is arguably as memorable as the rose windows of Gothic cathedral facades. At close quarters the detail on the glass elicits both a sensual and visual explosion. Thousands of life-size nails have been printed, using a raised silk-screen technique, onto the glass in the form of text from St John's Gospel and although the script is barely readable the nails are tangible (like Braille). This layer of glass is then doubled against another layer which has a random scattering of darker nails, rendering the text even less legible but magnifying the depth and texture of the surface. Beleschenko's contribution to this church, over 200 square metres of glass, is notable for its integration into the architects' scheme as well as its charismatic complexity.

The rest of the church's glass exterior is made from a clear glass, frosted in progressively denser panels. This progression, along the axis of the church, is reversed within the wooden shell of the building where the increasingly larger spacing between the maple louvres increases the light that reaches the altar. The vertical ribbing and warmer tones of the louvres are softening devices that contrast the interior with the exterior's more hard-edged appearance. (This also allows the kind of contemporary transparency that many new churches seek in the spirit of inclusivity.) Stone flooring and oak pews amplify the pale, honeyed internal features as does the full-wall reredos, a woven metallic (brass-copper hybrid) hanging whose warp and weft bears the insignia of a cross. The seeming detachment and the colouration of this screen bear a strong likeness to Japanese bamboo screens, although the scale of it doesn't indicate any temporality or movability.

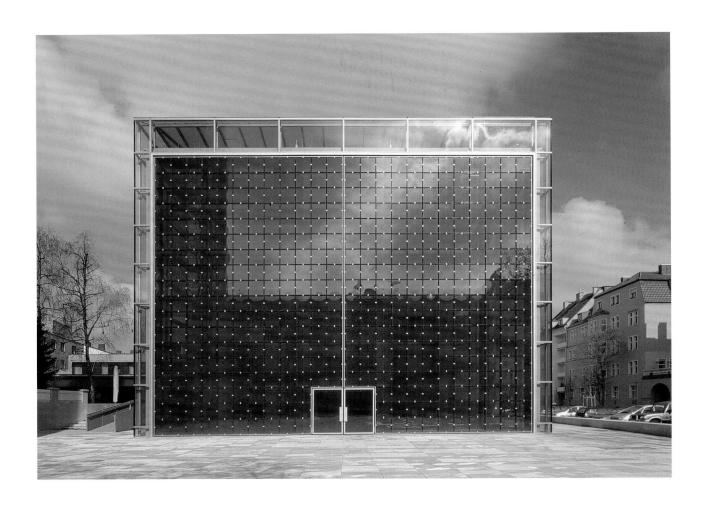

ABOVE Over 14 metres high, a grid of blue glass constitutes the Sacred Heart's front facade. Small dashes of metal fixtures prevent the surface from being a purely reflective screen and intimate the increased detail at closer proximity.

TOP RIGHT Pictorial nails are used as the component parts of lettering that spells out passages from the Gospel of St John.

BOTTOM RIGHT The cross-shaped nave echoes the cross woven into the reredos and holds the font at its centre. A gallery at the south end has capacity for the choir and organ while a wrap-around courtyard leads to ancillary rooms to the west.

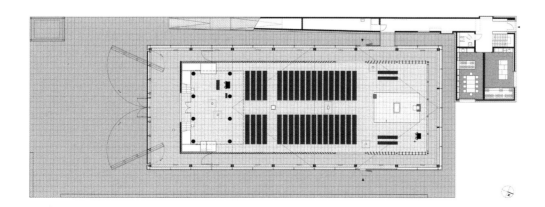

From the entrance (left) to the altar (right) the exterior glass shell is given an increasingly thick satin coating affecting light levels within the church and breaking down the monotony of its sidewalls. A separate bell tower is situated at the south corner of the front courtyard.

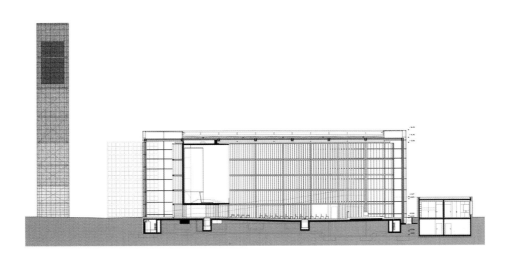

Rather, it towers monumentally over the resolutely human-scaled sanctuary furniture, and is even more dramatic by night when its award-winning lighting scheme creates the effect of an upward sunburst behind it. By night, the light from within the church is filtered through the maple and glass giving off an inviting glow to the urban community around it.

Some criticism has been directed at this competition-winning design for its lack of a traditional processional layout – like that of the previous church which had burnt down and as stipulated in the brief. Nevertheless, Sacred Heart offers another mode for liturgical procession around its louvred ambulatory, in the gap between the two structural layers and along which illuminated Stations of the Cross are positioned. It is also broad, spacious and neutral enough at its sanctuary to accommodate a variety of worship . A modest stage of 25 centimetres or so elevates the altar, lectern and preparation table and all elements are melded together in the same stone and set only at right angles. A gridded cage of the same brass-copper metal houses the tabernacle in a lyrical contrast to the blue and black nails that grid the facade. It is this sensibility, refined in a traditional aesthetic sense and yet Postmodern, that typifies this accomplished architectural project and does much to uphold the quality and stature of contemporary German church design.

TOP LEFT The church's most dramatic configuration involves swinging wide its front portals, revealing the inner shell of wooden louvres and creating a natural gathering place within its outspread plan.

BOTTOM LEFT The louvres lining both of the sidewalls gradually thin out towards the altar (right). All elements are strictly perpendicular including the bell tower that doubles the height of the church.

BELOW Outer glass panels join vertical load-bearing strips of glass, which together withstand high wind pressure and insulate the building thermodynamically.

RIGHT A straight broad nave lends its width to that of the cross that, by night, is given an extra dimension by backlighting through its woven texture.

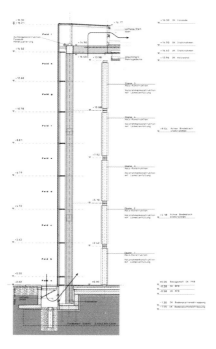

Church of Santa Maria

Álvaro Siza

Location: Marco de Canavezes,
Portugal
Completion date: 1996

RIGHT A small balcony curves around the
south-west corner extending the porch into the
church and prefixing the much larger curves of
the north wall and apse. The blonde wood of the
doors, chairs and flooring are a natural opposi-
tion to the cool white plaster.

BELOW A fairly traditional plan is overlaid with
the false arching north wall and the spaces
underneath the north-east and south-west
corners. Extra rooms including the sacristy are
hidden behind the north wall.

In the early 1990s urban development of the region around Porto in Portugal
necessitated the provision of a new church for the inhabitants of Marco de
Canavezes. Insistent on employing Álvaro Siza for the job, the local parish priest Fr
Nuno Higino sowed the seed for one of the most successful and revered churches
to be built in the last 20 – if not 50 – years. An instantaneous impression of the
church is its naturalness in the landscape. Siza managed to make an ultra modern
building look like it had occupied the site for centuries. Perhaps this is because he
utilised the traditional plan of a colonial-style church, with two towers either side
of the entrance, a rectangular plan and an altar that sits at the far end. Siza pared
this down so that the towers are circumscribed by the height of the roof and only
protrude in blank-faced blocks either side of the tall central doorway. The apse is
inverted so that where a traditional space would curve outwards, at Santa Maria
the apse curves into the church, forming two majestic fluted exterior walls at the
eastern end overlooking the conurbation. Siza was also careful to position the
church so that the rise and fall of the land around it affords additional crypt
spaces as well as a variety of approaches worthy of the best castles or cathedrals.
For example, a set of stairs curls around the lofty apse, and the towers of the western end dominate the built environment over which they preside.

From the northern approach the side wall of the church might be miscon-
strued as a sleek Modernist house with its row of high windows (where an upper
level might be), concealed entrances and a lower block of domestic proportions
(where, in fact, the sacristy joins the church). But round the corner from one of the
flanking 'towers', the entranceway, with its 10-metre-high door and row of bells in
an opening of the other tower, make clear the ecclesiastical character of this
design. A smaller, more functional set of doors offers immediate access to the
belfry side and the church. A large window in the opposite tower at ground level
mirrors the proportions of the doors and offers a view of the baptistery, as well as
a glimpse at the tenor and style of the main interior that does not eclipse the
impact of entering.

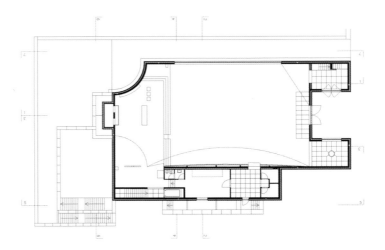

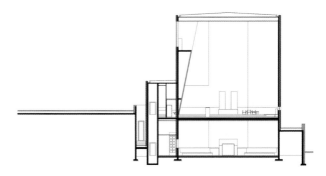

The western doors, for use on high days and holy days, mark out a symmetrical and centred elevation, and the long vertical strip is repeated at its eastern end in a kind of chimney flue that acts as a lightwell on to the altar area. However, this centralisation is not indicative of the interior that subverts and distorts this rule without seeming chaotic or unreasoned. At the south side, along whose axis one finds the everyday entrance, the wall is perpendicular and windowless except for a long narrow horizontal aperture looking out over the urban landscape. The north wall looms inwards in a large gracious curve, more bulbous at the top, almost as if the roof were caving in. Here three deep leaning windows – those that appear so flat and restrained from the outside – pull the light in across the ceiling and down into the church. The church does away with any ceiling- or wall-mounted lighting so the bare white plaster of this extraordinary interior volume magnifies and sensitises the natural light without distraction or compromise.

At the eastern end, the walls, which form the fluted bastion from the exterior curve into the sanctuary, focus attention on the altar; a simple white block raised up slightly on a platform of three steps. A wooden lectern is set into the steps, and wooden benches, a tabernacle and an almost T-shaped cross are placed around. The two blind windows that usher in the light from the well behind fall in symmetrical bands, a very slight gradation of light from top to bottom alluding to a heavenly source. The space that these bands form could also be read as the negative space around the lower half of a cross: the mind's eye can fill in the rest.

One of the apse curves is cut short before it reaches ground level and the space underneath it leads to the sacristy. A chest-height ribbon of yellow tiles circuits the church's east and south walls and lines the small baptistery providing continuity around the perimeter walls and preventing the white plaster becoming an overwhelming feature. Wooden floors (with stone flags around the entranceways) and wooden movable chairs convey a homeliness and warmth that make Santa Maria a comfortable place to be in as well as an inspiring and challenging one.

It must be a cliché to say that Siza makes good architecture look easy, but his church at Marco de Canavezes proves this a truism. To maximise this relatively small and uneven site with such a concise and elegant response is a rare thing. Although there is much to be said for ecclesiastical architecture that journeys and expresses a narrative or a symbol, an equally viable result can come from allowing a few apparently basic forms to speak for themselves.

ABOVE A band of tiling and a slit of window at chest height are the only details on the south wall. Beneath the church are public walkways, parking and a mortuary chapel.

ABOVE CENTRE Santa Maria's central axis is maintained by the altar and rear lightwells, but the symmetry is gently undermined by the ingress of the north wall.

ABOVE RIGHT A stoic trinity of windows subtracts from the curving north wall and sheds a diffuse light over the nave. The well added onto the east wall deflects light all the way to the mortuary chapel at subterranean level.

BOTTOM RIGHT At the western end Siza transforms the traditional twin towers and high central doors of so many colonial-period Portuguese churches into a paradigm of Modernist form.

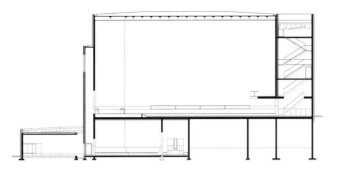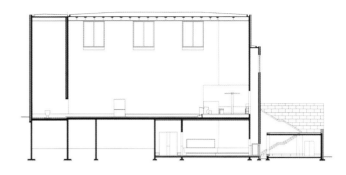

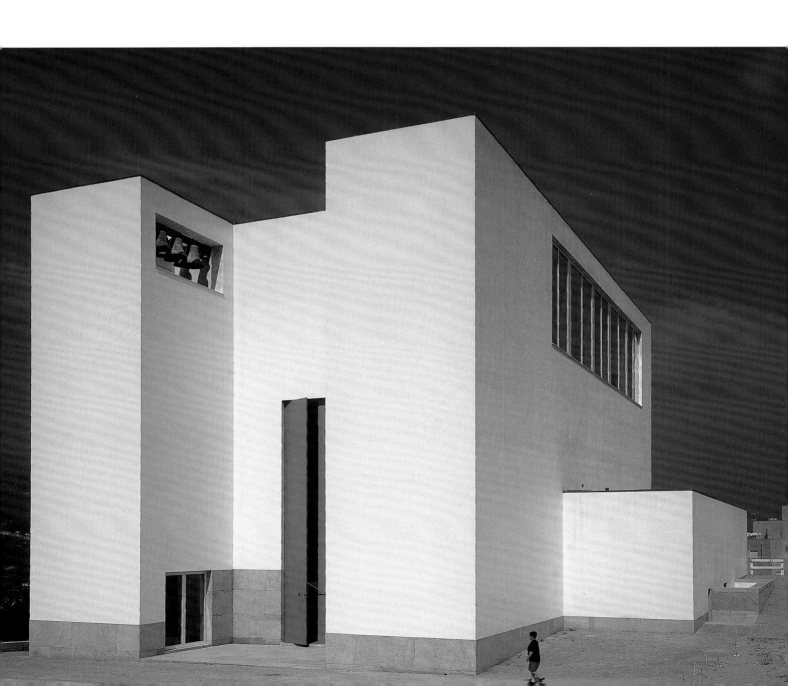

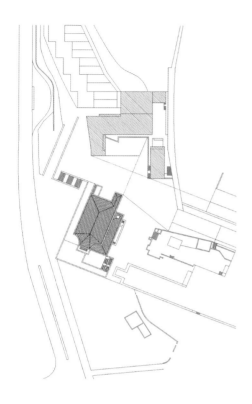

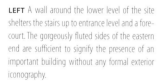

LEFT A wall around the lower level of the site shelters the stairs up to entrance level and a forecourt. The gorgeously fluted sides of the eastern end are sufficient to signify the presence of an important building without any formal exterior iconography.

ABOVE The church shoulders the sweep of the topography and overlooks its urban context with magnanimous poise.

TOP RIGHT Tiling and stone in and around the baptistery recall more traditional and vernacular styles and yet they sit well in Siza's contemporary design.

RIGHT Siza cuts away at the northern side of the main apse form creating a stronger perception of its depth and enlarging the sanctuary space.

JUBILEE CHURCH

Richard Meier & Partners

Location: Tor Tre Teste, Rome, Italy

Completion date: 2003

RIGHT At dusk the lights within the church contrast with the cool white of the exterior walls. The curved walls have a protective, sheltering character and echo centuries of vaulted church architecture.

In the bright Italian sun, Richard Meier's 'Jubilee Church', as it is now known, casts a strident if careful form in Tor Tre Teste, an area of 1970s housing estates just outside central Rome. The fiftieth church to be completed under the Vicariato's Millennium Project, Meier was selected from an impressive (and non-Christian) group of six, including Tadao Ando, Peter Eisenmann and Frank Gehry, who were invited to compete for the commission in 1996. The brief asked for 'a sign of the pilgrimage [to the See of Peter] for the Holy Year 2000, and of welcome by the Church of Rome [...] together with a role for expressed welcome for the communities in its neighbourhood' (L'architecttura, Cronache e Storia: p 71). That the Church of Rome chose Meier's entry showed both its seriousness and its generosity in developing fine new architecture in the capital's suburbs.

The triangular site tapers to a natural entry point at the eastern corner and the church is aligned with this axis; the adjoining community complex spreads to the north and an expansive forecourt broadens off to the south. Meier's signature handling of geometric forms is evident here: the design is based on four circles and a sequence of squares. The most distinctive elements are the three curved walls that hunker around each other to the south side. Formed as segments from three equal spheres, the tip of the largest curve hovers over the central entrance. The white cement, originally invented for the Olympic Stadium in Rome, was cast in situ into blocks, the intersecting pieces making visible the proportions which reference the church's window panels, doors and apertures. Beneath these curved forms are three separate doorways, shaded from southerly sunlight. From the centre outwards they lead to the main worship space, the baptistery and the Daily Chapel with confessionals. Access between the three is open, though the chapel has a short partition wall.

This capacious volume to one side of the church, with skylights in between each curved wall, creates a sense of height and grandeur while maintaining an enclosure that is relatively intimate and focused. The nave seats less than 300. The wall to the north side is also curved but only at its exterior face. Inside, a large part of this wall is rendered with long slats of warm-coloured hemlock, and the pews are of a similar hue but in beech. Chancel furniture is also pronounced in a warm marble, the altar a discrete oval vessel shape. These are positioned beneath varying white rectangular structures, which form a backdrop, and at times slim apertures reveal windows and landscaping behind. Above that the church has chosen a 19th-century crucifix in dark carved wood which stands out, perhaps a little too starkly.

Behind this screen the sacristy juts out beyond the edge of the west end of the building, creating a focal point for the approach from the west side as well as an indication of the angular structures within from the south side – from where the building appears most curvaceous. The fact that the church has its altar and sacristy at the west end is pragmatic rather than heretical. The aforementioned triangular site dictated the position of the entrance, and had Meier stuck with convention, keeping the altar in the east, the community would have had to walk round to the back of the church to enter.

A campanile rises up from the north side of the of the approach, loosely connected to the main church by intervening staircases, with a strip of bells descending down a slit in its front wall. It is reminiscent of campaniles by early Modernists

such as Rudolf Schwarz (for example, his Corpus Christi, Aachen, Germany, 1922), Fritz Metzger (St Karl, Lucerne, Switzerland, 1935), Alvar Aalto (Seinäjöki Church, Finland, 1960) and even Le Corbusier, whose boxy little campanile at Ste Maria de la Tourette (1953–60) truly broke with any convention of heavenward spires.

Beyond the campanile is the four-storey ancillary block, including priests' offices, living quarters, and conference, meeting and catechism rooms. A line of trees marks the northeast border of the site and small garden areas are also provided.

The flux between openness and enclosure, curved forms and straight, direct light and filtered is deftly and purposefully handled, only occasionally verging on something too intricate or complicated. Meier consciously attributes this sensibility to something that is 'fundamentally theological' – HG Gadamer's phrase from The Relevance of the Beautiful (Church Building p 24). There is a strong sense of the legacy of the Vatican's Second Council remit of 1964 in which it was decreed that altars in new churches should be made to stand proud of the east wall, bringing them closer to the laity and enlivening the liturgy. (It also stipulated that Mass be said or sung in the vernacular language.) This gave the impetus to experiment and modernise, and catholic church architecture has been some of the most startling in the last 40 years. This, in turn, has developed Catholic congregations' acceptance of such forms and produced a generic style of sorts that Meier has tapped into and over which he has laid the sophistication of a world-class architect.

LEFT An expansive paved courtyard sets off views of the distinctive curved elevation with the southern sun championing the polished white concrete. A slot at the bottom of the south side allows a little extra light to penetrate the chapel.

TOP LEFT The natural funnel created by this triangular site dictated the selection of an east end entrance, making for the unusual placement of the altar at the west.

TOP MIDDLE East section showing the curvature of the shell walls, framework suspending the glass-panelled ceiling, the adjoining four storeys for community use, and important iconographic detail such as the cup-shaped altar and offset perspectival treatment of the panel behind the cross.

TOP RIGHT The off-centre nave nevertheless sits elegantly under the arched south walls into which are tucked the Daily Chapel, confessionals (three small boxes) and baptistery (in front of the middle doorway). The curved walls, though broken up in parts, extend across the width of the complex with only the sacristy breaking the line to the west and the main entrance to the east.

RIGHT One wooden slatted wall provides some relief from Meier's predominantly bright white architecture as well as continuity between the wooden pews, off-white flooring and light-brown marble sanctuary furniture. The 19th-century crucifix is centred amid irregularly spaced blocks and apertures.

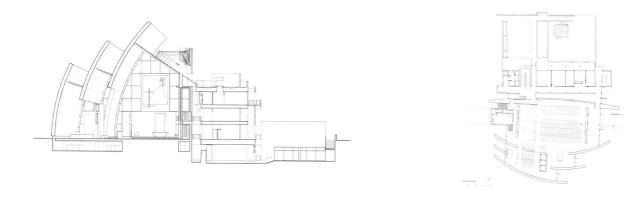

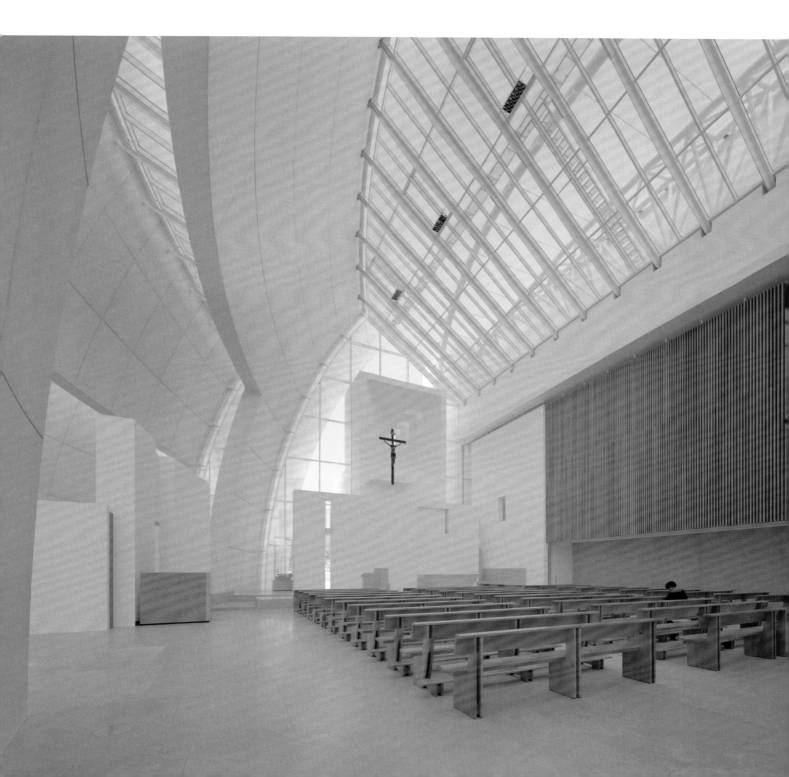

NOVÝ DVŮR MONASTERY

John Pawson
Location: Pilsen, Czech Republic
Completion date: 2004

RIGHT The presbytery has all the grandeur of a Gothic cathedral in its proportions and height without recourse to decoration or ornament- ation bar the precious iconography of the Order set on a central pedestal.

It was, arguably, more than mere serendipity that a group of Trappist monks should commission the 'high priest' of current minimalist design to build them a new monastery in rural Bohemia. Apart from the above metaphor used to describe John Pawson – the designer-cum-architect whose trademark projects include commercial ventures such as the Calvin Klein store in New York and his own impossibly minimalist house – the choice taken by the Cistercian Abbot of Sept-Fons in Burgundy was an astute and inspired one. The Abbot perceived the similarities between Pawson's architectural concerns and a 12th-century text by St Bernard of Clairvaux, which created a blueprint for building programmes for the Cistercian order. St Bernard sets out the practical requirements of the monastic building, but also describes the elements of design which embrace the monks' solitude, routine and prayerfulness and emphasises ascetic qualities of light, proportion, simplicity and clarity rather than the more materialistic concerns of monastic antecedents.

Pawson has all of this firmly under his belt. In his own house, the narrow stair-case, sandwiched closely between two high white walls and famously photographed with a burst of light at its zenith, looks more than a little like a stair-way to heaven; he does clever things with recessed apertures down which light is channelled softly and yet dramatically; and he is, some might say, obsessive about stowing away all the stuff of life, leaving his spaces clean and tidy and thus transferring all attention to forms and materials. So, although Pawson's work has been defined by the secular, if not atheist culture of minimalist design, the project was from the outset full of potential.

Returning to the Czech Republic since the fall of communism the new community of 40 monks acquired a site in a tiny and remote area of woodland between Pilsen and Karlsbad. A derelict cloister arrangement of buildings stood around a Baroque manor house, the only part of the complex sound enough to be restored. However, Pawson retained the footprint of the complex, and began the task of accommodating, among other things, the chapel, refectory, sleeping quarters, scriptorium, infirmary, laundry, kitchen and wine cellar.

Stories of the monks visiting Pawson to view preparatory drawings enliven the narrative of the monastery's progress, and the agreed designs are a very sure response to the remit of St Bernard together with a contemporary, though time-less, simplicity. The site slopes from the west to the east, and Pawson follows ecclesiastical tradition by maintaining the church's apse in the east; what is at ground level to the west (the former manor house, cloisters and courtyard) is the upper level at the east, allowing for a lower-ground-floor complex underneath the church space including the infirmary, kitchen, pharmacy, drying room, laun-dry, cloakroom and wine cellar. But it also affords Pawson the opportunity for one particularly spectacular hidden staircase. Behind the altar in the main church space the floor drops away to descend to a small door that leads out to the monks' cemetery and the adjoining lower-ground-floor wing. The stairs are flanked by flat sloping stonework, reminiscent of Egyptian mausoleums.

The end wall of the apse is a perfect semicircular cylinder and joins the sidewalls of the presbytery in a traditional Gothic form. But no vaulted arches or stained-glass windows are found here. Instead Pawson cuts two huge sym-metrical U-shapes into the walls behind which natural light is funnelled in

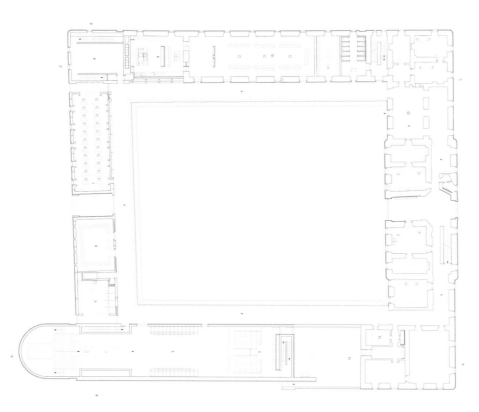

TOP LEFT Doing away with the usual pillar supports of cloisters, Pawson's white glazed walkways are an improbable feat of engineering.

CENTRE LEFT The church's semicircular apse protrudes from the northeast corner of the cloistered plan. The refectory is in the south wing and a scriptorium, chapter room and sacristy in the east.

ABOVE Pawson has maintained the footprint of the former buildings as well as something of the style of eastern European architecture. The sloping site is evident, allowing for two full floors through the lower half of the complex.

BOTTOM LEFT The monks' choir stalls in dark wood are a sensitive yet emphatic focus for the main church space. With light filtered through the squat U-shape bar above the panelling the contrast, though stark, is both a practical and aesthetic device.

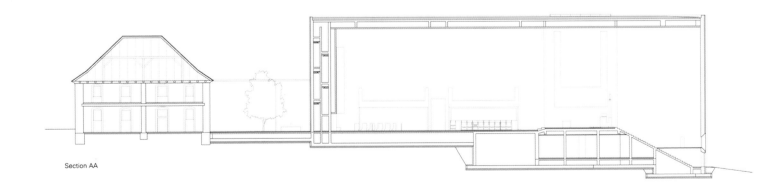

Section AA

deep vertical trenches. The bottom bar of the U-shape is much broader than the upward bars allowing plenty of light to reach the presbytery. On the outside of the building the shoulders of the funnel cut in to angle the light, but the curvature has been reversed to create a shallow but sheltering arch.

Moving backwards down the church the monks' choir is furnished with dark, stained-oak stalls and high panelling behind them. These are purposeful and quite luxuriant against the predominantly white walls, but they retain modesty in line with St Bernard's directives. Above them a similar U-shaped device allows in a constant light source at the monks' backs. A small number of seats are available for lay people at the back of the church. Pawson himself intends to return and maintain his friendship with the community, an indication of the strength of their hospitality and warmth, albeit a closed and private world.

Running alongside the church, around the east and south wings and interspersed between rooms of the old manor house, are long cloisters. Pawson chose to glaze the courtyard-facing apertures (traditionally left open to the elements) and, rather than interrupt their passage with framing or supports, the panels of glass are simply slotted between a low-rise wall at shin height and the overhanging edge of the barrel-vaulted cloister roof. The cloisters without pillars typify Pawson's uncompromising aesthetic: hidden structures of cantilevered steel girders add to the general lightness and dexterity of the complex.

Pawson's architecture at Nový Dvůr often succeeds through the details that are made to resonate by the surrounding simplicity. For instance, in the curved apse wall hovering above the altar an old sculpted figure of the Virgin Mary sits atop a tall slim pedestal. Only its head, shoulders and legs are distinguishable from a distance, but it is enough to make an expansive pictorial gesture and draws the eye to the tabernacle below it, a crucifix and two elegant iron candlesticks. The altar itself is a block of yellow Chinese granite of domestic proportions.

The impressiveness of the monastery's minimalist beauty is coupled with the surprisingly convincing practicality of the building. The care and deliberation that has so obviously been upheld by both monks and architect seems also to have been touched by prayer.

LEFT Behind the altar an unanticipated staircase descends to linking doors through to the infirmary in the east wing and the cemetery outside. It is suggestive of the great Egyptian monuments both in its form and in its allusions to a transition to life beyond mortality.

BOTTOM LEFT An intervening courtyard separates the old manor house from the church. The section shows the descending stairs behind the altar and the U-shaped light shafts.

BOTTOM RIGHT The angled in-turn of the light shafts deflects the light into the presbytery. The converse arch is visible on the outer wall to the left of this section.

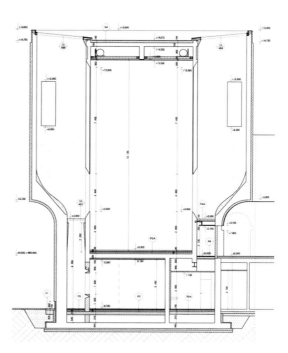

CATHEDRAL OF OUR LADY OF THE ANGELS

José Rafael Moneo

Location: Los Angeles, California, US

Completion date: 2002

RIGHT Creating the perfect cornerpost to the complex, the bell tower is configured so that various combinations of bells are seen from different angles.

As the website for the Cathedral of Our Lady of the Angels in Los Angeles points out, the 'Roman Catholic Church has never adopted one particular style of architecture […] There has always been an appreciation for the creative spirit indigenous to the local community' (OLA website). The Spanish architect Rafael Moneo may not be 'local', but Los Angeles' heritage certainly made him an appropriate candidate for the job. In fact, it might be hard to call any single culture in its current melting pot of inhabitants 'indigenous' to Los Angeles, nevertheless there's little doubt that the Catholic community, whose ancestors from the Spanish San Gabriel Mission founded the City in 1781, thrives today.

Earthquake damage to the 19th-century Saint Vibiana Cathedral rendered it beyond rescue. The job to create a new contemporary cathedral in downtown Los Angeles began in earnest in 1996 with the purchase of a 2.3-hectares site overlooking the Hollywood Freeway and the decision to commission Moneo. With a surfeit of expertise in urban municipal buildings, Moneo's confidence handling the site is evident and impressive. Likening the freeway to a 'river of transportation, the connection of people to each other', the cathedral complex sits on an axis that runs parallel to the 'river' – as does the Notre Dame to the Seine or the Houses of Parliament to the Thames – as if it were tapping into the momentum and dynamic. As well as significant community and residential buildings at the east end of the complex, the length and breadth of the site allows for plenty of open exterior space which Moneo handles with the same sophistication as the interior space. Indeed the transfer, or journey, from freeway to cathedral sanctuary is a foundational principal for the entire complex as the asymmetrical criss-cross of pathways and axes develops and unfolds unexpectedly.

Moneo chose to interpret the theme of journeying towards the light of God with white alabaster panels as the sole glazing material, giving the interior spaces a milky and serene light, evenly spread and always well illuminated with strong Californian sunlight. The altar is conventionally sited at the east end where the cathedral broadens expansively and a large alabaster window is divided into four sections by the intersection of the cross's sloping horizontal planes and incisive vertical bars. The sidewalls are not outer walls, but instead are flanked by side chapels and a clerestory whose high alabaster walls allow a double-filtered light into the main nave.

Other windows stretch up to a fluctuating ceiling level at the east end and immerse the sanctuary in light, and, together with the nave which tapers up and out to accommodate a large organ and choir, assure that the focus within the cathedral space is decisive without being grandiose. Moneo achieves much through thoughtful detailing which is integral to the whole – for instance, in the concentric circles formed by the cathedral's interior paving (they radiate from a centre point under the altar), or the panelling in the ceiling which accentuates the rise and fall of the roof planes. The cathedral has its own art consultant and a variety of commissions; the tapestry of saints or the bronze-cast doors are, perhaps, a more accurate indication of the church's commitment to the indigenous 'creative spirit'.

From the outside the cathedral has almost as much to see. The views from the surrounding four roads amass an array of spectacular planes, seemingly informal and irregular but underpinned by the gently tapering form of the cathedral that

extends through the plaza and landscaping. The entrance from Temple Street (the quieter side) leads under a campanile of 20 bells set into a deep wall that runs the length of the site and is planted with shrubs. A round fountain is prescient of the cathedral's full-immersion baptismal font and sets the initial marker for an alternative but nonetheless liturgically rooted journey into the complex. Tall palm trees intervene between the lower structures and the loftier heights of the east wall, and a wide plaza encourages a public realm of 'intermediating spaces', as the architect puts it.

The concrete is a specially mixed hue reminiscent of the early Californian mission buildings and of a deep enough tone to absorb light rather than reflect its glare. Against this, exterior glass boxes, which protect the alabaster and refract light to it, look dark – almost black – punctuating the structures seen from within, such as the cross on the east wall and angular windows. The bell tower also casts a purposeful profile at the northwest corner of the site. Separated from the cathedral in the manner of Giotto's Florentine masterpiece, its faceted vertical planes reveal different configurations of its 18 bells. The tower stands on its own specifically designed base isolators, as does the cathedral, to prevent against anything as large as an 8-point earthquake – a sobering but reassuring thought. The Cathedral of Our Lady of the Angels will be an important landmark for the people of Los Angeles for many years to come.

BELOW The unusual entrance at the southeast corner increases the sense of journeying towards the light-filled nave. Passing down the interior clerestory, private devotional chapels are easily accessible and tapered at idiosyncratic angles.

TOP RIGHT The site accommodates the cathedral at the highest end, a plaza and gardens in the middle, and auxillary buildings at the lowest end. The entrance is marked by a low, wide breach in the wall, under a cross and campanile.

BOTTOM RIGHT At its east end the scale of Moneo's cathedral reaches almost Gothic proportions. Yet the warm-hued concrete and clean lines prevent it from being domineering or pretentious.

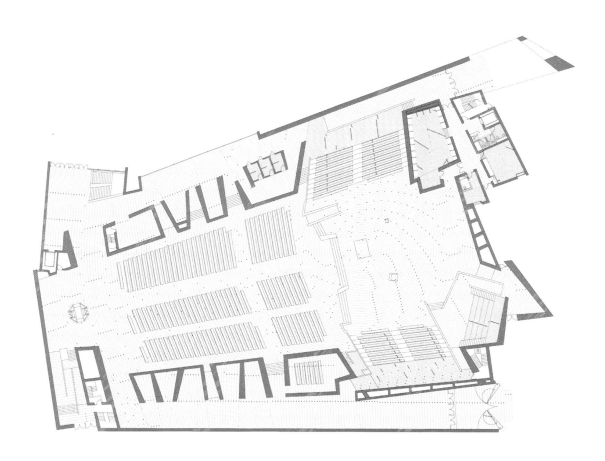

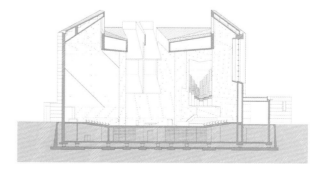

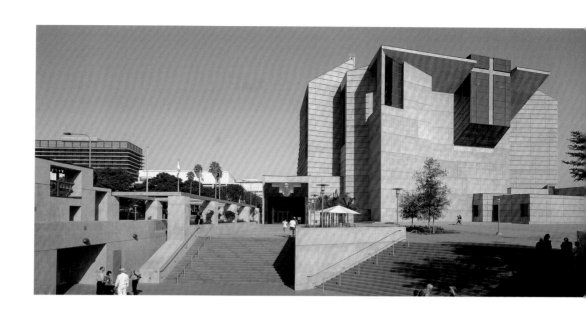

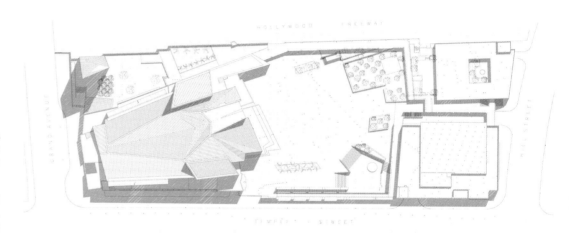

PREVIOUS SPREAD The rows of nave pews gently widen towards the sanctuary, which is an expansive space, flooded by light filtered through the white alabaster windows.

TOP LEFT The alabaster is secured in a diagonal formation around the cross at the east end. Moneo's architectural signature for this building would seem to be his ability to handle numerous angles and facets without losing any solidity or conviction.

BOTTOM LEFT Section A-A shows the breadth and height of the sanctuary and choir: compare the dimensions of the altar to those of the cross above it. The alabaster panels are ranged diagonally in the east window, a detail that is echoed in the sloping clerestory walls, the pitch and panelling of the roof and the downward slant of the composite parts of the cross.

TOP Two staircases lead up to the main doorway into the cathedral and across the plaza. The strong Californian sun casts stark shadows that emphasise the angularity of each facet.

ABOVE The kite-shaped pitch roof provides the central axis for the entire site with a dissecting axis cutting across the plaza from the round Gateway Pool and Waterfall. Irregular angles are fully played out in the autonomous bell tower that sits at the north corner of the site.

YANCEY CHAPEL

Samuel Mockbee and Rural Studio

Location: Sawyerville, Alabama, US

Completion date: 1996

In defiance of 'paper architecture', the kind of aloof design process that gives architects a bad name, the late Professor Samuel Mockbee taught his students at Auburn University the hands-on approach. Without fancy materials or middle-class budgets he also encouraged his students to work at a local level, building houses from scratch among small and disenfranchised communities. By 1992 Mockbee and his colleague DK Ruth had formalised this pedagogy and created Rural Studio, an architectural practice which has, with missionary zeal, gone out into the surrounding neighbourhoods of Hale County, Alabama, to make relevant, responsible and affordable buildings for and with its people. Sourcing materials from waste, recycling or surplus, and commandeering local labour and help in kind, Rural Studio's younger students helped construct houses while, by 1995, Mockbee challenged three fifth-year students – Steven Durden, Thomas Trethaway and Ruard Veltman – to build their first community project: a chapel for the village of Yancey. And if ever resources dictated the construction and style of a church this building would epitomise that functionality, while demonstrating that this need not preclude creativity and exuberance.

Disused dairy land was given over for the site and a local scrap merchant had a large number of tyres to dispose of. These tyres were used as building blocks, and then packed with earth to solidify them. They were stacked in a low, long wall that acts both as entry passage and church, forming a sunken shelter in the gentle lift of the land where a cattle trough once stood. The tyres bulbous forms were plastered in an adobe mud mix, a rich and sensuous texture that offsets the more mechanical features of the roof and its supports. From underneath the highest pitch of the roof, a view of the skeletal structure could be said, consciously or not, to resonate with the brutal simplicity of Christ's crucifixion. At the far end, where the tail of the central beam dips to the horizon between a cut in the wall, a quietly pronounced cross hangs in the light. In a sense, there are a hundred crosses in this chapel, testifying to the narrative of resurrection – wood salvaged from a previous building, the roof made of old corrugated iron shingles and paving stones lifted from a nearby stream.

Yet there is nothing apologetic about this architecture. A larger and taller version of the roof structure exists in Westport, Connecticut, where a 1960s church by Victor A Lundy appears from above like Concorde, with a great tall neck reaching up at one end. The Yancey Chapel roof is a calmer proposition, its peak is at best half the height of the surrounding trees, but it is still impressive and extremely graceful. Sheltering under its sweeping length it is hard to be certain about front or back, as both ends are open to the elements. There is a pulpit fashioned from reclaimed steel bars and concrete at one end which protrudes from a lower level on an old girder, its front an upright v-shape that occurs elsewhere in the chapel, mainly as a functional motif. Beyond the pulpit, as in most churches, the tempo changes to indicate the sanctuary space, and at Yancey there is a drop, a widening out, and wood flooring is introduced combined with the riverbed flagstones. There is also a vista and a canopy of trees that imbue these stepped platforms with a sense of protection and stillness.

At the opposite end of the chapel, a narrower passageway through the tyres, whose rising levels are capped with concrete slabs, brings you under a small curved-steel covering to an upright one which supports a water stoup.

ABOVE The chapel is aligned to the long axis of a former cattle trough, but the passage between the walls of mud-clad tyres and under the steeply pitched roof is well paced and proportioned. A combination of wood boards and stone paving in a formal arrangement at one end designates the sanctuary space.

Alternatively, small-scale baptisms could take place in this space. Such is the extent of the ecclesiastical furniture here, but for a building without doors, and with its gaping open section along the spine of the roof, it has to withstand a lack of security and inclement weather.

Few churches have been built with so little money that the constraints have not yet produced a familiar architectural vocabulary, even though a theology of asceticism and humility has been prevalent over the last 40 years in all denominations. While the church in the developed world still seeks solidarity with its brothers and sisters in less fortunate economies, this American prototype ought to teach a lesson about the broader value of education, as well as architecture of respect and dignity.

ABOVE A narrow entranceway to one side of the central roof beam magnifies the very tactile effect of the tyres in their overlapping courses.

LEFT Squares of old corrugated tin cover a structure that doesn't conceal its base materials. Tyres, mud, wood, stone, concrete and rusty steel sit easily in this once agricultural landscape.

CHAPEL OF ST IGNATIUS

Many architects' claim that light is a guiding material which informs and forms the structures they envisage – not only is its manipulation and entry into a building an infinitely interesting aspect of architectural skill, but for religious projects the potency of its symbolic and atmospheric qualities make it a chief concern. However, few architects can claim to have gone to the ingenious lengths deployed by Steven Holl Architects at the Chapel of St Ignatius in Seattle. Expressly in awe of the way light 'presents us with a psychological and transcendental realm of the phenomena of architecture' (from Anchoring, cited in Church Builders 1997, p 187). Holl has tried, almost literally, to bottle the stuff. Early sketches for St Ignatius and its community of Jesuit Christians on campus at Seattle University show seven tightly packed conical structures – or 'bottles' as Holl calls them – within a rectangle. Each bottle bends its top towards a different angle so that light enters from all compass directions. In the completed chapel each bottle has different-coloured stained glass so that various parts of the building are marked out by coloured light.

In order to accommodate this formula within an integrated single building, boxier shapes are built around the bottles giving solid parameters and flat exterior planes, though at roof height the topography is a jumble of curves and angled windows. The building wears its Postmodernity on its sleeve: the slabs of concrete which were poured on site and then hoisted into place are left unrendered and the embedded pick-pocket points that the lifting crane attaches to are left visible (though covered with cast bronze plugs) as testimony to the chapel's elaborate construction.

A campanile at one end of the site typifies this conjunction of straight and curved forms. A tall sharp corner piece (to the square pond in front of the chapel), its top end tails off in a long elegant curve shielding the bells and crucifix. These patterns resemble more traditional ecclesiastical forms like those of large cathedral crypts inside the chapel where sections of roof descend to low-slung arches and others rise high. It is a useful strategy for carving up otherwise grand volumes in a manner more akin to the Jesuit's ethos and for emphasising the transition between different liturgical programmes.

A broad path leads past the water in front of the chapel to the southwest corner where a large unit of Alaskan yellow cedar reveals two doors, the smaller door for every day use and the larger one next to it for ceremonial use. More intriguingly, seven small oval-shaped windows are hand-carved into the doors and radiate in a scattered formation, a recapitulation of the seven irregular bottles.

The axis of entry follows a straight line from the doors, but a large narthex is positioned to the east of this 'corridor'. Lit generously by two large south-facing windows it creates an open and informal gathering space: icons of St Ignatius have been placed here as well as devotional furniture and a carpet designed by Holl. Other ancillary rooms lead off the narthex, and its light bottle has a green lens and a red baffle. The baptistery is set at the next junction along the entry axis and is again well lit by a frosted-glass panel behind the font. The lens in this section is clear and the baffle white – the only 'colourless' section of the building. The bronze bowl of the font is inscribed with a text from the 5th-century St John Lateran Basilica, and other detailing includes a protruding casket of holy oils whose subtle colouration is richly attractive in this simple configuration.

Steven Holl Architects
Location: Seattle, Washington, US
Completion date: 1997

LEFT The complementary colours of yellow and blue are evident here where the light is filtered past a yellow lens and the blue baffle reflects and opposes it. A careful balance is struck between forms heralded by light and those grounded to the dark polished floor.

ABOVE A simple, long rectangular site, Holl's curvy roof structure is built around seven 'bottles' that filter light in from all directions. A stain added to the concrete exterior walls articulates the upright forms.

TOP RIGHT The decision to keep the outer shell perpendicular instead of curving to the form of the bottles maintains a solemnity and order. The small bumps on the chapel's walls are the points at which the crane that hoisted the concrete slabs into place was attached.

BOTTOM RIGHT The long side elevations indicate the frequent placement of different-sized windows in the walls. Almost sandwiched in between the jigsaw of slabs of concrete they permit an even spread of natural light.

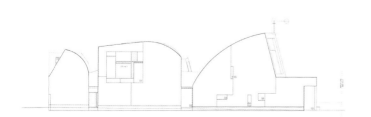
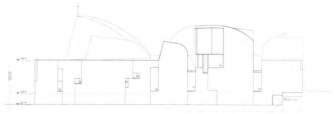

One stretch of the main nave leads at an angle from the baptistery between two sections of pews. It is a dramatic processional route and yet the frequent tilt and fall of ceiling height and walls retains something of the feel of a series of domestic rooms. The interior plastering lends itself to this too in that it has been scumbled in opposite directions making up an irregular patchwork of texture in the way a wallpaper might. The lighting here is also slightly dimmer so that the focus is instantaneously directed at the more concentrated areas of light: the yellow and blue pairings of lens and baffle that fall behind perpendicular envelopes of wall, and the hand-blown light shades which pepper the ceiling and form ghostly shapes around low-watt bulbs.

The chancel furniture is made from the same combination of materials as the doors – yellow cedar and bronze – and creates strong accents on the raised platform and against the pale walls. One central panel behind the altar is covered in a patina of gold leaf and an old Austrian corpus Christi has been mounted on a new cedar cross. Although, in this instance, the constituent elements are held in an appropriate composition and none dominates, nor does the whole seem overloaded or trite, the same might not be said of the side chapel dedicated to the Blessed Sacrament. Here, the interior design has been left to a local Seattle artist whose attempts at a contemporary take on Christian texts and symbols fails to make either a cohesive environment (it is at odds with Holl's style which unifies the rest of the building) or a challenging one. If the general trend for involving artists again in ecclesiastical design and architecture is to flourish in the way it should, proper consultation and curatorial advice needs to be undertaken; prayers stamped into the beeswax walls are, quite frankly, too self-conscious to aid visitors' contemplation.

TOP LEFT Two doors for different occasions are carved of Alaskan yellow cedar and trimmed in bronze. The seven ovals are the only real exterior decoration and are especially visual at night when the light from within attracts passers-by.

BOTTOM LEFT The intersections of straight lines and curves relate one part of the building to another without being too obvious or showy.

RIGHT Looking up one of the bottles to its blue lens it is evident that Holl has achieved a practical and playful solution to a concept that taxes many architects.

While the intermediate fenestration admits powerful ribs of light, they also highlight the precise curves of the ceiling and walls. The cross is dominant but perhaps too nondescript to be of much symbolic value.

HARAJYUKU CHURCH

Ciel Rouge Création
Location: Tokyo, Japan
Completion date: 2005

'Their concepts have been perfected from complimentary viewpoints based on the extremes of earth and sky with the image of space at the centre resembling a landscape.' Thus claims the unretiring 'information' section of Ciel Rouge Création's website which, to give the benefit of the doubt, might prove that sometimes modesty is lost in translation. But 'perfected' concepts aside, the 'image of space at the centre resembling a landscape' is a fitting if slightly confusing one-liner that describes one of the French-Japanese partnership's latest projects, a new Church at Harajyuku in the Aoyama district of Tokyo. The undulating marcel wave ceiling gives the feeling the church was built under the side of a hill, like a secret headquarters, its white walls reminiscent of the sophisticated lair within which an enemy of James Bond might reside.

But this is a church for a community whose children have already been catered for by Ciel Rouge Création in the kindergarten on the neighbouring site, and common practice in Japan dictates a church to sister the school. A 1904 church destroyed during the Second World War, and after that a wooden church destroyed by an earthquake, had previously occupied the site. The pastor and congregation of Harajyuku's United Church of Christ in Japan stipulated a building that would bring visitors to its doors by sheer force of character, a welcoming entrance and a non-exclusive aura.

The facades at either end of the church resemble the forecourt landscaping of the kindergarten that is set on a lower level to the northwest of the church. One entrance to the east rises up almost from the edge of the kerb, its roofline sloping at a low angle. To the west, the roof meets the walls at its peak and an angular bell tower (an upright triangular prism) is set apart and cut with voids the shape of long crosses. Smaller triangles tumble down the side of the tower in a visual simile of chiming bells. An aluminium fence directs people to a rear entranceway.

Both east and west ends of the church introduce the forms that dominate the interior. A trio of amorphous arches is cut out from the thin metal skin and deeper into the concrete under whose contours the glazed east entranceway fits. From the doorway the central arch above is visibly repeated in the cross-section of contours, which develops beyond as an intersected tunnel, right the way through the church. Inside, these white curving contours fall in equal sections some 3 metres wide, and the narrower gaps in between are glazed in clear glass straddling over the congregation's heads, one falling plumb centre behind the altar. Small balconies, walkways and benches nestle in the stepped cavities of the walls, and long horizontal shutters can be opened or closed to adapt the acoustics for which the subtleties of the curving walls have been modulated.

The worshipping is focused across this sliced-up tunnel so that there is an overriding sense that things are happening in a sideways fashion. Indeed the pews are only five rows deep, but spread at least three times as far widthways. Spaces behind the pews under the lowest curve of the ceiling/walls are partitioned off to provide ample facilities, such as baby rooms and an audio suite.

The sanctuary space, raised on a platform and bowed at the front to follow the semicircle of pews around it, never seems very far away because of the shallow depth of the roughly east–west axis (more precisely, the altar lies to the northeast). The altar and two side pedestals are moulded in a long oval shape and

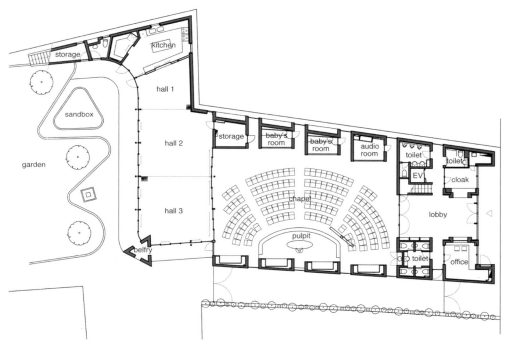

ABOVE The bold eastern entrance gives tempting glimpses into the cavernous structure of the church. The sense of levity and playfulness is carried through both the exterior and interior, maximising the impact on passers-by.

LEFT The outline of the kindergarten's front garden is an echo of the vertical shapes at each end of the church. The six modular sections of the structure make convenient rooms for a welcoming and hospitable church.

RIGHT The bell tower marks the corner of the church's site, which abuts and complements that of the kindergarten. Small triangles are worked into the surfaces of both the bell tower and the church, a perfect Trinitarian sign.

smaller cylinders respectively, their plastic shine a 21st-century substitute for gold or silver. The impracticality of so much white in a busy and youthful church is symptomatic of Ciel Rouge's optimistic architecture but will surely prove an effort to keep pristine, even in Japan's ultra-hygienic society.

A large white cross stands at very close quarters to one front row of pews and although it is not wide enough to really disrupt anyone's view of the Eucharistic act, it dominates the nave in a strangely inappropriate way. No Christian would deny the centrality of the crucifixion in the life of a church, but this slick, unadulterated symbol barely hints at a theological truth. Claims that the cross can be read as a mast of a ship are, frankly, tenuous, as are the claims for the seven days of creation being implicit in the six vertical sections of the tunnel plus the bell tower. Such symbolising, even if spelt out in so many words, is an implausible gesture at the great narratives of the Old and New Testaments, even if it is one that many architects over the centuries have fallen foul of.

While this church is, arguably, too disparate in its parts and too self-conscious an attempt at significance, something is redeemed by the simple spectacle of its curving interior shell, the abundance of light from all directions, the splashes of kindergarten colour among the chairs and the very context of Tokyo architecture. Why not worship in a place that is comparable to contemporary fashions in secular architecture? If the context of Tokyo life determines what is and what is not suitable architectural language for this church, we can appreciate how direct and integrated a response Ciel Rouge's is. Some church architects of the early 20th century understood that it would take time for congregations to become comfortable with 'technologically inspired architectural form' (Rudolf Schwarz cited in Schnell, 1974: 37). But their persistence as well as their sensitivity about 'a gradual imbuement and enrichment of this form in the service of God' ensures (for us now) a legacy of contextualised and localised churches. Harajyuku Church would seem to reflect the zeitgeist of current Japanese design, but remains in peril of seeming anachronistic and impractical in the future.

LEFT Shiny white materials used for the altar and pedestals as well as the seating are a contemporary take on ecclesiastical furnishings as well as being a signature feature of Ciel Rouge's recent work.

RIGHT A traditional pitched roof accommodates the high-arched interior as well as further spaces in the cavity between the walls and roof.

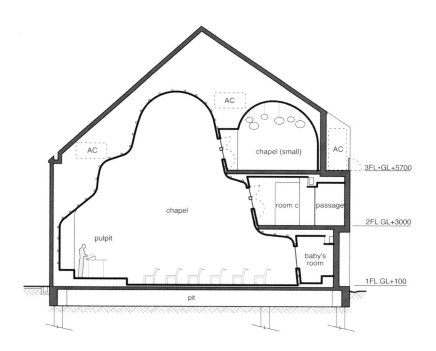

ABOVE By night the interior space is illumined and dramatised by the lifting archway over the east entrance. The traditional pitch of the exterior roof hides the interior curves of the ceiling.

RIGHT The unusual axis of worship gives the church a shallow depth so that the whole congregation is relatively near to the sanctuary. It also creates a feeling of breadth, both physically and in an analogy to the congregation's wish for inclusivity.

SACRED HEART CATHOLIC CHURCH AND PARISH CENTRE

The materials with which we build our churches can speak volumes about social, cultural and economic values, as well as eliciting a metaphorical eloquence by means of a certain patina, grain of wood or hue of stone. Early Modernist architects working in Germany in the 1920s and 1930s understood this well and used industrial materials like steel and concrete to devise completely new ecclesiastical forms, despite being warned by a church hierarchy that the materials were 'unworthy of a church building' (see Schnell, 1974: 37). Auguste Perret's Notre Dame du Raincy (1923) in France is often heralded as the first concrete church, and Otto Bartning's church at Essen in West Germany was boldly named the Steel Church (1928). Further north, in Saarbrücken, Gottfried Böhm brought some of his father Dominikus Böhm's more radical and unrealised plans to fruition in the Church of St Albert (1955), a buttressed round construction in reinforced concrete with a bell tower reminiscent of water towers in the region.

Such striking local precedents must have been seminal to Lamott Architekten, a Stuttgart-based firm, who were commissioned to build a new complex (including church, kindergarten and community centre) at Völklingen just a few kilosmetres outside of Saarbrücken. The complex is largely built of concrete but the architects' use of steel (the town's former industry) is concentrated and potent. Various planes are decked in larch, and walls of glass reveal courtyards and passageways. Shallow areas of water contribute to the interchange of secular and religious space. The steel (prerusted sheets of Corten) is used to envelope the church almost reverentially – even the huge wide doors are fabricated from steel – making a clear statement about embracing the local industrial heritage and celebrating it.

Lamott Architekten also combines materials to offset colour and texture in ways that break up the fairly simple L-shape plan. One side houses the meeting rooms and kindergarten, the other, at right angles to it, the church. A courtyard between three concrete facades is planted with lavender, paved in grey pebbles and framed by a grey and black ambulatory. These are complemented with the burnished red steel, red bricks around the lavender bed and the warm horizontal slats of larch that run across walls and ceilings. Entering over a flat wooden bridge the doors to the church are composed of a patchwork of smaller sheets of rusted steel and the middle row bears the subtle imprint of lines from the Book of Revelation. These are etched more legibly in large block capitals on the interior set of glass doors. That this detail relies on text rather than imagery is an indication of the architects' desire to relate to the contemporary anxiety over traditional iconography or of simply finding imagery unsuited to the Modernist context. Either way, the rows of scripture constitute a very literal boundary – marking the entrance to a place to contemplate scripture – as well as a more abstract and fluid screen.

At right angles to the entranceway and narthex, the main body of the church is a fairly traditional composition within a broad rectangle. The font, altar, lectern and priest's pew are all cast in concrete with minimal details. Pews are a dark stained wood and are arranged either side of the sanctuary as well as in the nave. The south wall is a three-tier screen of steel sheets suspended above the ground with light admitted through glazing at the bottom and the top. This wall continues beyond the adjoining east glass wall and, in another L-shape, runs

Lamott Architekten
Location: Völklingen, Germany
Completion date: 2001

LEFT The glass walls of both the east and north sides of the church are shadowed by steel and concrete walls. Much of the ceiling and roof surfaces are planked in larch while the bare simplicity of detailing, like the rows of round unshaded light bulbs, adds to the church's stringently contemporary style.

behind it leaving a gap of about 1.5 metres onto which natural light falls through a pergola of larch, and in which a very simple wooden cross stands. The effect, from the pews of the church, is a sophisticated layering of materials, light and lines. The cross is barely noticeable at first and there is, arguably, something not entirely theologically right about its separation from the congregation. But the overall patterning and colouration of this east wall is so attractive and change-able that it is as if the cross actually underpins all of its complexity.

Although the church is only one element of a site whose other parts are not expressly religious, it might be argued that this Catholic building has understated its definition to the point of detachment: the self-consciousness of replaying Modernist and Internationalist architectural styles can detract attention away from the poignancy of building a forum for worship, communion and prayer. But ultimately, Sacred Heart has sufficient beauty and composure to herald in the sacred in a discrete and localised voice.

BELOW Two glass walls admit plenty of daylight while the east wall is a complex layering of reflections and shadows. The passage between the glass and the steel accommodates a slender wooden cross, positioned in line with one side of the altar.

TOP RIGHT The impressive outswing of the steel doors creates a step change between the courtyard and the church. Simple etched lettering scatters lines from the Book of Revelation across the congregation's path as they enter and leave.

BOTTOM RIGHT Two interlocking T-shapes fit around a central courtyard with the church at the southeast corner of the site. Areas of shallow water, overhanging platforms and long, wide windows borrow from the vocabulary of the Internationalist style.

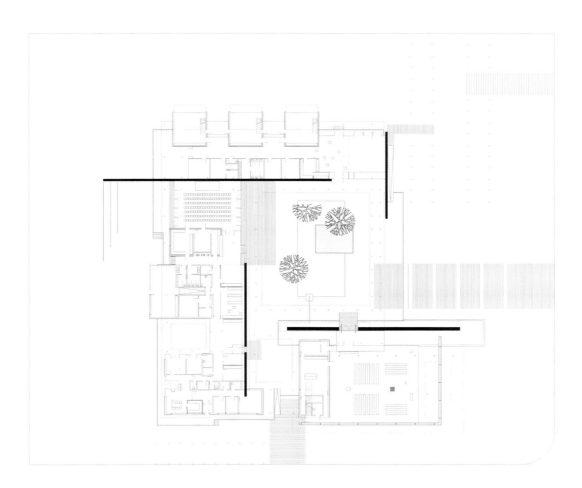

FAITH HOUSE

Tony Fretton Architects
Location: Poole, Dorset, UK
Completion date: 2002

RIGHT An informal ring of silver birch trunks set against walls of polished concrete adds a very deliberate reference to the environment at Faith House. It provides an intimate arena where a few people could gather for a short liturgical act or chairs can be introduced for solitary contemplation.

Strictly speaking Faith House is not a church. Built in memory of Faith Lees, a founder of Holton Lee, her name is nevertheless an accurate indication of the broad remit of this building. A centre of holistic care for disabled people, Holton Lee commissioned Faith House as a space where visitors of any or no faith can find quiet and meditative surroundings. Positioned at the highest point of the complex, albeit in a flat English landscape, Faith House sits at the edge of the grounds on the cusp of a semi-agricultural vista, marking both a boundary and a beginning.

A self-confessed aetheist, Tony Fretton might have been an unlikely candidate for a religious commission. But the practice's track record for working with galleries and artists – which includes the Lisson Gallery and the Camden Arts Centre both in London, as well as a number of artists' and collectors' houses – is among the most impressive in the UK and Faith House was only one part of a larger commission to build artists' studios and a performing arts centre. It was, then, an enlightened decision taken by the Holton Lee Charitable Trust to ask Fretton to extend his capability for simple but very beautiful buildings (usually on small budgets) to a place for spiritual focus.

From the approach its proportions are distinctive, as is its flat, grassed roof. From left to right three equally sized oblongs reveal the entrance, a glass wall and a wall of red cedar boards. Through both the entranceway and the glass wall there is a view through the adjoining rooms and out to the horizon. This permeability gives Faith House a sense of both modesty and confidence. This is a welcoming space, simple enough to be able to immediately gauge its scope, not something that most churches, with their private vestries and chapels, aspire to.

On entering via a cedar-boarded porch, there are two routes into its two main rooms: one, a small square-plan 'quiet room' in which a ring of floor-to-ceiling silver birch tree trunks stand; and the other, a much larger 'assembly room' flooded with light from the south-facing wall of three tall windows and doors that look out onto the landscape. There is a history of fine Modern church building that uses this dignified play on nature, both in terms of using untimbered wood and of the outlook onto a natural vista which acts as the iconography of a building: it stretches back to EG Asplund and Sigurd Lewerentz's 1940 Woodland Cemetery in Stockholm, Siren Architects' Otaniemi Chapel (1957) and, more recently, Richard MacCormac's Chapel at Fitzwilliam College, Cambridge (1991), and Fretton's contribution sits well in this lineage. The only criticism that might be levelled at this kind of architectural device is one that comes with the territory of preferencing contemporary spirituality over traditional religion; it is difficult to resolve whether Faith House lacks a theological backbone, or whether its overall achievement as, simply, a good building to be in is a theological assertion in itself.

Despite its budget (only £150,000), the permutations of materials piece together a rich sequence of transparent portals, intimate enclosures and brightly lit open space, lending an ease of transition – both visual and physical – from indoor to outdoor. Movement between rooms might be more difficult for larger groups of people, in the instance of any communal liturgical activity, but the building seems to respond appropriately to the type of nonconformist use its visitors are likely to want. The quiet room, for example, is really only big enough for a handful of people at a time, and as such it invites solace and stillness.

Murals by the artist Diego Ferrari of overhead views of a canopy of trees, birds of prey in flight and a summers' sky are to be added to the ceilings of the quiet room, lobby and porches. The commissioning process and designs were funded under the 'Art for Architecture' scheme which pioneered exceptional collaborations between artist and architects before falling foul of the UK government's funding cuts in 2004. Holton Lee is currently trying to complete a fund-raising effort to have the murals painted.

The mural depicting a canopy of trees complete with bursts of light between branches and leaves is destined for the sun porch that leads onto the garden areas. It is a sophisticated but light-hearted architectural segue from artifice to nature but the building's grass roof and low energy fabrication methods ensure that there are also serious environmental moves here too. As such, this kind of building is a talisman for sensible rural architecture and, in this age of increasing environmental responsibility, it should and will set precedents for community and church buildings alike. Moreover, the more established theology that a church building should be fit for social and community use as well as for worship, which Peter Hammond and others in the UK pushed for in the 1960s, seems now to be all too often mistranslated into buildings where function overrides aesthetic. Against this unfortunate scenario, Faith House sets a standard for quality and beauty that most of our ancillary church buildings fail to reach.

ABOVE LEFT In a complex of old farm buildings, Holton Lee overlooks the Dorset coast and Poole Harbour. Three equal-sized oblongs form the front facade, two of which allow views right through the building to the landscape on the other side.

BELOW LEFT The three distinct units relate to each other with a classical harmony. Each has its own texture when seen from afar – the birch trees on the left, the fenestration in the middle unit and the open air of the sun porch on the right.

RIGHT The sun porch on the west side of the building joins the assembly room with its tall French windows. The red cedar wood cladding is a distinctly warm hue against the blue and green of the sky and landscape in which it sits. One of Diego Ferrari's murals will be on the ceiling of the porch.

BELOW Under the now defunct but nonetheless highly successful scheme 'Art for Architecture', Tony Fretton Architects collaborated with the painter Diego Ferrari to commission murals for the ceilings in all but the assembly room of Faith House. Ferrari's slightly tongue-in-cheek imagery is due to be completed in 2007.

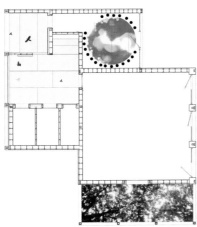

KOREAN PRESBYTERIAN CHURCH OF NEW YORK

Greg Lynn, Douglas Garofalo, Michael McInturf
Location: Long Island City, New York, US
Completion date: 1998

A thriving Korean Presbyterian community from Long Island City in New York purchased this former 1930s Knickerbocker Laundry to house their worship and community activities. Architects Greg Lynn, Douglas Garofalo and Michael McInturf teamed up to take on a complete refit, incorporating a worship area to seat 2,500, a library and classrooms, meeting rooms, a cafeteria and day-care centre, and a 600-seat wedding chapel.

Like many Christian immigrant populations, the Korean community in New York are accustomed to converting churches from buildings with a variety of histories and, arguably, this contributes to a style of architecture in which the Knickerbocker Laundry might fit. The commission sought to conflate an authentic Korean Presbyterian church template with something bold and iconic. The three collaborating architects all share a reputation for using innovative digital techniques for design and fabrication, and their appointment to this particular project was always going to create media interest. The level of ambition, of both the worshipping community in taking on a building that would seat over 2000, and the architects' response to the brief, matched expectations but reactions from the architectural press on completion were mixed.

The main worship space adopts a utilitarian and rather conservative approach with gently tiered pews in metal grey and maroon facing a stage-like chancel, and would be featureless were it not for some unremarkable furniture and a pipe organ. The interest is in the structure of the walls and ceiling which stray from the perpendicular shell of the original building into almost organic forms, forms which, we are assured, could not be designed without the aid of new technology. At regular intervals the sections of wall follow a sequence of wide-tapered angles, buttressing out to the ceiling where the apex is lit by a scattering of hundreds of small sunken spotlights.

These repeated angular forms are used throughout the interior, and are at their most effective in the smaller hallways where at close quarters the jutting walls are more dramatic and playful. On the exterior of the building huge angular 'ears' fit one inside another, and create a tunnel into which the main entrance stairway ascends. This metal-clad structure, another product of computer-aided design, affords views through its intersecting shells out to the Manhattan skyline. But it is an awkward adjunct, a form that it is hard to fathom a good reason for, and without wanting to dismiss the potential for using such technology altogether, the merits for applying it to this particular job are questionable.

The front facade retains the strongest indication of the Laundry's former aesthetic (there are also some Art Deco curves to be found on the walls of the car park) and its tri-part sections have been treated with some restraint. A white cross is picked out of the central section's glass framework, a tried and tested device. An all too frequent feature of US culture, serried ranks of car parking spaces dominate the surrounding landscape.

In 1922 Rudolf Schwarz completed the church of Corpus Christi in Aachen. Quickly nick-named 'the factory', its simplicity is breathtaking. It is neither featureless nor dull. Schwarz knew how to handle empty walls, the importance of good proportions – be it for factory or church – and the integrity of straight lines. The New York Presbyterian Church is a testament to architecture which consciously diverts from the ubiquitous 'good-taste' of Modernism's straight lines, but by only

Sequences of angular sidewalls taper to a low
axial apex in the ceiling. Seating, by contrast, is
quite formal and conventional.

LEFT The unusual progression of ear-like appendages to one end of the former Laundry, in which a wide staircase ascends, reinforces the sense of this project's fearlessness in taking on an old industrial footprint.

ABOVE RIGHT The environment within the staircase's enveloping structure is as near as the architects get to grandeur, in the traditional and ecclesiastical sense of the word. Views to the west and the skyline of Manhattan make it a good place for convivial loitering on the way out.

BELOW RIGHT The incorporation of nonperpendicular forms extends to foyers and corridors and is a generous intervention that gives the interlocking spaces as much credence as the adjoining meeting rooms and worship spaces.

BELOW Two entrances at the north and the south filter the congregation into the main worship space. The irregular angles of the structure enveloping the north staircase are repeated in the walls separating the worship area from the corridor to ancillary rooms in the south part of the building.

RIGHT ABOVE A new entrance, glazing and an undulating roof give an impressive exterior composition, albeit one that lacks an obvious beginning and end. It is clear that the building has high potential for servicing thousands of people at a time, but as a religious environment it will, for many, lack lustre.

RIGHT BELOW Gently modulating ceiling and roof structures are evidence of the architects' preference for a Postmodern augmentation of a 1930s industrial shell.

partially hiding or augmenting the industrial building with irregular angles and biomorphic forms what's left is neither one thing nor another.

Given the ambitiousness of the architects' scheme – though arguably not ambitious enough – and the willingness of this Christian community to recycle an old building, this is more than standard fare for large American congregations whose rapid growth has necessitated vast and impersonal barn-like spaces. But the history of nonconformist church architecture, particularly in America, is much richer than this foray into a 21st-century vocabulary and obvious templates for simple utilitarian design might have made more sense of this industrial footprint, to a more convincing religious effect.

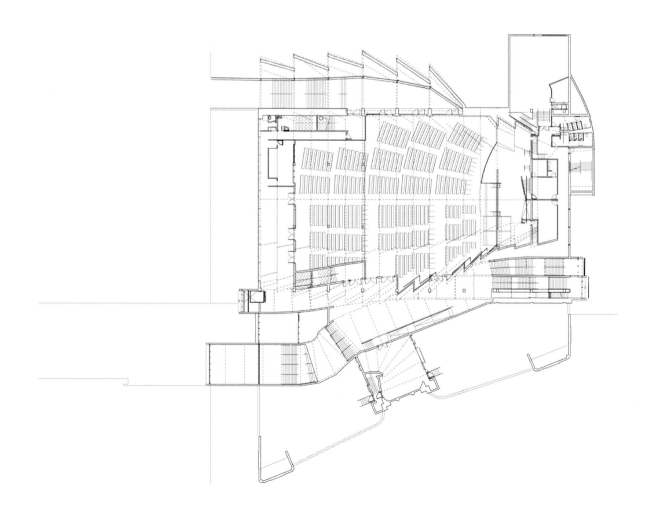

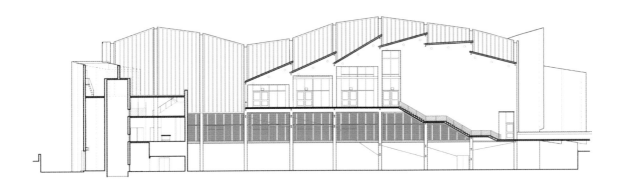

ANTIOCH BAPTIST CHURCH

Rural Studio

Location: Perry County, Alabama, US

Completion date: 2002

The rapidity with which timber churches sprang up in southern America during the last couple of centuries will almost certainly spawn a flux of maintenance problems for the descendents of the faithful communities who built them. One such church in Perry County, Alabama, was quaking in its foundations to the extent that, by the turn of the millennium, the congregation had dwindled to a scant four families. Realising this detriment, the down-sliding relationship between the fabric of the church and its mission, along with the need for a rest-room and baptismal font, the congregation welcomed a team of four thesis-year students from Auburn University over the county border. Under the auspices of Rural Studio and the late Samuel Mockbee's challenging system of requiring his architecture students to complete self-build projects with the poorer neighbour-hoods in their vicinity, Gabe Michaud, Jared Fulton, Marion McElroy and Bill Nauck undertook to restore the church to good working order.

Without ado, the old building was dismantled and a new foundation laid. By working on the limited budgets of both studentship and congregation, and with the ingrained ethos of Mockbee's environmentally responsible attitude, Rural Studio managed to salvage the majority of the existing church's materials for the job – wood panelling, corrugated iron, joists and tongue-and-groove boards. The students also built a small interim chapel for the congregation so that they could continue to worship on Sundays.

What rose, phoenix-like, from the site of the Antioch Baptist Church is some-thing considerably firmer on its feet, equally modest, but with a sense of signifi-cance and grace. A long sloping roofline that pitches up again at one end is its most distinctive exterior feature and holds it in good stead against the back-drop of surrounding forestry. The length runs east to west and so the height of the end walls allows liberal stretches of windows above and around the wood panelling. Another section of fenestration runs along the length of the pews and down to floor level so that a clear view onto the graveyard is afforded from a seated position.

A box-like wooden structure juts out at both ends, accommodating the preacher's room and restroom at the east end of the church and the baptistery at the west end. The box at the east end is narrower than the width of the main body of the church and creates a corridor to one side of it through which an entranceway is forged. A steeply sloping sidewall intensifies the approach, and the glazed doorway makes visible the trees on the other side of the site. Being Baptist by denomination, the font is a full-immersion pool set into the floor under a lifting section of wooden boards (where the pulpit is normally), and is tiled in black with orange highlights on each step. The black tiles are a good aesthetic choice, picking up on the black metal trusses and window frames while also determining some theological significance about the baptismal moment.

What is impressive about this church is the combination of a highly dexterous and sensitive re-use of the materials at hand, along with the muted innovation and careful contemporaneousness of its design. The handcrafted trusses, which form a neat rhythmic structure supporting the flat wooden ceiling, show recep-tiveness to traditional techniques, and details in the arrangement of furniture and fenestration reveal an intimate knowledge of the congregation's needs. On the other hand Rural Studio has adapted a clean Modernist style with considerable

The church has good proportions with plenty of
scope for the existing congregation to grow again.
Ceiling trusses mimic simple barn roof structures
yet the building as a whole remains sensible to
the ecclesiastical tradition of the Baptists.

conviction; the obtuse angles of the church in profile evoke the pitch of agricultural barn roofs while the use of stripes in the corrugated metal, the wood boards and the grey breeze blocks compose a sequence of texture and tone that would not go unnoticed in a fashionable urban context. The church also appears to float about 15 centimetres off the ground on the south side to where the site slopes, giving it some semblance of a mobile unit, a church that could, fittingly, really go places.

It is a testament to Rural Studio and the School of Architecture at Auburn that four students can pull off such an accomplishment, not least because they do it on a fraction of the budget that most new churches are built with. But, it also demonstrates what can be achieved with a plot of land, a broken building and a high level of engagement with the worshipping congregation.

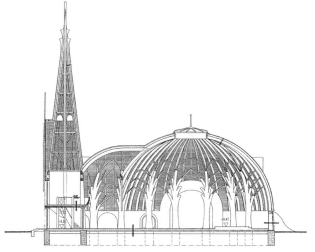

ABOVE Makovecz's organicism is relatively understated here in the use of a fairly classical roof structure and the more contemporary look of the white concrete.

LEFT A medieval looking wooden framework is given, almost literally, a new twist and concrete supporting pillars take on the form of trees with their pollarded branches and thickening trunks.

St Stephen's Church

Of all the architects featured in this book, the Hungarian Imre Makovecz is perhaps the most experienced in ecclesiastical work. By the 1960s, Makovecz had stoically reintroduced a more organic quality into municipal buildings as a reaction to the abundance of poor-quality Modernist work in Hungary (a stance which lost him his job with the state in the 1970s). In doing so he has evolved a language of rich cultural symbolism, which he has utilised in church and mortuary buildings to unrivalled effect. Earlier churches than St Stephen's, like those at Siófok and at Paks (both in Hungary), draw deeply on the wealth of native Hungarian cultures (Magyar, Scythian and Celtic) whose symbolism and imagery can be transcribed into universal and timeless forms: two S-shapes form the plan at Paks, and a mask-like pair of wings fronts the church at Siófok. Plant and animal forms, eyes as windows, seraphic wings, primal geometrical decorative motifs and mythical allusions are conflated in fantastical creations. And although there is a sense of paganism or perhaps pantheism about Makovecz's churches, the prevalent Christian theme always underscores this and brings a continuity to religious traditions over the centuries.

Százhalmobatta is a large town to the southwest of Budapest whose name derives from the Hungarian for 'a hundred mounds' of some 4000 years ago. The Roman Catholic Church of St Stephen occupies the site of these burial mounds, which required careful excavation before the build could begin. Roman remains can also be found and a more recent revival of the Serbian population together with a significant 18th-century Serbian-Orthodox Church in the town. Today, St Stephen's sits in a landscaped park area amid modern industrialised development. Makovecz has brought much of this into play, and bases the main rotund forms on those of the burial mounds. As with much of his previous work, the church has a weighty gravitational relation to the earth as well as seeming to rise from it, with quasi-phoenix-like characteristics.

What is more unusual for Makovecz at Százhalmobatta is the integration of severe exterior white walls, where normally his church's exterior skins are clad in wood and slate. There are two that sandwich the softer 'mounds' of the main church between them, and one that dissects at a tangent the sister 'mound', under which lies a chapel and rectory. The walls do not support a roof structure and neither is there any glazing in the windows; they simply introduce the idea of Roman Classicism into the mix and frame the typically Makoveczian curves between their sturdy arms.

The entranceway, as is again typical in a Makovecz church, is centred under the tower and a wooden framework around the door uses Art-Nouveau curves derivative of trees. The roof of the church, tiled in slate, swoops to a low level at the front and two tree trunks support its arc. Stripped of bark, though with some branches intact, they stand like sentry guards to the tower whose composition of wings, fork and golden disc sits at roof level, while the tower's shingled surface tapers inwards and soars upwards.

Without detracting from the dominant expression of the church, a circular mound of earth attaches to the north side almost entirely covering the rectory and chapel. With its shorter Roman wall dissecting its plan and another atrium of light permitted through the circular window at its centre, the complex (which was paid for by the citizens of Százhalmobatta) meets contemporary standards of

Imre Makovecz
Location: Százhalmobatta, Hungary
Completion date: 1998

provision. Whether the priest of St Stephen's appreciates living in a subterranean Makoveczian world is another matter.

The church interior is formed around the main cupola built entirely on a pinewood frame and supported by concrete pillars that mimic the branching tree trunks at the entrance. In fact, together in the round, they look like fine upturned feathers brushing against the walls of the dome instead of carrying its weight. A small glazed cupola at the top lets in some light while the rest floods from the southwesterly orientation of the doors and ground-level windows. Makovecz frequently maximises the impact of a transition from light to dark, exterior to interior, and at St Stephen's there is contrast between the dark and slightly forbidding shingled roof that dominates its profile and the warm wood and white-washed concrete inside. But, more than just a shift in tone and colour, the interior at St Stephen's is an upturned cradle, conducive to traditional worship patterns and the communion of Christians under one roof, whereas the exterior is almost warrior-like in its defensive walls, armoured shell and iconic facade.

The walls beneath the cupola switch to white concrete forming a perimeter that segues to pale white floorstones and increases the dominance of the roof elements. In contrast, the pine seating for the congregation and for the priests brings the wooden colouration to floor level as well as a rather monstrance-shaped pine reredos marking the altar and sanctuary. By Makovecz's standards this coupling of wood and whitewash is uncomplicated, although no less distinctive for it, and proves that his persistent translation of almost medieval-looking forms can still be powerful, enriching and new.

LEFT High white walls, like rejuvenated sections of a Roman citadel, flank the bulbous roof of the church. Together with Makovecz's signature concoction of pre-Christian and Christian symbols, the church expresses the ancient significance of this 4,000-year-old burial ground.

RIGHT Makovecz's uses of animal forms, together with strong decorative and symbolic motifs, are always compiled in an extremely distinctive feature.

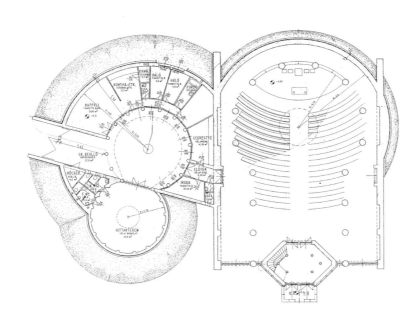

ABOVE The Church itself looks as if it is raised upon a burial mound, more so the area to the west side of the church which is built under a flatter dome of earth and bisected by another staunch wall.

OPPOSITE TOP LEFT Entering under the bell tower the white concrete underside of the interior springs up in tree-shaped supports on which the large cupola rests.

OPPOSITE TOP RIGHT The sanctuary is relatively undefined in that its furniture and scale are compliant with the congregation. A tall wooden structure behind the altar derives its decorative forms from the rest of the church and carries a small crucifix at its apex.

OPPOSITE BOTTOM Three circles and three straight lines overlap within the complex of St Stephen's. The design for the interior pews forms a wing-shaped plan typical of Makovecz's use of animal forms.

THE CHRIST PAVILION

**Meinhard von Gerkan and
Joachim Zais**

Location: EXPO 2000, Hanover,
and Volkenroda Monastery,
Thuringia, Germany
Completion date: 2000

Putting Christianity on display is not something that normally comes to mind when we think of seminal reasons for building a church. But exhibition fairs, be they for trade or for culture, are a contemporary phenomenon we cannot ignore and, if churches are to be taken seriously as 'players' in contemporary life, then opportunities to exhibit at such fairs should not be dismissed lightly. For all the ensuing controversy, London's Millennium Dome made one such an attempt when it commissioned Eva Jiricna to create a Faith Zone. An earlier precedent won greater acclaim when, in 1997, the Catholic and Protestant churches in Germany united to invite submissions for a competition to build a pavilion of the Christian faith for the Hanover fair EXPO 2000. Meinhard von Gerkan and Joachim Zais of the German practice GMP Architekten won the commission with a design that adapts the old cloister form into a new manifestation as well as treating the exhibitory values inherent in the scheme with a light and innovative touch. GMP is an established practice with a breadth of experience in urban architecture – including Berlin-Tegel Airport and a number of large exhibition pavilions – and the Christ Pavilion depends on this mode of architecture, on structural simplicity and transparency. Its framework is of steel crosses, and glass is used as a building block, banked against marble in the church space and sandwiching layers of all manner of everyday objects in the cloister sections.

At EXPO 2000 a colonnade of bare steel and glazed tower formed additional distinctive elements to the pavilion, ones that, again, carried characteristics that overlapped the idioms of ecclesiastical architecture and exhibition design. Post-EXPO 2000 the pavilion's life does not include these or the crypt: the church and the cloisters were dissembled and moved wholesale to a nearby monastery. Inaugurated in 2001, the Brotherhood of Jesus, a German Protestant community in Volkenroda, Thuringia, welcomed the travelling church while they make headway restoring their old Cistercian cloisters.

A large square basin of water mirrors the pavilion (at both the EXPO site and at the monastery), doubling the impact of its cubic facade and the patchwork of textures behind glass. The church is visible from all approaches, rising to twice the height of the enwrapping cloisters, and composed of squares in white marble laminated to glass. Each square component, in both the church and the cloisters, is dissected into four again with a cross-shape of a thinner steel framework, so that the complex is built entirely around the unit of a square cross.

On entering the cloisters from the side of the water basin they diverge around a rectangular plan. The church sits in the north half of this, forming a small, protected courtyard. Crossing the courtyard are three tall steel doors to the church. But the transfer from the water basin to the church will be, for many, a less direct route via the cloisters which are distracting, not to say mesmerising in their detail. Worldly textures are created in a layer (only about 4 centimetres deep) between two sheets of glass. From the natural world shells, feathers, poppy heads, coal, bamboo and wood, among other things, are stacked high with museum-like clarity. From the man-made world ephemera such as cigarette lighters, cogs, syringes, tea strainers and light bulbs jostle for space in this visual slice of mass production. As showcases they are a brilliant reductive metaphor of the complexity that exists between man and nature, and as a cloister in which Christians might move around or dwell for longer they are stimulating and challenging while having a meditative capacity too.

LEFT 18-metre steel columns break into finned crosses in the ceiling where there are skylights, but much daylight permeates the church through the glass and marble walls.

RIGHT Variations in the choice of objects, natural and man-made, sandwiched between glasses refract and distort light inside the cloisters.

BELOW The steel pillars within the taller church block reach up to skylights in the flat roof and are interspaced between portals opening into the cloisters.

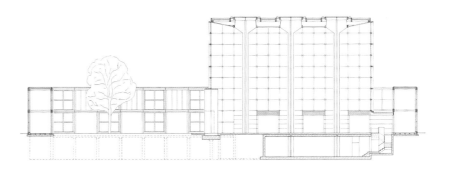

Ansicht v.d. Plaza

Hofansicht der Kirche

Längsschnitt

ABOVE LEFT AND RIGHT These sections show how all the elements take their measure from a single square unit. While the pavilion was at EXPO 2000 it included a tower (seen here) that incorporated a cross within it.

LEFT A darker stripe around the perimeter of the church's interior gives clarity to its floor elements including the portals that reveal one section of the cloister glass. Every unit relates to another, either in its size or by the use of square crosses.

RIGHT One side of the water basin in front of the complex acts as a pathway towards the entrance at the centre of the cloisters. Reflections of the multitextured panels add an illusory height to this otherwise ground-hugging building.

BELOW The superficial treatment of the church and cloisters masks the simplicity of the grid on which they are laid out.

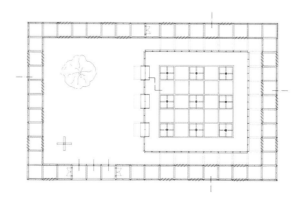

ABOVE An extraordinary array of colouration and patterning makes a display of worldly things, open to different permutations of meanings and allusions, and acts as a compelling incentive to walk around the whole cloister.

RIGHT The cloisters form a courtyard in front of the church space where a trinity of equal-sized doors are harbingers of the rational divisions of space within.

FAR RIGHT In its new home at the monastery of Volkenroda the Christ Pavilion resonates with the changes in architectural styles around it as well as retaining its own distinctive autonomy.

Inside the church the white marble cube is divided up by nine equally spaced steel pillars while squares of polished exposed concrete demarcate the floor. The pillars – whose cross-section is formed of four L-shapes that back-to-back form another square cross – span outwards at ceiling height, each within a square unit of skylight. Otherwise, daylight is evenly spread through the high marble walls. Only a small portion of the floor space (two of the concrete squares) is adapted for traditional worship with minimalist oak benches for pews, and on a low dais are the altar, lectern and priests' chairs, which are also hewn from the same pale wood. In a large glass case at the back of the dais the 'Georgs-Kruzifix', on loan from a Cologne museum, hangs on a brushed stainless-steel cross. It is the only concession to an actual historical element (the glass case deliberately quoting contemporary museum design) and succeeds on the strength and potency of this. The rest of the floor space is unoccupied, which extends the cloister idea into the church itself, as if GMP was intent on providing more fluid and transitory modes of architecture for worship and meditation. The continuity between the cloisters and the church is also maintained by large square portals in the church allowing sight of one panel of the layered cloister glass. The fact that all these elements are grounded at floor level accentuates the simplicity and drama of the rising steel columns against the white marble.

GMP's adherence to Modernist strictures gives this pavilion a sharp aesthetic edge that is both attractive to contemporary audiences in the context of an exhibition and autonomous when situated in the wider complex of the monastery at Volkenroda. It augments its contemporary relevance with the gently humorous detailing of the glass-entrapped objects, a humour that is befitting of trade fairs and monasteries alike.

Select Bibliography

BOOKS

Hammond, Peter, *Towards a Church Architecture*, Architectural Press (London), 1962

Heathcote, Edwin and Iona Spens *Church Builders*, Academy Editions (London), 1997

Maguire, Robert and Keith Murray, *Modern Churches of the World*, Studio Vista (London), 1965

Marion, Jean-Luc, *God Without Being*, The University of Chicago Press (Chicago) 1991

Schnell, Hugo, *Twentieth Century Church Architecture in Germany*, Verlag Schnell & Steiner (Munich), 1974

Stock, Wolfgang Jean, (ed) *European Church Architecture 1950–2000*, Prestel (Munich), 2002

PERIODICALS

Teller, Matthew, 'Architecture – Built to Impress', *The Independent*, London, 26 February 2005

Heathcote, Edwin, 'St Mary of the Angels', *Church Building*, no 72, Nov/Dec 2001, p 4

'Questions and Answers' *Church Building*, no 86, Mar/Apr 2004, p 24

'The Customer's Intentions', *L'architecttura*, Cronache e Storia, no 484 (Rome), p 71

URLS

http://www.bbc.co.uk/radio3/architecture/risingstars.shtml
http://www.olacathedral.org/cathedral/arch/overview

OTHER

Wiederin, Gerold, 2001, press release